MILITARY
ARCHITECTURE

MILITARY ARCHITECTURE

THE ART OF DEFENCE FROM EARLIEST TIMES
TO THE ATLANTIC WALL

BY

QUENTIN HUGHES

BEAUFORT

TO
THE LATE GENERAL ROBERT NICOLAS
WHO KNEW SO MUCH ABOUT FORTIFICATIONS
AND WAS ALWAYS WILLING TO SHARE
HIS KNOWLEDGE

British Library Cataloguing in Publication Data

Hughes, Quentin
    Military Architecture: the art of defence from earliest
    times to the Atlantic wall. – 2nd. ed.
    1. Fortifications. Architectural features, to 1945
    I. title
    725.18

    ISBN 1–85512–008–9

First published in 1974
Revised and expanded second edition
published in Great Britain 1991 by
Beaufort Publishing Ltd
PO Box 22, Liphook, Hants
GU30 7PJ

Designed by Tony Garrett
Typeset by Inforum Typesetting, Portsmouth
Printed and bound in Great Britain by
The Bath Press, Avon

Contents

Acknowledgements

I wish to express my thanks to the many people who have helped me in the preparation of this book.

In particular I am indebted to Their Excellencies the Ambassadors to Malta of France, Italy and West Germany, Brigadier Paul Ward, Captain I Drummond, RN and the staff at the library of the Royal Engineers' Institution, Major R A Bartelot, RA and the staff of the Royal Artillery Institution, Captain P Truttman and his colleagues in the French army at Thionville and Metz, Captain G Koppert and his associates in the Dutch army at Utrecht, Mr William Allcorn, Mr and Mrs R Blijstra, Mr Aulis Blomstedt, Professor J P Bonta, Mr David Dean, Dr C J Duffy, Mr J V H Eames, Lieutenant-Colonel Francisco Fornals, Mrs Eva Friis, Dr De Pasquale and Chevalier Joseph Galea at the Royal Malta Library, Kolonel Dr Robert Gils, Mr Anthony Kemp, Professor Edmund Malachowicz, Mr F S Mallia, Major General J R Matthys, Général Robert Nicolas, Dr Simon Pepper, Commander Charles Robbins, USN, Brigadier A Samut-Tagliaferro, and Father Marius Zerafa at the National Museum in Valletta, Mr Caruana Dingli at the Department of the Environment, Malta, Mr R Vella Bonavita, Dr Paul Xuereb, Mr John Mangion, Mr Frans Attard and students in the Department of Architecture at the Royal University of Malta. Mr David Braithwaite has painstakingly read and advised me on the original text.

The photographs of Chester (p17), Restormel Castle (p19), Deal (p83), St Mawes and Pendennis Castles (p85) were kindly supplied by Aerofilms Ltd; those of the Tower of London (p20), Caerlaverock (p37), Claypotts (p82) and Fort Tilbury (p137) by the Department of the Environment; Verdala Palace (p81) by Mr D M Wrightson; Fort Popton (p193) by BP Ltd; Castello di San Marcos (p134) by United States National Parks Service; Monbeltrán (p47), Medina del Campo (p47) and Coca (p48) by Mr Alberto Weissmüller from his book *Castles from the Heart of Spain*, Barrie & Jenkins, London 1969 and Fort George (p139) by *The Scotsman*.

Finally I am most grateful to Mr Carmel Gatt and Mr Anton Valentino for help with the numerous line drawings in the text, to Mr Ian Hunter for preparing some of the photographs, to Miss Maria Cremona, now Mrs Galea, for interpreting my notes and typing my manuscript, to Miss Michele Rice for transferring all the material meticulously onto the computer and to Mrs Juliet Jamieson for her help in correcting this book.

Preface

'Military engineering,' wrote the eminent seventeenth century marshal Vauban, 'is a business beyond our strength; it embraces too many things for a man to be able to make himself perfectly master of it.' In the succeeding three centuries the complexity of the art has increased threefold. What has been difficult to practise is as difficult to describe and write about. Perhaps this is why there is no comprehensive survey of the subject in any language, and why this book can only attempt to demonstrate the scope of the subject. There are many over-simplifications and numerous omissions and for this I apologise, making only the excuse that with so massive a subject the references have had to be selective.

The main fascination of military architecture lies in its honesty. Admittedly there are elements of facadism applied purely for their psychological impact, like the ornate decoration of fortified gates and the rusticated walls which suggest a strength greater than they possess, but military architecture is essentially functional architecture; it has always had to be. For its efficient function it required an integrity of plan and section, the use of appropriate first rate materials and craftsmanship, and the strongest and most resistant forms of construction.

Its fascination also lies in its sculptural quality. It was Lendy who wrote, 'a thorough engineer sees his fortress completely modelled on a plateau, a hill, a plain, or a rock, just as a sculptor sees his statue in a block of marble; nay, more, he also makes the best of nature's resources.'

Equally one can say that its fascination lies in its very changing nature. Fontenelle called it the most difficult of all arts, 'since it does not afford to men of ordinary capacity the convenience of the application of certain fixed rules, but demands at every moment the natural and improved parts of a lofty genius.' Not subject to caprice or fashion, it has changed of necessity and has been forced to change in order to survive. It is an art with few vagaries. Nevertheless there have been rules and a pattern of evolution which is easier for us to see looking at the subject in retrospect. If a genius like Vauban could write, 'the art of fortifying does not consist in rules and systems, but solely in good sense and experience', other lesser mortals were in dire need of guidelines. One is reminded of the prisoner who scrawled on the walls of his cell, 'Stone walls and iron bars do not a prison make, *but they sure help.*'

The evolution of military architecture is moulded by the weapons used against it and by those used in its support. Gradually weapons assumed a position of importance far in excess of the actual structure of the fort, and changes in fortification have been largely the consequence of improvements that have been made in weaponry. From earliest times the gun has in its various forms been the decisive factor in fortification. Its impact has been affected by its range, its energy and its mobility. Up to the fourteenth century the ancient and medieval ballistae were the main weapons of attack and defence, and engineers evolved with no great difficulty defences of sufficient strength to withstand attack. Soon the artillery cannon began to usurp the position of importance. By 1327 it was being used in siege warfare, and at the battle of Crecy in 1346 was in action in the field. The efficiency of the cannon and of other weapons was then built up with ever-increasing momentum: wheeled artillery, flintlock muskets in 1521, mortars in 1543, the socket bayonet in 1702, the simplification and standardisation of gun parts by Gribauval in 1763 which soon led to mass production, shrapnel fire in 1810, explosive shells from 1826, breech-loading guns in the 1850s, machine-guns in the 1870s, high explosive shells in 1885, quick-firing guns two years later and the magazine rifle in the following year, and the introduction of smokeless powder by 1890. From stone projectiles, the missiles changed to cast iron shot fired from smooth-bore ordnance, and finally to the introduction of missiles for rifled guns in 1859. The result was that muzzle energy inreased at a phenomenal rate which coupled with an increased weight of projectiles and a greater penetrating power, changed the pattern of war. The effective breaching range of a gun was increased from a mere 350 metres (380yds) in the case of a 20-pounder in the sixteenth century to some 3500 metres (3800yds) by the end of the nineteenth.

Throughout history there was a continual swing in the balance of the superiority of attack and defence. From a situation during the middle ages when defences were clearly superior and castles safe, an equilibrium was reached between attack and defence in the middle years of the sixteenth century, to be superseded by a superiority of attack over defence as a result of Vauban's innovations towards the end of the seventeenth century. From then on the situation fluctuated; sometimes the defences were proof against assault and in other periods they crumbled with surprising rapidity.

The trace or outline of a fortification was the result of the pressures imposed upon it, and as pressures changed so did the shape of the trace. Before 1480 height, thickness and solidity were sufficient barriers to aggression, but the invention of gunpowder rapidly changed the situation. In the old castles frontal fire, consisting of projectiles dropped from the walls or stone missiles thrown directly forward, was usually sufficient reply to any attack. By the early sixteenth century it became necessary to introduce a bastion system of defence, where the ground in front of a fortress was criss-crossed with fire through which any attacker must pass. As the range of weapons increased, defences had to be spread further out into the countryside. As the striking power of missiles increased, defences had to be designed with a reduced profile and curved or angled surfaces to deflect their blows. The defences were thus thrown farther and farther out like an explosion, the parts fragmented and yet mutually related. The enlarged circumference and the high cost of building militated against the use of concentric circles of continuous fortifications stretching out like ripples in a pool. Detached forts became a substitute for a continuous enceinte. So the pattern was elaborated.

But an introduction is not the place to tell the story. The body of the text and the illustrations related to it must do that. A word of warning is necessary, however, before a reader unaccustomed to the subject ventures into the text. 'As among seamen,' wrote Sir William Chambers, 'there is a technical language, of which no admiral could be ignorant, without appearing ridiculous; so in architecture, and the professions connected herewith, there are particular modes of expression and terms of art, of which an architect must by no means be ignorant.' Over the centuries military architecture has evolved a language of its own. In order to express succinctly the intricate techniques which have been introduced into the art it was necessary to evolve a large number of specialist words. An explanation of these is necessary if the subject is to be understood. For this reason a glossary has been included near the end of the book which should be sufficient to explain the words used in the text. The contents of the bibliography have created a more difficult problem. Books and articles on military architecture fill many volumes. Only those which have been found relevant to the writing of this book have been included, in the hope that they may provide sources of reference for those who wish to study further.

I close the introduction with a reminder that this subject is not of a warlike and provocative nature, rather it is the very essence of peaceful co-existence. Fortresses were designed to maintain authority, not to usurp it. Military architecture is the art of defence, not of attack. Permanent fortifications are in essence non-aggressive and unprovocative.

Quentin Hughes
Malta 1972

This new edition contains all the material of the original edition to which has been added about a third more text and many new illustrations to help fill some of the gaps which have appeared to me on rereading my original work. Since 1972 there has been a renewed interest in the subject in Britain and throughout the western world. New societies have sprung up to safeguard remaining monuments of fortification to promote an ever-widening interest in the subject of military architecture. Many new books and articles have been published, some of which have provided me with additional information to help expand this new edition. But the subject is vast and large quantities of documentary material still lie largely untouched in the libraries of Europe and the United States for future researchers to investigate with profit. This small book merely touches the fringe of the subject and can be no more than a meagre introduction to military architecture.

Quentin Hughes
Liverpool 1989

The Ancient World

From earliest times man has learnt to protect himself by artificial means. Unlike other animals which depend upon the slow evolution of natural protective devices, he has learnt to clothe his naked body, to warm himself by fire, to protect himself with weapons and secure himself and his possessions with an artificial protective screen which may be termed military architecture.

By the third millennium some cities in Mesopotamia were being fortified, mainly those of the smaller nations in an attempt to ward off the aggressive Assyrians. Walls of brick and stone were built thick and high in a bid to out-top the scaling ladders of attackers. Correspondingly the Assyrians pushed forward the techniques of attack and siege warfare. They breached walls and gates, tunnelled under them in order to make them collapse, scaled them with ladders and carried ramparts by direct assault. In these ways the Assyrians co-ordinated their techniques of attack. Large cumbersome battering-rams, about 5 metres

Walls of Mycenae (below) *and the fortified walls of Tiryns; after Perrot and Chipiez.*

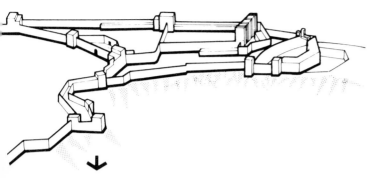

A reconstruction of the Castello Eurialo (Euryalus fort) at Syracuse by Luigi Mauceri.

Underground passages leading to the ditch in the Castello Eurialo.

(16ft) long, running on six wheels, and resembling some ancient tank, were surmounted by a round turret about 6 metres (20ft) high from which archers could give covering fire. The head of the ram could pierce the joints in masonry and, by leverage, could slowly cause a wall to crumble.

GREEK WARFARE

In ancient Greece the stronger cities were placed high on invulnerable sites. The fortifications of Mycenae and Tiryns both date from about 1500 BC. At Mycenae the acropolis, on a naturally strong hillside, was surrounded by a wall of massive hewn masonry, a continuous enceinte without towers. The stronghold was approached from the lower city by a ramp and a passage leading through a double system of gateways; the impressive capital Gate of the Lions, with its monolithic jambs, marked the first entrance to the acropolis. The plan form of the citadel was irregular as

the walls followed the naturally strong line of the ridge.

At Tiryns the hill rose in two stages, enveloped in a cyclopean masonry wall some 9 metres thick and about 20 metres high (30ft × 65ft). It was a long finger of a city with a crosswall cutting off the citadel on the high ground from the lower ward. High massive walls along the escarpment were the defence of this stronghold. The path was a ramp fashioned so that visitors were forced to expose the right side of their bodies unprotected by their shields as they approached the city walls. Only if he passed through three gateways, each at right angles to the last and with no space in which to charge, could any assailant penetrate the main rooms of the palace.

The Euryalus fort, standing on the western edge of a limestone ridge five miles from the centre of Syracuse, is probably the most complete Greek fortress remaining. It was begun by Dionysius I (405–367

Castello Eurialo; massive abutments supported the ballistae.

A mobile Roman tower illustrated in a sixteenth century edition of Vegetius.

BC) but the work was spread over a long period. Modifications were probably still being undertaken by Archimedes when the Romans under Marcellus besieged the fort and sacked the city in 212 BC. Commanding the plains and the road to the centre of Sicily, the fortress projected from the extremity of the town walls like a 'broad nail' along the high salient ridge. Facing the probable direction of attack there were three deep ditches, the centre and the innermost being inter-connected by a series of underground passages probably designed to facilitate the removal of any earth on which attackers might attempt to cross the ditches, and so contrived that an enemy penetrating the subterranean passages was constantly forced to turn to his right thus exposing the unprotected part of his body. There were outworks between the ditches and a bold triangular ravelin was poised above the scarp of the inner ditch. Behind this ravelin stood five huge towers capable of housing heavy ballistae which could pour a devastating fire on to the extremity of the outer ditch. Beyond the ballistae lay the keep, a further enclosure containing the fort's wells and a strong tower at the junction with the city walls.

The development of the techniques of attack and defence went forward apace. Syracuse is credited with the invention of the catapult in 399 BC, a device which could throw stones and arrows with considerable force. The performance of this weapon was improved by the discovery of the principle of exploiting torsion, which was probably applied to catapults as early as 330 BC. Like many weapons of war its introduction frightened people and a contemporary writer, seeing catapult artillery in action for the first time, cried 'Man's martial valour is of no avail any more!' It was the moral effect of artillery which was most telling. As later, with the introduction of gunpowder, the possession of large artillery pieces improved the morale of troops and demoralised the enemy. But ancient artillery was also very accurate, and arrow-shooting and stone-throwing catapults could operate effectively up to about 400–500 metres (1300–1650ft). In an assault their main purpose was to neutralise the defence so that rams could be pushed forward to destroy the walls. In an attack artillery could be used to kill the defenders on a wall, to stop dead a sally from a town and for counter-battery work against machines mounted on the towers of a besieged town. In defence

A precarious method of attacking an enemy fortress; after Vegetius, 1585.

artillery provided covering fire in support of sallies and, placed in elevated situations on towers, was effective in counter-battery work against besiegers' weapons. Already the principle of the tactical handling of artillery was emerging in a manner which has remained operative to this day.

The siege of Tyre by the army of Alexander the Great in 332 BC is a classic and well-recorded example of the outstanding ingenuity displayed by both attack and defence. Alexander benefited from the army reorganisation carried out by his father, Philip of Macedon, his build-up of elaborate siege machinery and the employment of first rate military engineers, but Tyre was a tough nut to crack. The Tyrians withdrew into their stronghold, a city perched on the edge of the sea and providing no firm ground for the erection of the Greeks' engines of attack. There seemed little to fear: Alexander had no navy then available, relief was expected from the Persian fleet and the city was considered impregnable. Alexander however was determined upon its capture and pushed forward his siege with painstaking care and detailed planning. A mole, some 66 metres (216ft) wide, was built out towards the island site of the city and piles were driven into the muddy shore. As the mole was pushed nearer to the city walls, its workmen were constantly harassed by archers and slingers operating from their

*Reconstruction of a stone-throwing onager
by Viollet-le-Duc.*

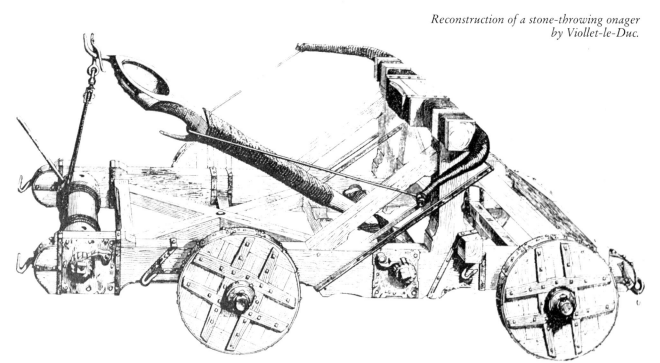

*Reconstruction of a stone-throwing onager
by Viollet-le-Duc.*

lofty positions. The Greeks retaliated by building two tall towers from which they suspended sails and the hides of animals wetted by seawater and soaked in vinegar in an attempt to make them fireproof, but the Tyrians fitted up a fireship filled with combustibles and with two masts projecting from its prow from which were suspended other highly inflammable materials. By loading the stern of the fireship its bows were made to rise high and, caught by the wind, the ship sped towards the mole, ramming the base of the towers which were soon ablaze. The defenders were either consumed by the flames or leapt to their deaths. Swimmers and divers then pulled up the stakes which protected the outer face of the mole and, in the heavy seas which followed, its stonework was swept away. Undeterred, Alexander ordered a new mole to be constructed. It was to be wider and to have more room for the employment of artillery. The Greeks next brought up ships and the investment of the city began, but the navy's task was not easy. In manoeuvring close to the city walls the ships ran on to underwater obstacles, and at anchor their cables were cut by daring commando raids from the town. During the heat of midday the ships themselves were attacked and many sunk by platoons of marines operating from small boats. At night the Greeks retaliated by bombarding the city from floating batteries, but a sudden storm tore their planks apart and many of the heavily armed soldiers fell into the sea.

The assault on the walls finally began from the Greek towers and their artillery on the mole. But the citizens were equally ingenious. Leather bags filled with wet seaweed were suspended from the ramparts to absorb the blows from the large rocks which were flung against the walls. Great revolving machines, like flails, were placed on the walls and when these flails were rapidly rotated they intercepted the darts and missiles, deflecting them from the city. Grappling hooks on long ropes swung out to tear the Greek soldiers from their towers and drop their mangled bodies on the rocks below. Other soldiers were entangled in nets. Red hot sand poured from the battlements penetrated the armour of the assault troops causing them, in removing it, to expose themselves to the arrows of the defenders.

There were times when Alexander considered abandoning the siege, but finally he ordered the great assault, a combined operation from the sea and the mole. Ships with drawbridges, similar in concept to modern infantry landing craft, carried marines into the initial attack. Stone-throwers bombarded and quaked the city walls and arrow-firing catapults put down a barrage of covering fire for the Greek assault battalions. The force of the attack was irresistible. Breaches opened and the Greeks poured into the city. There was no mercy shown. Buildings were put to the flame and their defenders to the sword; 8000 fell at their posts and a further 2000 were crucified as a gesture to appease Alexander's wrath; 30,000 were sold into slavery. The siege had lasted from the middle of January until the middle of July, six months of concentrated attack and defence.

The defensive system of the Greek cities developed slowly over the years and with it came the emergence in embryo of two basic systems of design. The first was the idea of making a curtain wall less vulnerable by placing along it, at intervals, projecting towers from which flanking fire could be poured across the front of the vulnerable curtain. The distance between each pair of towers was dictated by the effective range of the weapons used to flank them. As the towers were pushed forward they became as vulnerable as previously the curtain walls had been and towers were thus designed to support each other so that adjoining towers could always fire on troops assaulting any particular tower. Towers began to be shaped so as to deflect the shot of besiegers' artillery.

By the fourth century BC there was a major revolution in Greek siege technique, largely occasioned by the introduction of the catapult. Towers were built higher so that a defender's artillery could outrange that of an attacker, and larger so that heavier and more numerous artillery pieces could be sited for defence. The casemate was introduced, a chamber within a tower which protected the artillery piece from bad weather, for catapults were susceptible to damp conditions. The pieces fired arrows through slits in the walls and their crews were protected by the masonry of the towers. The difficulty in using this sort of layout was always the restriction it imposed upon manoeuvrability and observation. For this reason the Greeks tended to use circular or semi-circular towers at the most exposed positions of the defensive wall. But they also built towers of pentagonal shape pointed towards the front like the later bastion. These had the advantage that an attacker's shot glanced off their oblique fronts. But because of their pointed shape no artillery in them could fire directly forward, so the towers had to be adequately flanked from their neighbours.

The distinction between these angled towers and the true bastion introduced by Italian engineers at the end of the fifteenth century should be clearly understood. The true bastion was designed so that its faces were elongated from the flanks of its adjoining bastions and it was therefore fully protected by flanking fire. On the other hand the Greek towers were merely pointed to deflect projectiles. This is a misunderstanding which has dogged many of the arguments about the origin of the bastion and has caused at least one writer to suggest that the bastion was invented by the military engineer of the Knights of St John at Rhodes about 1496, when, in fact, his work merely consisted of a Greek-type tower transmitted by succeeding generations of Romans, Byzantines and Saracens to the Knights at Rhodes.

There were ancient Greek examples of superimposed casemates where towers could bring a maximum of defensive fire to bear on any threatened front. This was really the birth of the idea which developed into those nineteenth century multi-gun artillery towers which can still be seen in places like Linz and Verona.

The first development then was the introduction of a system of flanking fire from well-designed projecting towers for the defence of a city wall. It is not necessarily a Greek invention, but certainly Greek engineers utilised this method of defence.

The second development, which has remained one of the basic principles to the present day, was the idea of defence in depth. It is known that at the siege of Syracuse between 213 and 211 BC Archimedes placed his military engines in front of the main wall of the city and had them covered by outworks. This increased their range and effectiveness against assaulting troops and allowed defenders on the outermost city walls to provide covering fire to ensure protection of the artillery. This was the basis of concentric defence which was fully utilised in the Theodosian Walls of Constantinople, the crusader castles in the Holy Land and the frontier forts of Edward I in Wales. The outworks were important and had to be strong. They were adequately provided with ditches, palisades and minefields. Pots filled with seaweed sufficiently compacted to withstand a man's weight, but which would collapse under the weight of an attacker's machines, were buried in the ground. The anti-tank trap is a modern equivalent. The use of all these devices became common practice under the Romans who, if not brilliant technical innovators, were extremely clever at adapting others' ideas.

Only large powerful cities and strategic strongholds could afford to ring themselves with defensive walls. Villages had to withstand threats as best they could, and it may be that the apparently haphazard irregular planning of some ancient villages was the result of a conscious attempt to confuse and bewilder any attacker who penetrated them. The Second World War demonstrated the difficulty of permeating dense urban areas and the comparative ease with which house-to-houses fighting could hold up an apparently more powerful attacker. Witness the four-week survival of the Jews in the Warsaw ghetto against great German superiority in equipment. Villages and small towns were often designed with a series of cul-de-sacs and alleys running at right angles to each other and terminating at a distance of one building-depth from the outer houses of the town. The latter, a continuous block of buildings constructed with blank outer walls, formed a dense defensive belt against attack from the surrounding countryside. Plato hints at this form of design where, by constantly closing the vista of town streets, strangers penetrating the maze were left confused. Thucydides describes how the Thebans lost their way in the narrow streets of Plataea and were surrounded by the villagers who, knowing all the intricacies of their town's layout, were able, unseen, to break through the party walls of their own houses to destroy the attackers. Remnants of this pattern of defence, both the unwindowed outer walls of houses and the apparent confusion of the cul-de-sac system, can be seen today in some of the villages of Malta.

ROMAN DEFENCES

The manner in which the Romans defended their towns is evident from numerous excavations and in the writings of two important authors on the art of fortification, Vitruvius and Vegetius. Neither author possessed much originality and both drew heavily on Greek inspiration but their writings are important for they contain firsthand knowledge of the aims and ideas of the Roman military engineer. Vitruvius was the first man to write about the use of symbolism as a means of promoting defence, such as the psychological impact of using architectural devices such as the caryatid – women with burdens placed upon their heads were to show to posterity the punishment and humiliation which would be meted out to those who failed to defend their city and who conspired with an enemy. Similarly, there had been the representation of captive Persians to arouse patriotism for the defence of freedom among the Greek states. Just as the dangers of defeat could be represented by architectural devices, a feeling of strength could be imparted to a defensive system in order to deter an attacker. The deterrent effect of military architecture has always been one of its most attractive constituents. The Romans often applied rusticated masonry to the towers which flanked the entrances to their towns. Not that rusticated stonework is stronger than ashlar; it is in fact weaker and more liable to be prised apart by attackers' rams,

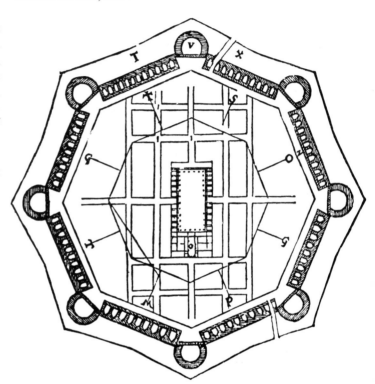

The fortifications of a Roman town by Vitruvius; after Daniele Barbaro, 1567.

but its rugged quality gives the appearance of power; it looks stronger.

Vitruvius stated the principle which had been applied on the approach route to the citadel at Tiryns. 'As troops approach,' he wrote, 'their right side will be next to the wall and will not be protected by their shields.' His most important recommendation was that, in order to be most easily defensible, a city should be round in plan. An angular city, because its walls could obscure an attack from the view of some of its defenders, helped an enemy. This suggestion was entirely at variance with Roman usage where the square or rectangular plan became the almost universal solution for fortresses and marching camps. Vitruvius took the principle even further, suggesting that towers also should be round so that an enemy could be seen from several sides. Towers were to be placed a bowshot apart and curtain walls were to be separated from towers by removable wooden planks so that, should attackers gain a foothold on one of the curtains, they would not be able to exploit this by passing their troops around the circuit of the walls. Each tower could be isolated and become a strongpoint even if surrounded by the enemy. Also, round or

A nineteenth century drawing of the Roman gate, the Porta Nigra at Trèves.

polygonal towers were better than square ones because the angles of square towers could be broken by battering-rams. In the case of round surfaces, even when rams were driven wedge-fashioned towards the centre, they could not significantly damage the masonry. To further strengthen the defences, foundations were to be run out at right angles to the walls like the teeth of a comb.

Vitruvius' tenth book was about military machines and from this can be gathered much knowledge on the artillery of the ancient world. He described the sizes of catapults or scorpions and the methods of stringing and tuning them. He described the capstans, drums, blocks and pulleys of the giant ballistae and he outlined the method of using battering-rams and similar machines. There were machines for boring holes, others for scaling walls. A large wheeled tower, twenty storeys high, had an archers' gallery round each storey. Also there was a tortoise whose purpose was filling ditches in order to make it possible to breach the main wall of a besieged city. To resist blows and ward off fire the tortoise was covered with a double layer of stitched rawhide stuffed with seaweed or straw soaked in vinegar. The tortoise designed by Hegator of Byzantium was an immense affair weighing 218,000 kilos (215 tons), controlled by 100 men and fitted with an iron-pointed ram to breach walls. By the fourth century AD a new weapon, the onager, a single-armed military engine capable of throwing large stones with great accuracy, was in use.

ROMAN FORTRESSES

Two of the greatest sieges in the history of the Roman army, at Avaricum and Alesia, were undertaken by Caesar in his campaign to subjugate Gaul between 58 and 50 BC. A reliable account of Roman siege methods described by Caesar himself has survived. Basically the procedure consisted of constructing a double belt of fortifications, the inner one completely enclosing the enemy city and sufficiently strong to prevent its forces breaking out; the outer belt was directed towards the open country in order to deny help from a relief force and to safeguard the rear of the besieging army.

Roman fortresses were of two kinds, the marching camp and the legionary fortress, and both were based on a gridiron plan of streets. In a legionary fortress the two main streets met at right angles in the centre of the fortress in front of the *principia* or head-

The Roman walls at Portchester; plan.

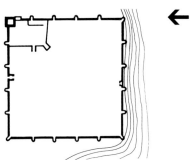

Model in the Grosvenor Museum of the Roman fortress at Chester.

quarters of the legion, and at the extremities of the streets stood the city gates. The legionary fortress, from which many of the planned Roman towns developed, was surrounded by a rectangular or square enceinte with its corners slightly rounded, its walls sometimes punctuated at regular intervals by towers and its gateways supported by pairs of strong towers with casemates. The ramparts were sufficiently wide and deep for the employment of artillery. The plan was therefore quite different from Vitruvius' ideal circular solution for a city. Novaesium (Neuss) on the Rhine opposite Düsseldorf is the most completely excavated example and in Britain there are other fine remains at Chester and Caerleon. The earthen ramparts at Chester were some 8.5 metres (28ft) wide at the base and 5.5 metres (18ft) high to the terreplein, which was sufficiently wide for the easy movement of troops protected by an ample parapet. The construction of a legionary fortress was reinforced by turf laid on logs which were strapped together. At a later date an outer skin of stone was applied to form a more permanent defence line and towers were inserted at intervals. Beyond the ramparts lay a ditch, usually with a steep counterscarp, augmented by a thorn hedge barrier so that enemy troops penetrating the

ditch would find their retreat impeded by sharp thorns as they stood exposed to retaliatory fire from the walls.

The other type of Roman fortress, either an auxiliary fort or a marching camp, was usually smaller, although laid out in the same basic gridiron plan and surrounded by a rectangular rampart. Marching camps protected the legions in hostile countries. Turf ramparts about 1.5 metres (5ft) high, thrown up from the material of an encircling ditch, provided a protective screen for an encamped legion sheltered in its leather tents. The gateways were usually protected by a curved extension, a device which developed in the seventeenth century into the hornwork of the Vauban period, intended to force any attackers to approach the camp on an oblique line with their right sides exposed to the defenders' fire.

Auxiliary forts were placed at vulnerable points in the countryside to ward off sudden attack. Two of the best groups exist in Britain. Along the east and south coasts from Norfolk to Hampshire, a chain of forts, called the 'forts of the Saxon Shore', nine of which have survived, were constructed in the third century AD. This was the first major coastal defence system in Britain, all the forts being placed at strategic points such as harbours or river mouths. The forts

Portchester Castle.

were mostly rectangular in plan, surrounded by high massive stone walls with circular towers projecting at intervals and sufficiently large for mounting ballistae. Portchester, near Portsmouth, is a well-preserved example. Once a large square Roman fort, the sides of which measured nearly 180 metres (590ft), it had twenty rounded towers placed at regular intervals, each one hollow with floors of timber capable of carrying light ballistae, and open to the interior of the fort. The towers at the corners were set diagonally. In the early middle ages, possibly in the reign of Henry I, a large square keep and its attendant castle were built into the north-west corner of this Roman fort.

The south coast forts were originally thought to be part of a defensive system constructed against Saxon sea raiders, but a recent theory has been advanced which suggests that they may have been built by Carausius, a Roman naval officer who had mutinied against imperial rule and wished to protect himself against a possible Roman counter-attack by the fleet of Maximian.

HADRIAN'S WALL

In the north of Britain there remains the most dramatic expression of Roman defensive architecture. Hadrian's Wall marks the northernmost limit of the Roman Empire. In about the year 122 the emperor ordered the construction of this mighty barrier stretching from coast to coast, over 120 kilometres (75 miles) long and some 4.5 metres (15ft) high, with a 2-metre (6.5ft) parapet originally designed to be about 3 metres (10ft) wide. In front, where the ground was particularly vulnerable to an attack, a ditch some 8 metres (26ft) wide, dug to an average depth of 2.7 metres (9ft), gave further protection. Guardrooms or milecastles were placed every mile along the wall with two guard turrets between each. Behind the wall ran a military road for the rapid movement of garrison troops stationed in seventeen strategic forts stretching from Newcastle to the Solway Firth.

These latter forts were rectangular in plan and straddled the wall so that their northern front projected into the open country beyond. The gates were strongly fortified by supporting artillery towers, two of which lay astride the wall. This was the solution in forts like Benwell and Chesters, though others had their northern walls formed from the wall itself. At each end the two coasts were guarded by watchtowers and protected by additional forts to prevent an enemy outflanking the wall.

CHAPTER TWO

Castles of the Middle Ages

The battle of Adrianpole was fought in 378. Not only was it the most fearful defeat suffered by the Roman army for nearly six hundred years, but it saw the demise of the Roman infantry and changed the whole pattern of warfare. Cavalry, forerunner of the armoured knights of the middle ages and the crusades, became the main striking force of an army in the field. Infantry, its role now subordinated, garrisoned the forts and castles in the years that followed. Infantry soldiers began to discard their heavy armour which was no match against the terrific impact of the mail-clad horse and rider. The power of the infantry soldier did not return until, in the fourteenth and early fifteenth centuries, he developed a means of defending himself with missiles. It will be recalled that English archers at Crecy and Agincourt were able to break a powerful cavalry charge before it could get near to them: at Laupen in 1339 Swiss pikemen, using long pointed weapons which outreached the horsemen's swords and maces, perfected an alternative method of breaking the power of cavalry.

NORMAN STRONGHOLDS

In the meantime a new system of defence was evolved. Mobile armour was used to break an enemy, and feudal castles (that is, strongholds held by an occupying power) were used to hold down a subjugated race. This is what happened in Britain. William the Conquerer's cavalry, admittedly with considerable difficulty, finally shattered the English infantry at Hastings and William's followers then set in train a systematic occupation of the country. Hundreds of castles of subjugation were built. At first these Norman strongholds consisted of a motte and bailey, the motte being a mound of earth surrounded by a protective wooden palisade which, with the passage of time and the availability of money, was rebuilt as a strong stone wall, then called a shell keep. There are many well-preserved examples, among the best being Launceston and Restormel castles in the west country. The

Restormel Castle.

Tower of London. (Crown Copyright)

motte became the strongroom of the castle, a prison for captives and a safe retreat for its lord. When built of stone it was fireproof. The bailey was more spacious, providing accommodation in peacetime and a refuge for animals and tenants in time of attack. The building of this type of castle at Hastings is illustrated on the Bayeux tapestry.

The massive square stone keeps are among the glories of Norman architecture, built so strongly that many have survived almost intact. The construction of the main ones was supervised by Gundulf, Bishop of Rochester from 1077 to 1108. He had taken part in a crusade and possibly had seen the Byzantine citadel at Saône, for its dimensions are close to those of the Tower of London's White Tower and the heavy buttresses resemble those at Colchester. The White Tower, now the central core of the Tower of London, was built by William the Conqueror to protect and con-

trol the city. Approximately square in plan, its battlements rise to a height of 27.5 metres (90ft), the walls some 4.5 metres (15ft) thick at the base. To further strengthen this structure a thick crosswall was constructed the full height of the building, and a second massive wall cuts off from the rest of the keep the chapel of St John and its crypts, the apsidal projection of which can be seen on the outside of the building.

Rochester Castle on the old Roman road from the coast to London is mentioned in the Domesday Book. Part of the castle was built by Gundulf about 1087 but the dominant keep-tower, the most splendid in Britain, was added about 1127 during the reign of Henry I. Rochester Castle was involved in three major sieges and still stands today. King John's siege of 1215 was described by a contemporary chronicler as follows: 'Our age has not known a siege so hard pressed nor so strongly resisted.' During the

The Norman keep at Rochester Castle.

Barons' Wars it resisted siege engines until relieved by the king. The keep is square, 21.3 metres (70ft) across at ground level, strengthened by a splayed base, and measuring 34.5 metres (113ft) to the top of the parapet. The corners are strengthened by towers which rise a further 3.6 metres (12ft). Originally timber hoarding was cantilevered and roofed over so that archers could fire and drop missiles from a protected position. Like the Tower of London it has an internal crosswall which divides the interior.

Dover Castle, called by Matthew Paris in the thirteenth century 'the key to England', is on a naturally strong site guarding the harbour. Probably the strongest castle in the country, its main buildings date from the reign of Henry II (1154–89). It was immensely expensive, costing about £7000 (the royal revenue was then only £10,000 a year) and only rivalled by Richard I's castle at Château-Gaillard. The keep, built between 1181 and 1188, was designed by Maurice the Engineer who may also have been responsible for Newcastle-on-Tyne keep. Although conservative in design, the general concept of Dover Castle is advanced. It was the first castle in western Europe which convincingly employed a concentric system of defence. This system, consisting of two independent defensive walls, had been used on the Theodosian Line at Constantinople in the fifth century. At Dover the inner curtain probably begun in 1185, overshadows the outer curtain, whose defenders were thus covered from above. The outer curtain, thrust forward, took the brunt of an attack and held it at arm's length from the stronghold. Flanking towers project at intervals along both curtain walls, a device re-introduced by Henry II at Orford Castle but used much earlier by the Romans at places like Portchester.

Many of the Norman keeps were retained in castles which grew around them, and some were modified and embellished to provide more up to date accommodation. Of these latter Kenilworth is an example. It has aptly been described as looking like a burnt out factory, but it must have been magnificent in its heyday, embellished by the Earl of Leicester and containing John of Gaunt's hall which, after Westminster, was the finest in the land. A richly ornamental garden gave a sense of spaciousness conducive to gracious living. Kenilworth Castle dates from Norman times. The great square keep was once stark and forbidding, with small slits piercing its thick masonry. Leicester cut generous windows in it to throw sunlight into the interior and parliamentarians blew out its rear wall when it succumbed, like so many English castles, to the cannon of the Civil War.

SWABIAN CASTLES IN ITALY

Few kings, except perhaps Edward I of England, have rivalled Frederick II as castle-builders. Hohenstaufen Emperor of the West and King of Sicily, Frederick in the year 1220, initiated a policy of pulling down all private castles in his domain in Italy and building a series of magnificent royal strongholds. Interested in architecture himself, his Swabian castles show a consistency which he may have inspired for they are clear statements of regal power, well-proportioned and symmetrical in plan. Castel del Monte in Apulia is the most beautiful. The octagonal castle, with its eight sturdy octagonal towers projecting clearly beyond the curtain wall, was intended to act as a central keep on high ground surrounded by a second peripheral curtain wall which was never built. Frederick's love of classical art is reflected not only in the symmetry of the plan, but in the pilastered and pedimented main doorway. There may also have been some influence from the Holy Land as the emperor undertook a crusade in 1227. There are French affinities too, especially in the similarity of the plan form to that of the castle at Boulogne (1231), Castel del Monte dating from about 1240. Some eight years later Frederick began the castle at Prato, a square plan with massive

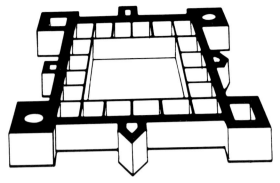

Above and right: *Castello dell'Imperatore at Prato.*

Below: *Castel del Monte.*

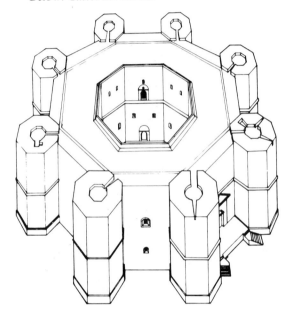

square corner towers and intermediate curtain towers, two of which are pointed or angular-shaped, perhaps a conscious revival of Greek and Roman forms. The tops of the walls and towers are battlemented, their parapets pierced by crenelles and protected by Guelph merlons of a later period, showing a characteristic zigzag silhouette against the sky.

In south-eastern Italy there are other castles of the period built by Frederick, at Bari, Trani, Lucera, Termoli and Gioia del Colle, but their original outlines are partly obscured by later building. In troubled Sicily, seething with disorder, Frederick built his main strong castles – Syracuse, Augusta and, most imposing of all, the Castello Ursino at Catania. Catania, designed by Lentini and begun in 1239, combined the comfort of a royal residence with the requirements of defence. Symmetrical and mathematically precise, a vaulted perimeter of thick walls enclosed a square courtyard. There are four corner circular towers, and four semi-circular towers are placed centrally on the curtain walls. The concept is clearly Roman, but all of Frederick's castles show affinities to both Byzantine and Saracenic fortresses in the Middle East. Whether

the Italian examples were derivative or shared a common source has not yet been convincingly established.

THE CRUSADER CASTLES

Although the First Crusade began in 1095 most of the significant castle-building in the Holy Land was undertaken later and was an extension of twelfth and thirteenth century architectural concepts in France. The influence of Byzantine castles must not, however, be underestimated, for Constantinople lay in the path of Godfrey of Bouillon's First Crusade. Its fortifications stood intact with a landline dating from the time of Theodosius II (408–50), unbreached for a thousand years until it finally fell to the Turks in 1453. The Theodosian Walls stretched unbroken from the Golden Horn to the Sea of Marmara, a concentric line of defences pierced by seven main gates. The line was extremely strong, consisting of a main inner wall 4.5 metres thick and 12 metres high (15ft × 39ft), with 96 projecting battlemented towers, some square, some octagonal, rising to a height of 18 metres (59ft). There was an open space, then the second wall between 7.5 and 9 metres (25–30ft) high flanked by ten square

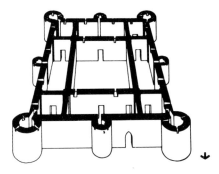

Castello Ursino at Catania in Sicily.

towers, an outer esplanade 12 metres wide and a final defensive parapet. Beyond this lay the ditch, 18 metres wide and 6 metres deep (59ft × 20ft), normally kept dry but capable of being flooded at short notice from the city's water supply. It was a most complex design of interrelated defences, each supporting its neighbour. There was nothing like it in the west and the city must have been a revelation to the crusader armies.

In the early years of the crusades the Franks, backed by a large army, had the initiative, but their strategy was poor. With their minds set upon the psychological victory of the capture of Jerusalem, both Aleppo and Damascus, a constant threat to their flank, were left unsubdued. Energy was dissipated and the christians carved out an impossibly shaped kingdom some 800 kilometres (500 miles) long and rarely more than 80 to 96 kilometres (50–60 miles) wide. The long

flank, instead of resting on the inhospitable sands of the desert, became in the years that followed a springboard for counter-attack by the Saracens. After the initial christian enthusiasm there was a continuous shortage of manpower, alleviated only temporarily by the army of the Third Crusade. Thus immense and strong fortifications were demonstrated to be prerequisite to holding the new kingdom. The castles constructed by the Templar and Hospitaller knights were the most powerful buildings of their time and they revolutionised military thinking in the west. The square keep was developed into a stronghold consisting of two or more linked towers, both a last line of defence in the event of a siege, and a highly protected core against any mutinous uprising of a mercenary garrison. The keep was ringed by concentric lines of curtain walls studded with round towers of deep

Le Krak des Chevaliers; an aerial reconstruction by Sauvageot.

salient capable of flanking the vulnerable curtains. Three or more tiers rose one above the other so that the archers with their now efficient bows could pour a devastating fire on an enemy. The old Greco-Roman device of exposing invaders to a series of right-angled turns in order to penetrate a castle gate was used. Machicolation was systematically developed into a corbelled timber parapet with holes in its floor through which stones and red-hot material could be dropped on the attackers. Finally, the castle was thought of as a device for providing both active and passive defence. Posterns were provided so that the garrison could sally out and harass besiegers when they least expected it.

In peacetime the castles became the business and administrative centres of the land, controlling large, highly efficient farms. In wartime their careful siting gave them control over each vulnerable pass and coastal anchorage, so that the castles stood like a chain along the length of the Holy Land. They were often grouped for interdependence and sited so that signals could be passed with great rapidity from one to another.

The greatest was Krak des Chevaliers, stronghold of the Knights of St John. It stood on a naturally defensible spur, watching over the Homs Gap. Only to the south was it vulnerable to direct assault and against this stood a massive keep of three linked towers standing above the castle's main reservoir, a deep water-filled moat. The knights took over an older castle on the same site and modified it in the 1140s, but the main work of construction was carried on after the earthquake of 1202 when complete redesigning took place. The plan was concentric with

View of Krak from the south-west; after Rey.

Margat Castle from the south-east; after Rey.

Edward I's castle at Rhuddlan.

two tiers of curtain walls interspersed between projecting towers. The bases of the inner walls were further strengthened by a massive talus where the masonry was sloped outwards as protection against mining. The main entrance was in the eastern wall, approached up the steep scarp by a zigzag path which exposed an enemy to a barrage of missiles from the high walls. Each line of defence was supported by one above. 'A fortress, like a spiral spring, should offer more resistance the more it is compressed.' Krak was immensely strong and was never fairly taken. The Saracens attacked on at least twelve occasions and by 1271 it was held by no more than a skeleton garrison. Even then it fell as a result of cunning rather than by direct assault. A forged letter purporting to have come from the knights' headquarters induced its commander to lay down his arms and surrender his castle.

Krak, according to T E Lawrence, was 'the most wholly admirable castle in the world'. There were many other significant bastions in the Holy Land, but there is only space for two references. Margat lies on the Syrian coast. An irregular fortress of considerable size, in 1186 it became the property of the Knights of St John who turned it into their headquarters. Its system of defence is less easily read than Krak, but the castle consists basically of a triangular citadel with a double perimeter of walls. Two of its corners are joined to an outer ward which is only partly concentric. Saône is more impressive, its walled enclosure occupying about 5 hectares (12½ acres) on a narrow spit of land running from north-east to south-west and dropping on three sides into deep gorges. The ground is conveniently bisected to form a lower bailey on the promontory and an upper bailey with a keep formed from the old Byzantine castle. The north-east front is of necessity more strongly defended and here there is another deep ditch cut across the peninsula, with a tall needle of rock which rises 27 metres (89ft) from the bed of the 18-metre (60ft) wide ditch to support the bridge leading to the main gate. It is indeed forbidding and was only captured by Saladin in 1188 after heavy bombardment with mangonels against a garrison far too depleted to hold so large a perimeter.

In 1291 the knights withdrew to their base camp at Acre and, before a devastating attack, with all the paraphernalia of siege warfare, they made their last

stand. After six weeks of siege they surrendered and withdrew for ever from the Holy Land.

THE EDWARDIAN CASTLES IN WALES

The great works of Edward I in Wales are a culmination of the long line of development from Roman and Byzantine times. Like the Doric order, by fine adjustments over generations the medieval fortress was brought to a kind of perfection. Edward was probably the greatest castle-builder in the middle ages and his North Wales castles formed the greatest fortification of that period. It was an expensive undertaking and one marvels at the organisational ability of the English Crown. Some money had to be borrowed from Italian banks but, to keep the undertaking in perspective, one should realise that it was to cost more to maintain the English army in the field with its naval support, marines and crossbowmen, than it did to build the Welsh castles at Conway, Caernarvon, Harlech, Criccieth and Bere. As a crusader he had strengthened the defences of Acre and, probably on his return home in 1273, had commissioned James of St George from Savoy to carry out his projects. His work in Britain falls into three periods. In the initial campaign to bottle up the Welsh in their mountain fastness, Edward ordered the building of castles and towns to secure his

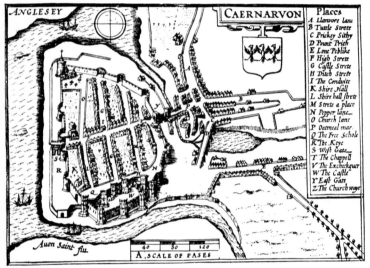

Caernarvon Castle from the river.

John Speed's map of the town and castle at Caernarvon, 1610.

reach the central room but could not easily attack the defenders in the gallery. Rhuddlan Castle was begun in the same year and work continued without pause until 1282. It was built on the river so that it could be supplied from the sea, and it consisted of a high lozenge-shaped inner ward with east and west gateways at the angles of the curtains, buttressed by pairs of large drum towers. Lower walls in the moat surrounded the outer ward, providing the advanced battlements of a concentric design. To the south-west the river covered the rear of the castle but because of the slope of the ground the outer walls are here too far forward to receive effective cover from the battlements of the inner ward.

War broke out again in 1282 and it took time for Edward to starve the Welsh into submission. He then began the systematic planting of English boroughs deep in the Welsh hinterland: Conway, Caernarvon, Denbigh, Criccieth and, in 1284, Harlech, the most impressive of all. Some, like Criccieth, were adaptations of earlier Welsh castles. Most of the remaining work at Criccieth dates from its Welsh occupation, although the two drum towers of the inner ward were strengthened and heightened by the English. Caernarvon, begun in 1283 and still unfinished by 1323, was planned as a seat of royal government and a palace for the Prince of Wales after the English abandoned the idea of using Rhuddlan as their capital in Wales. Caernarvon Castle has a strange plan. Its walls follow a long irregular contour interspersed by towers and give support to a gridiron fortified colonial town. The curtain walls are high, sometimes splayed at the base, and a crosswall originally divided

lines of communication. He had control of the sea and could victual his castles from ships. Flint, Rhuddlan and Aberystwyth were all in the first contract. In most cases, like Flint, the scheme envisaged a strong citadel attached to a walled town which was laid out on a geometrical grid plan. The town was for colonists attracted by adventure, favourable taxation laws and other inducements. The townspeople served the garrison and the garrison defended the town. It was a basic colonial solution adopted by both Edward and Saint Louis in the French Wars.

Flint was begun in 1277, a square castle with four corner towers, one of which was much larger than the others and was detached from the curtain wall so that it acted as a defensible keep. In some respects it was similar to the donjon at the Château de Coucy, built half a century earlier, massive and impressive. However, it had a strange feature, for there appear to have been two concentric walls leaving a circular central space not directly accessible to a peripheral gallery above it, so that anyone breaking into the tower might

Harlech Castle.

what is now optimistically described as an inner and outer ward. Supporting fire was provided from the battlements of the high towers and, from a curious feature, a number of additional small towers which rose even higher within the core of the main towers. The Eagle Tower has three of these devices. The proportions of the octagonal towers, and the way in which striped masonry of dark and light stones has been used, are so reminiscent of Constantinople that one must accept that the linear quality of Caernarvon is modelled on the New Rome.

Caernarvon certainly set out to impress. Its bulk must have towered above the low, single-storey Welsh cottages in the vicinity, making it look invulnerable. Edward appears to have been interested in history and the heritage of his realm and royal descent. He referred, from time to time, to Arthurian legend. In choosing Caernarvon he chose the site near an ancient Roman fortress, Segontium, memorably described by Welsh poets in the *Mabinogion* as a place of gold and magnificence. It would seem plausible that, at his new Welsh capital, Caernarvon, he should try to link the place symbolically with a noble past, particularly to those massive walls of Theodosius which protected the Roman Christian capital at Constantinople from assault by the infidels.

Conway, with its walled town, stands on the river's edge. Also designed by James of St George, it was started in 1283, ready to receive its garrison in only two years and almost completed in five. It was very expensive, with building costs running in the region of £6000 a year. One can appreciate the expenditure poured out by the English exchequer in this

programme of holding down Wales. By 1285 Conway alone was employing 1500 builders; it was the most costly of all Edward's castles in Wales.

Using Conway as a springboard, Edward I, in the year 1283, passed his army along the coast to Harlech. With them went masons and quarrymen for the construction of this majestic castle, for Harlech represents the summit of medieval castle-building. Perched on a craggy site, it looks out over the bay of Cardigan to the towers of Criccieth, clearly visible on the opposite shore. Its plan is symmetrical on an east–west axis. It consists of a commodious inner ward containing the main garrison accommodation surrounded by a high curtain wall between three and four metres thick. From the corners project circular towers with turrets, similar to those at Caernarvon, rising within the towers on the north and south fronts. The outer ward is narrow and its battlements, which follow the perimeter of the main curtain, are kept low so that the tiers of fire are closely integrated. On the east face a great bulk of masonry encases the entrance to the inner ward, and this was to become the characteristic keep-gatehouse of the English castle. The concept was not entirely new; in embryo it can be seen in the Porta Nigra at Trier and the gatehouses of Roman towns in Britain. James of St George had used it earlier at Rhuddlan and in a modified form at Caernarvon. And the idea of placing a citadel in the forefront of the attack, and yet capable of complete isolation from the remainder of the fortress, was seen at Krak des Chevaliers. But the essence of the English keep-gatehouse is in the idea of creating an active defence by pushing the headquarters into the forefront of the battle so that the commander can witness and be fully informed of the progress of the assault. His living and fighting accommodation were therefore provided in this building. In addition to one portcullis on the main gate another was probably provided at the rear of the

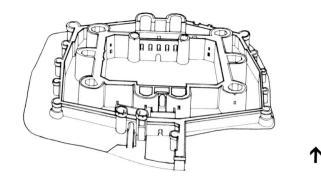

Beaumaris Castle.

keep-gatehouse so that it could be completely isolated from troops in the rest of the castle. This was always a useful precaution against the possibility of mutiny. Psychologically the keep-gatehouse imposes a feeling of strength at the point most vulnerable to attack and emphasises the age-old theory of the effect of deterrence. This device appears to have worked at Harlech for in 1294 the castle was besieged by Prince Madog whose forces were repulsed by a garrison of thirty-seven soldiers. The immense expenditure of between £8000 and £9000, on this one building was thereby justified.

Beaumaris Castle belongs to the third period,

after the Welsh Revolt. It was begun in 1295 and the outer curtain was added in 1316 by Nicholas de Derneford, certainly carrying out St George's original design. Beaumaris is somewhat similar in plan to Harlech, although the site is very different. Low down on the shore, on a flat site, it watches the northern entrance to the Menai Straits. Because of the threat of attack both from the land and along the narrow coastal strip from the sea, Beaumaris duplicates the keep-gatehouse and additional semi-circular towers are introduced mid-way along the curtain on the east and west sides, equal in size and strength to the four corner ones. The moat originally went right round the castle

Harlech Castle, showing the arcs of fire available to the defending crossbowmen.

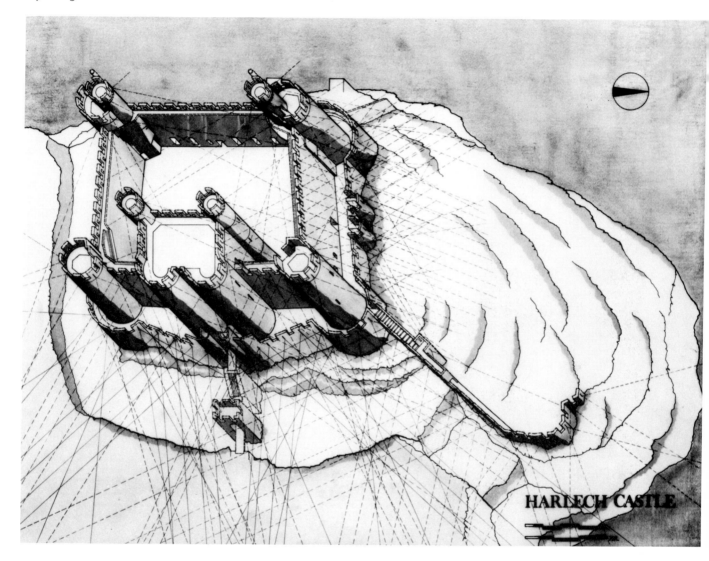

and the low outer battlements were provided with flanking fire from smaller regularly placed towers. Except for the little dock, built for the safe anchorage of English ships, and the position of the northern gate, the plan has an almost perfect symmetry.

Although mostly designed by the Savoyard military engineer, James of St George, it can be seen that the North Wales castles differed amongst themselves both in shape and size. Caernarvon, as one would expect from its status, was large, but Beaumaris was largest of all. However, in spite of the variations, two basic types of castle emerge. Conway, Caernarvon and Harlech were built high with impressive

single outer walls, with turrets rising higher still. The reason for this was because, near at hand and within range, lay high ground from which an enemy might bombard the castle. High walls hid most of the interior from a spying enemy and usually the main apartments and royal accommodation were placed behind the outer walls that faced the threat, thus screening them from view. If the castle walls reached the height of the nearby hills, the defenders could reply with a firepower as effective as that which could be mounted by the attackers.

Flint, the earliest of the castles, is in a different category and Builth was mainly earthworks.

Beaumaris Castle, showing the archers' arcs of fire on one side of the castle only. It must be realised that there was a similar arrangement of firepaths on the far side of the castle not shown in this drawing.

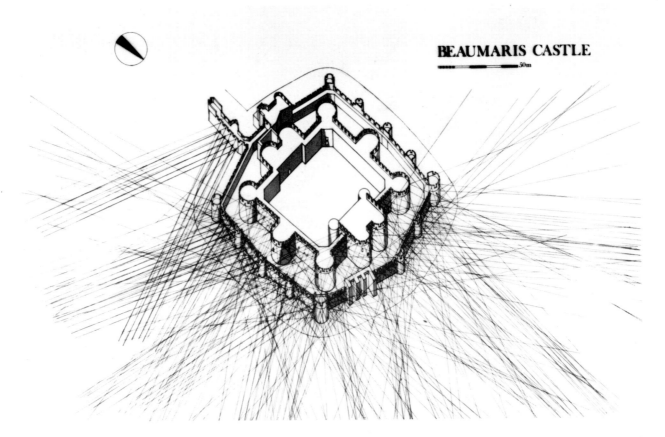

BEAUMARIS CASTLE

50m

The other basic type had concentric walls. Although in theory they provided positions for archers on the inner, higher walls to give covering fire to their more exposed colleagues on the outer walls, it is uncertain whether the concentric system was originally developed in order to provide a coordinated defensive system, or was merely a succession of barriers which allowed the defenders to fall back, stage by stage, leaving killing ground between the walls where an attacker would perish.

Aberystwyth, Rhuddlan, Harlech and Beaumaris are concentric and their plans show a steady development to the final solution at Beaumaris where the idea of an active defence is fully realised with carefully laid out firepaths so that missile defence and passive masonry are fully integrated. By using a model crossbow similar in size to that used to defend the Welsh castles it has been possible to plot accurately the arc of fire from every embrasure on some of these castles, bearing in mind that the width of the opening

is not the same as the arc of fire which is determined by the shoulder width of an archer plus his upheld bow.

The survey drawings show how Conway, depending for strength upon its rock base and high walls, had most of the firing positions placed high up, leaving dead ground below the castle walls which could only be covered by an archer exposing himself or by dropping objects on an attacker. These were limited by the difficulty of carrying them up to the battlements and storing them there where they would occupy valuable space. By experiment it was proved that an object dropped from the battlements took so long to descend that an attacker would have had time to move away and avoid it. Therefore, stones, oil or Greek Fire would have been saved and only used at a crucial stage in battle when the foot of the walls and towers was teeming with attackers.

In contrast, Harlech has a more carefully planned system of fire with firepaths criss-crossing to

Caerphilly Castle.

cover the approaches and, in particular, the ditch. The trouble there was the high ground behind the castle so the inner walls had to be built high and stiffened at that front by a keep-gatehouse. As a result there is not a good configuration of inner and outer walls, the inner walls being too high to permit archers to give covering fire without exposing themselves, and then only ineffectual plunging fire against smaller targets. Also, there was dead ground in front of some of the walls where an enemy could hide and prepare an assault.

Beaumaris shows the solution fully thought out with the ground in front criss-crossed by crossbow firepaths and with hardly a foot of ground left uncovered. The inner walls are not too high, for there is no high ground within range, and the killing space is adequate and covered. The firepaths have been worked out logically and completely. However, one must remember that, although all these firing positions were provided, the garrison of a Welsh castle often had

no more than fifteen crossbowmen. Their weapons were slow to load but could be loaded by others and stacked ready for use. It still meant that, during a siege, the archers would have had to move to threatened positions, leaving other embrasures unoccupied, but with the happy realisation that it took more time for an attacker to shift the direction of his attack than for a defender to move into a position to resist it.

CAERPHILLY CASTLE

Caerphilly is not one of the royal castles built for the control of Wales. Lying in the south of the country, it belonged to Gilbert de Clare, ninth Earl of Gloucester, and son-in-law of Edward I. It took a long time to build and is therefore more complex and less articulate than Harlech and Beaumaris. Probably James of St George was involved in the work for the inner castle bears some resemblance to Beaumaris. It has an

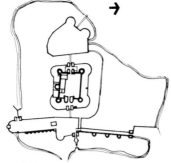

Caerphilly Castle.

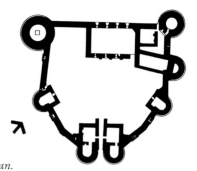

The great barrage at Caerphilly.

Kildrummy Castle; plan.

approximately square inner ward with four corner towers and a powerful keep-gatehouse on the east face capable of being cut off by portcullis from both inside and out. There is an outer battlemented ward surrounded by a moat, so the defence system was concentric. On the west side there is another keep-gatehouse which provided supporting fire for the west gate in the outer battlements, buttressed between two further drum towers. One suggestion is that at some date the castle was turned round and the western gatehouse defences built on what became the new front; for protecting them is a further defensive system called a hornwork, with its own gateway and drawbridge spanning a further moat. The ground to the north and south was flooded to provide an impenetrable barrier some 150 metres (500ft) across. In order to do this the great barrage, a triumph of engineering, was constructed across the whole eastern face of the castle, forming a front of over 250 metres (820ft). The barrage consisted of a double wall with towers and massive

buttresses and, behind these, wide platforms or terrepleins for the outermost defence of the castle. It was a truly formidable concept. Although thrice attacked, on each occasion Caerphilly Castle held out.

EDWARD I IN SCOTLAND

By 1296 Edward had conquered Scotland. Wallace's revolt of the following year was cracked at Falkirk and the English began to consolidate their position by the construction of castles in a manner they were already adopting in Wales. James of St George went north in 1302 and in the following year he was probably engaged on the design of the great keep-gatehouse at Kildrummy Castle which, both in shape and scale, is not dissimilar from Harlech. The castle is now badly damaged but it seems clear that the general layout of the enceinte predates the English occupation and probably drew direct inspiration from France. The present plan is almost semi-circular with a keep-gatehouse in the centre of the semi-circle and large

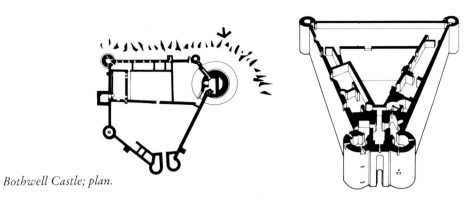

Bothwell Castle; plan.

Left and below:
Caerlaverock Castle.
(Crown Copyright)

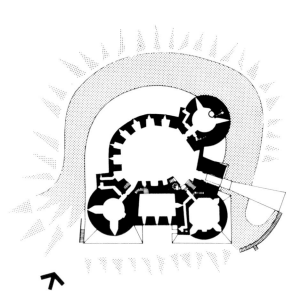

Castell Coch.

drum towers at the north and west corners, the latter being more pronounced and reminiscent of the donjon at Coucy. The connection is easy to establish, for Alexander II of Scotland married Marie de Coucy in 1239. The similarity with the donjon tower at Bothwell Castle, also thirteenth century, is even more pronounced. Here the tower is much larger than its neighbours and is partially isolated from the inner ward by a segment of moat constructed inside the castle.

Caerlaverock Castle is the third important Scottish example dating from the thirteenth century. It links the semi-circular plan of Kildrummy and the asymmetrical but pointed solution at Bothwell to form a perfect equilateral triangle with a powerful keep-gatehouse at one apex.

Caerlaverock is well preserved, its curtains and towers rising directly from the waters of the moat. This is no concentric design. It was begun in 1290 and successfully besieged by the English in 1300 who held it until 1312. The keep-gatehouse, the western curtain and the southern tower date from the period of the original castle. The eastern tower and the other curtains are mainly fourteenth century and perhaps the evidence is too scant to prove that they stood upon earlier foundations, and that the castle was originally triangular.

CASTLE-BUILDING

Throughout Britain castle-building was incessant in the fourteenth and fifteenth centuries, the need for heavy fortification slowly giving way to the provision of more comfortable living accommodation.

Although an almost entirely nineteenth century structure, Castell Coch, near Cardiff, is interesting for it successfully reproduces, certainly on the outside, the characteristics of an early fourteenth century Welsh castle. It was restored in 1875 with imagination and artistic licence, but with considerable integrity, by the Marquess of Bute and his architect

Bodiam Castle.

William Burges. It stands on a hillock and has an almost round courtyard with circular towers on the north, east and south faces. The entrance gate and drawbridge lead between the first two towers with the southern tower acting as a keep. The main hall and living accommodation lie between the keep and the southern or kitchen tower.

Bodiam Castle in Sussex is a fine representative example from the late fourteenth century. It was built in 1385 to defend the countryside from French naval raids, the river Rother being navigable as far as Bodiam bridge. The castle plan is rectangular with four corner drum towers 9 metres (30ft) in diameter rising to a height of over 18 metres (59ft), thus

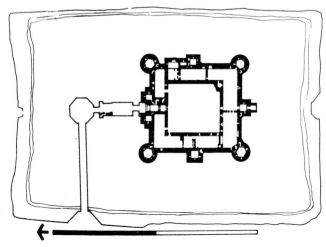

Carcassonne; plan.

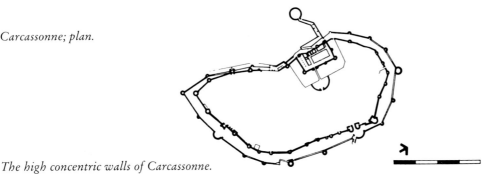

The high concentric walls of Carcassonne.

dominating the lower curtain wall which is further supported by rectangular towers in the middle of three sides and an elaborate keep-gatehouse on the fourth. The castle stands in a wide moat and was approached by narrow bridges and a walkway which swung at right angles in front of the keep-gatehouse in order to expose the unshielded sides of attackers in true classical manner.

FRENCH CASTLES

In France the tradition of castle-building goes back earlier than in Britain. The Franks had carried their ideas with them to the Holy Land and embodied them in the castles of the crusaders. Swabian kings had taken them to Italy and the Normans brought their tradition to England and later to Scotland. In France there

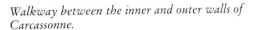

Walkway between the inner and outer walls of Carcassonne.

The citadel at Carcassonne.

still stands the innumerable remains of castles and fortified towns dating from the eleventh century onwards.

Carcassonne is the finest remaining example of a town defended by concentric walls of fortifications but has been elaborately restored by Viollet-le-Duc in the nineteenth century. The core of the inner rampart dates back to the fifth century and was erected by Visigoths. Outside this lies an open passage, or esplanade, some 8 metres (26ft) wide and then the outer rampart, battlemented and lower. The ground, clear of scrub and trees, drops away so that the city stands on a clearly defined natural plateau. Round, square and semi-circular towers with turret roofs project from both curtain walls at regular intervals. There are only two gates to the city, guarded by drawbridge, portcullis and bartizan, and the defence is strengthened by a high-walled citadel.

Aigues-Mortes is also thirteenth century. It was laid out by Louis IX in 1240 on the Rhone delta to

Opposite: *The donjon at Loches.*

Left: *The Tower of Constance at Aigues-Mortes.*

Below: *The walls of Aigues-Mortes.*

form a base camp for troops embarking on the crusade. The town is approximately rectangular in plan, with streets crossing at right angles. It has a high curtain wall punctuated at regular intervals by towers which rise above the ramparts of the curtain and are topped by additional slender turrets like those found at Caernarvon. Where the streets terminate at the town walls the towers are coupled in Roman fashion to accommodate additional garrisons at these vulnerable points. At one corner stands the massive Tower of Constance, a typical French donjon, built between 1241 and 1250 as a safe residence for the king. Isolated from the two walls, which are in any case later in date, it is an almost solid chunk of masonry pierced by very thin arrow slits and with two fine gothic vaulted rooms some 12 metres (40ft) high scooped out of its interior. The present battlements date from the seventeenth century. The walls of the town were constructed after Louis' death in 1270 by his son Philip the Bold and carried out by a Genoese contractor

Château-Gaillard; plan.

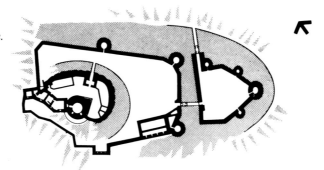

Drum towers of the château at Angers.

called Boccanegra. Their splendid preservation is largely due to the fact that the town lay on the deserted sandhills of the river delta.

Loches has one of the most impressive donjons in France. The castle was begun soon after 987 by the Comte d'Anjou as part of a policy to place fortresses at strategic points in order to consolidate his conquests in Touraine. Like most early designs the donjon is rectangular. Constructed of rubble masonry with an inner and outer dressing of cut stones, it rises to an awe inspiring height of 37 metres (120ft). Its sides are now flanked by tall slender semi-circular buttresses which were added towards the end of the eleventh century. They appear to provide little additional strength to the mighty keep, but perhaps they did if their dressed masonry penetrated deeply into the rubble wall. In the twelfth century Loches was in the hands of the English who built the main enceinte. In the following century three beautiful and strangely shaped towers, each formed like an almond, were attached to stiffen the defence.

Château-Gaillard was built by Richard

Coeur de Lion in his French domain. It stands ruined on a finger of land rising from precipitous cliffs 90 metres (300ft) above a bend on the River Seine. Begun in 1196 when the traditional square and rectangular keeps of the French castles like Langeais and Beaugency were being replaced by polygonal or circular ones, Château-Gaillard displayed the latest techniques in military architecture. Probably it was partly designed by Richard who knew the crusader castles, for there are similarities with Saône. The castle consists of a V-shaped forward bailey on the edge of the spur, separated by ditch and drawbridge from the middle bailey which forms the outer fortification of a concentric design supported by the vastly thick segmentally buttressed walls of the inner bailey, and the steeply battered and buttressed walls of the great circular keep or donjon.

In 1203 it was attacked by the French and surrendered after a bitter siege; an unusual circumstance for so powerful a fortress in the age when castles could be considered impregnable. But the attack was both painstaking and audacious. All the

Château de Coucy; after Viollet-le-Duc.

traditional tools of the besieger were utilised, including siege-towers, battering-rams, scaling-ladders and ballistae. Every type of projectile available was thrown at the walls of the castle, supplies were cut off and the garrison were starving. Four hundred women and children were sent out from the walls but the French, acting correctly within the rules of war, refused to accept these refugees who spent a miserable winter sandwiched between the opposing lines and so reduced by starvation that having eaten the dogs they consumed their own children. In the spring, missile engines and sappers resumed the attack, a tower collapsed from mining and the French captured the middle bailey. The English were now bottled up in the inner bailey and the strong donjon. Eventually, the walls fractured by mines and shattered by catapults, a breech was made sufficiently large to allow the French troops to pour in for the final attack and the garrison surrendered.

Farther south the château at Angers was unsurpassed in its expression of power and self-sufficiency. Seventeen large drum towers, splayed out at their base, were built along the curtain of St Louis' castle between the years 1228 and 1238. They must once have looked even more daunting, for before the Wars of Religion they rose two storeys higher dressed by machicolations and pepper-pot roofs. The whole concept is a remembrance of the past for, although more closely spaced, the drum towers are strongly reminiscent of Roman usage in such places as Portchester.

The castle at Coucy was destroyed by the Germans in the First World War, but it is known from drawings and engravings and is important because of the great influence it exerted on later building. It was constructed between 1225 and 1240 on the edge of a high cliff 46 metres (150ft) above the valley of the Aisne. Here the French abandoned the concentric system of defence for a castle of enceinte with powerful curtains, depending for their defence upon even more powerful circular flanking towers. The upper castle, an irregular quadrilateral with corner towers, had as its core a great circular donjon 32 metres (105ft) in diameter with walls 7.5 metres (25ft) thick at the base, completely surrounded by its own moat which isolated it from the rest of the castle. Inside it had three rooms, one above another, each vaulted from a central column; the structure stood over 60 metres (200ft) high.

Josselin in Brittany is the epitome of the French medieval castle. Three of its nine giant cylindrical towers rise from the rocky banks of the river, savage and awesome. Once they were topped by a *chemin de ronde* from which projectiles could be dropped upon anyone foolish enough to attack the base of the castle. This projecting gallery originally continued along the top of the curtain wall making it higher than it is at present. The main structure on the south-west river facade is late fourteenth century.

Pierrefonds near Compiègne in northern France has been much altered in the restoration by Viollet-le-Duc, but the main walls and towers and the general external appearance are a faithful restoration of what once existed. In spite of the liberties taken in the restoration of the interior and the outworks, the castle gives a remarkably true impression of what such a fortress must have looked like at the height of its power. It was begun towards the end of the fourteenth century and completed early in the following century, one of a group of castles acquired or constructed by the Comte de Vâlois to form a vast military area threatening Paris. It was eventually restored under the personal initiative of Napoleon III, that remarkable ruler with a flair for architectural aggrandisement. Viollet began work in 1857 and when criticised about the far-reaching nature of his restoration called it 'a fine lesson in popular history'. The plan forms an irregular parallelogram perched high on a commanding

The château at Josselin.

site. It combined the provision of ample luxurious apartments with the need for security. Thick walls, regular towers, the double system of concentric defence and the ability to pass troops rapidly from point to point so as to be able to reinforce any menaced position were all incorporated. Tiers of machicolations on the towers and the curtains walls provided four stages of defence one above the other.

SPANISH CASTLES

In Spain war raged up and down the peninsula for centuries as the christians tried to expel the Moors. The reconquest began in 718 but it took some 200 years to reach the Douro river, a distance of only 200 kilometres (130 miles). It was not until 1492 with the surrender of Granada that the Moors were finally expelled. There was also a struggle within a struggle, for the unification of Leon and Castile with Aragon, when

christian fought christian. Most of the great castles lie in Castile and differ from those in France and England, for feudalism was never so strongly entrenched, and the buildings were required more for the garrisoning of troops than for the living accommodation of the lord.

Mombeltrán, near Avila in the Kingdom of Castile, probably dates from the thirteenth century; it has a square plan with concentric defences and one considerably enlarged corner tower acting as donjon, similar to Flint and Bothwell.

La Mota at Medina del Campo is a large well-preserved brick castle, trapezoidal in plan, with part of the central core of its concentric defences dating from the thirteenth century and the rest of the building begun in 1440 and completed about 1479. From this last period dates the great square tower which rises to more than twice the height of the inner

Pierrefonds; after Viollet-le-Duc.

Below: *Mobeltrán; from Alberto Weissmüller.*

Bottom: *Medina del Campo; from Alberto Weissmüller.*

curtain wall of the battlemented and towered outer enceinte. By the time this part was built cannon and handguns were in regular use and gunloops were provided all along the battlements in passages on two floors.

    In the province of Segovia, Coca is also late, built in the fifteenth century by the Archbishop of Seville as a giant castle-palace. It is a sort of brick caricature of Harlech, but less symmetrical as the keep-gatehouse is replaced by a traditional corner keep representing a castle in miniature. Everything is over-exaggerated, the talus, used at Krak, now occupies most of the surface of the outer walls and towers and the battlements drip rich Arab *mudéjar* decoration. There are gunports for heavy cannon, some placed a metre above the floor of the dry moat and others facing out from above the line of the talus in the thick curtain walls and the hexagonal corner

Coca; from Alberto Weissmüller.

Coca; plan.

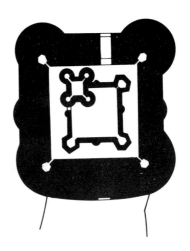

The tower at Bitonto.

towers. Altogether one gets the impression that Coca was designed for its effect rather than for its efficiency under siege conditions.

ITALIAN CASTLES AND FORTIFIED TOWNS

In Italy can be traced a gradual regression in military effectiveness from the powerful modelling of Frederick's Norman castles to the florid exuberant manifestations in late medieval castles like Sirmione. Little wonder that these card-like structures fell apart so disastrously under the impact of explosive-powered cannon at the end of the fifteenth century. It was the Italians too, realising the deficiencies of their late medieval castles, who were the first to carry out major reformation in the art of fortification throughout the first half of the sixteenth century. In the interim the Italian peninsula, like other parts of Europe, bristled with castles too numerous to cover in any detail. A selection will illustrate some of the main characteristics.

The tower at Bitonto built about 1384 is a plain freestanding drum 16 metres (53ft) in diameter and 24 metres (79ft) high. There were once many in this area of Apulia. In character it seems to have come straight from the Norman fortresses. Gaunt and forbidding, thick-walled and powerful, it is as though a corner tower of Frederick's castle at Catania had been detached to stand ground on its own.

Lucera, built between 1263 and 1283, is still the great medieval castle of enceinte. Almost rectangular

Rectangular towers on the east front of Lucera Castle.

in plan it stands high on a spur looking out over the plain of Foggia and is separated from the town by a deep ditch. The castle has a great courtyard enclosed within a curtain wall, punctuated at close intervals by powerful rectangular towers. The land front facing the ditch has seven sharp-angled towers spaced between the drum towers which act as pivots to the eastern and western corners of the fortress.

Towered walls at Lucera enclosed a fortress, but towns too needed to be defended and the enceinte system was also applied to them. In the thirteenth century there were many walled towns in Italy, though most have now been pulled down or replaced by later fortifications. Montagnana near Padua still has

its complete circuit of walls with a circumference of nearly two kilometres (over a mile). These were probably begun by Ezzelino il Monaco shortly after he captured the town in 1242 and were continued until his death in 1256. By that time the high square towers of the Castello San Zeno, which supported the town walls and acted as a citadel, had been completed in stone. Work on improvement and restoration continued for another century and probably much of the present city walls dates from 1360; they were designed by Franceschin de Schici.

Monteriggioni near Siena is Montagnana in miniature. Built in the thirteenth century, its complete circuit of curtain wall punctuated by square towers at

Opposite: *The towers of San Gimignano*

Below: *The town walls and the Castello di S Zeno at Montagnana.*

Bottom: *The walled town of Monteriggioni near Siena.*

regular intervals encircles a small hilltop town. It was mentioned by Dante in the *Inferno*. Nearby San Gimignano is also walled but its defensive character is emphasised by innumerable embattled towers rising like diminitive skyscrapers and giving the town a unique flavour. In the fourteenth century when most of these towers were built to protect their owners against civil strife and display an arrogant expression of power there were already many such towers in central Italy. Bologna once had clusters of these tall thin rectangular towers, although only three famous ones remain.

The Este Castle at Ferrara is typical of fourteenth century Italian military architecture. Built to provide palatial accommodation for a rich noble family, it was constructed on a square plan surrounding a central courtyard and approached through four battle-

Entrance to the Este Castle at Ferrara.

The fortified dock at Sirmione.

mented gateways guarded by porcullis and draw-bridge. Its corners are reinforced by square towers, the lower courses of which splay out to give additional strength and thickness at foundation level and at the same time make attack across the enveloping moat a hazardous undertaking. The curtain walls and the towers are topped with traditional Italian machicolation composed of corbelled brick ribs projecting from the vertical surface of the wall and joined by semi-circular arches. Behind these lie the holes through which boiling oil and other combustibles could be dropped on assailants. The upper storeys of the walls and towers are later additions.

Characteristic of all these Italian castles, which in their hundreds still dot the countryside, are high walls topped by elaborate machicolations and stiffened by rectangular or square towers. Most towns

Sirmione Castle on Lake Garda.

in the north have their examples. The once forbidding exterior of the castello at Mantua has been weakened by the introduction of later windows and the pantile roofs which cover the jagged edges of the fifteenth century crenellations. Sirmione, which stands on a spit of land jutting into the waters of Lake Garda, is a splendid example of the late medieval phase. It is a brick castle and was built by the Scaligeri in the fifteenth century. The waters of the lake are channelled to form an effective moat and it even has its own dock surrounded by a crenellated defensive wall. Its walls and towers are extremely high and although thick and strong they give all the appearance of having been cut from cardboard.

By the middle of the fifteenth century many of the Italian military engineers resorted again to the use of the round drum tower as a better means of deflecting projectiles, especially with the threat of the explosive cannon. The Castello Orsini at Bracciano north of Rome was begun in 1470 and completed in fifteen years. It has an irregular pentagonal plan with two main courtyards and its walls are stiffened by means of cylindrical towers. Its walls and towers, however, are still high, menacing in appearance but vulnerable to bombardment. The round tower of the fortress at Roveretto built in 1488 was also very tall, but it gained a degree of security from its almost impregnable site.

Gradually the engineers began to appreciate the advantages of lowering the profile and rounding the edges of the new fortresses so as to present a minimum target to a besieger's artillery. Early attempts to offset the effect of cannon fire, both by the introduction of counter-batteries and the reduction in height of castle buildings, are to be found in the work of the last decades of the fifteenth century in the Romagna, the Marche and Lazio. Strength still depended on mass, gunports were few and small, and round drum towers were immensely broad, often being steeply splayed out towards their bases from string courses sometimes more than halfway up their total height. The round towers consequently left large areas of dead ground which could not be covered from the small gunports.

Imola (1472–73) has this immensely stolid appearance, but probably the rocca at Senigalia built about 1480 was the most classic expression of this type of fortress. It has a low squat symmetrical form,

The Rocca at Senigalia.

s'Gravensteen at Ghent.

s'Gravensteen; plan.

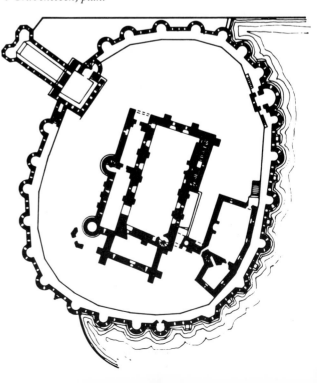

The Imperial Castle at Nürnberg; plan.

The Sinweh Tower in the Imperial Castle at Nürnberg.

square, with massive corner drum towers whose scale is emphasised by the close spacing of the ribs in the machicolations: the base of the towers was still intended to be protected by these devices. The towers and the curtain wall rise to the same height and form a continuous solid platform for the defending artillery. Forli (1481–83) is similar but it still retains the traditional keep or mastio abutting one wall of its quadrangular plan. At Sarzana near La Spezia both the town bastion and the fort built by the Florentines in 1487 follow this pattern.

Already gunpowder was seen to be affecting the medieval castles of Italy, but before discussing its full significance, there are other areas of Europe which require passing reference. In north-western Europe there are many fine examples of castles and fortified towns still well-preserved.

CASTLES AND FORTIFIED TOWNS IN NORTH-WESTERN EUROPE

Vulnerable Belgium, lying in the path of powerful armies, is full of strong castles but probably the most powerful is the castle of the Counts of Flanders, s'Gravensteen at Ghent. It was begun in its present form in 1180 by Philip of Alsace who had seen service in the Holy Land and well knew the crusader castles of Syria. The keep, which is Philip's work, is a large thick-walled rectangular structure braced externally with buttresses and with walls which are in places 1.7 metres (5.5ft) thick. It stands in the middle of an elliptical enceinte which rises from the waters of the moat, strengthened by twenty-four turrets constructed like buttresses.

The banks of the Rhine, which has always been the most strongly fortified river in Europe, are studded with castles and fortifications. They present a varied picture as each German state tended to develop its own characteristics. Some, like Eltz on the Moselle, display a continuous process of building from the twelfth to the sixteenth centuries.

Farther to the north-east the golden age of the Hohenstaufen monarchy is displayed in the Imperial Castle at Nürnberg. It was a rich complex of buildings originating from the tall round Sinweh Tower built about 1200. At first this stronghold of the Holy Roman Empire protected the town, a mere huddle of houses which clustered around the base of

Below: *The Klingentor and town walls, Rothenburg on the Tauber.*

Bottom: *The Pulver Turm at Rothenburg on the Tauber.*   *The Grüner Turm at Dinkelsbühl.*

The Muiderslot.

the powerful castle, but later as in so many European towns the position was reversed and the strong walled town succoured the castle which was gradually relegated to the task of acting as a citadel. The town of Nürnberg was encircled by a double bank of strong fortified walls punctuated and reinforced with powerful drum towers so that its concentric system of defence could deter any attack. Early in the fifteenth century during the Hussite Wars the fortifications on the north and west sides were strengthened and the Imperial Castle was incorporated into the town's defences. The programme of improving and strengthening the defences was continued into the sixteenth century when the burghers availed themselves of the latest Italian techniques and employed an Italian military engineer, Antoni Fazuni Maltese, to lay out imposing bastions in the Italian manner between 1538 and 1545.

Some medieval walled towns still stand intact. Dinkelsbuhl has a complete circuit of walls, four fortified gates and some eighteen additional tall thin towers placed at intervals straddling the town's walls. Rothenburg on the Tauber is similarly defended. The town's walls and towers date from the thirteenth and fourteenth centuries with additions like the Spitaltor, a strong circular sixteenth century bastion, designed for artillery and containing two oval inner courtyards. Built in 1572, Rothenburg remains to this day a typical sixteenth century German fortified town.

THE SQUARE CASTLE PLAN

The square castle with four corner drum towers has always been one of the most simple, direct and effective defensive statements. From the castles of Frederick in Sicily, to Edward I's great castle at Harlech, to fourteenth century Bodiam and fifteenth century Imola and Senigalia, to sixteenth century Civitavecchia, this plan form persisted and became, with the substitution of triangular bastions for drum towers, one of the most popular solutions to fortress design. L'Aquila in the sixteenth century and the innumerable colonial forts constructed in the seventeenth and eighteenth centuries are typical examples. It was a well-tried solution which has since withstood the test of time.

Muiden Castle in Holland is of this progeny. The original castle was built in 1285 so that the square plan with the round corner towers is close in date to Harlech, but there is no concentric system. In 1386 the castle was rebuilt on its original foundations. It was restored between 1895 and 1948. The building is in brick and is surrounded, like all fortifications in Holland, by water defences. The curtain walls are high but the corner towers are considerably higher, topped by steep-pitched conical roofs. The square gatehouse in the centre of one curtain is approached over the moat by a bridge. The main living accommodation lies on the far side of a generous courtyard, its roofs rising at ridge level higher than the battlements of the adjoining towers.

CHAPTER THREE
Renaissance Fortifications

The medieval world perfected a type of defence which was normally resistant to direct attack. Height and thickness of wall were vital for a small garrison to hold off a large invading force. This was the supreme age of the castle, whose invulnerability was to collapse before the onslaught of gunpowder, mining and cannon. Here is the great change which signals the Renaissance and one of the major problems whose solution taxed its greatest thinkers.

The large stock of medieval castles had to be drastically modified or rebuilt rapidly to face the threat of gunpowder. A vast capital investment was involved. If towers could be cut down and strengthened they could provide gun platforms for the garrison artillery to reply effectively to a bombardment.

RAGUSA AND RHODES

Not all the gun platforms were cut down, particularly if there was high ground in the vicinity. Military engineers continued to match height with height as they had done at Conway and Caernarvon, and which they

Ragusa: the curtain wall and towers on the landfront.

were to do on the land front of that magnificent walled town, Dubrovnik (Ragusa). This front consists of a high curtain wall interspersed with square medieval towers. At the south-east corner of the fortifications there stands the tall, machicolated Minceta Tower. Although an independent republic, Ragusa, a christian stronghold on the edge of a Turkish-held land mass, depended for much of its expertise on Italian designers. In 1463, Michelozzo from Florence built a broad, encircling lower tower with a sloping parapet and embrasures for cannon with, in front of each square tower, a semi-circular gun platform joined by a lower curtain wall. This was, in effect, an extension of the medieval concentric system into the age of gunpowder artillery.

After evacuating the Holy Land the Knights of St John in 1309 took over 'that pleasant green island', Rhodes, and fortified it strongly. They also built powerful forts on nearby Cos and on the Turkish

Ragusa: the Minceta Tower.

mainland at Bodrum. There they sat under the Turkish nose, in sight of enemy territory. In May 1453, Constantinople fell to the Turks; Rhodes felt even more isolated.

In addition to building outlying castles, the Knights fortified their headquarters with a single, high curtain wall, spaced square towers and a lower walkway or berm, all forming a great curve around the town and the commercial harbour, in front of which the walls were less robust, pierced by a splendid medieval Water Gate. The galley port, containing their striking force – for they were by then a formidable naval power – lay up the coast to the north, protected by the round tower of Fort St Nicholas at the end of a long narrow mole. At the entrance to the commercial port stood two other towers and booms were later drawn between all these towers.

Useless attacks occurred in 1440, when the Turks lost twelve of their fourteen vessels, and in 1443, but pressure was building up and the first serious assault came in 1480 when the Turks lay siege to Rhodes. The Knights and their troops managed to

The walls of Rhodes: part of the land defences; after Gabriel.

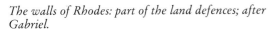

Rhodes. A model of the coastal fort of St Nicholas.

hold out until they gained protection from the autumn gales. However, in 1522 the Knights were again attacked and, after a bitter siege and a memorable resistance, they surrendered the place and were permitted to march out with honour, eventually taking up their abode on Malta.

Steeped in a long tradition of fortress-building, their fortifications on Rhodes are particularly interesting in the development of defences to both use and counter explosive artillery. They show the transition from the medieval world to an age of gunpowder.

The coastal fort of St Nicholas had its original round tower strengthened by first one and later two envelopes by the grand master, Pierre D'Aubusson, to provide tiers of fire; and perhaps, by its shape and successful role in the first siege, it may have inspired Henry VIII of England to build his coastal forts in 1539.

In the north-west corner of the walled town the grand master built his palace, so devastated in the siege of 1522 that subsequently it was rebuilt by Mussolini in a somewhat magnificent style. Adjoining the palace were the streets of the Convent, reserved for the knights and separated from the rest of the town by a high, fortified wall. Referred to as the *Collachio*, in its seclusion dwelt the knights of the various language groups that made up the Order of St John. Each language group was to show national or regional characteristics in the design of its living accommodation, called *auberges* or hotels. This same individuality is apparent in the development of the fortifications where each language group was apportioned a sector to defend.

After the siege of 1480 it was clear that the landward defences would have to be strengthened. The main walls were thickened, built up to provide a wide terreplein behind the parapets where guns could be mounted and men moved freely and fast to any threatened sector. Then, and not necessarily in this order, they constructed the highly original Bulwark of Auvergne, a large pentagonal gun platform with guns enfilading the town walls and firing forward. Some authors have called it an early bastion which it was not for its outer faces could not be flanked. It was merely a large variation on the popular semi-circular gun platform or low drum tower. To strengthen the gates, so-called ravelins which were really irregularly-shaped gun platforms set lower down than the walls, were pushed forward into the ditch. The one in front of the Tower of Italy forms a semi-circular ring like some of Henry VIII's forts.

With the building of the terreplein it was necessary to provide gun embrasures and to slope back the battlements to deflect shot. Those in front of the Post of England were curved, similar to those on the Sangallo Bastion at Rome and the fort at Salses, and similar to the parapets soon to be built on the coastal forts in England. Part of the Post of Italy was defended by serrated walls, *en cremaillère*, to concentrate flanking fire on the end of the line and the sea shore. At the Post of Germany, on the north-west corner, a caponier projects boldly into the ditch. Its date is uncertain as it is difficult to know what repairs and additions were made by the Turks after the siege of 1522, but it is tempting to believe that this was a Knights' caponier.

Finally, and most important, in front of the Posts of Italy, England and Aragon, the centre of which was to bear the full brunt of the Turkish attack in 1522, where the ditch had been cut from the solid rock, a long, second outer ditch was dug leaving tenailles of rock to keep the Turks off and protect the base of the inner walls and cover the walkway. This must have been a mighty undertaking with a double dry ditch cut from solid rock.

The fortifications of Rhodes formed a formidable barrier against which the Turks, with fine artillery, although finally victorious, were to lose, it is

Below: *Rhodes: the Amboise Gate and the Bulwark of Auvergne beyond; after Gabriel.*

Bottom: *The land front at Rhodes shwoing both ditches and the tenaille of rock between them; after Gabriel.*

Reconstruction of a fifteenth century breech-loading gun firing through an embrasure at Mondavio.

said, some 90,000 men out of a total force of 300,000. The many large cannon balls which still lie on the ground at Rhodes give some idea of the power of artillery at that time.

FACTORS OF CHANGE: THE IMPACT OF GUNPOWDER

The two basic testing grounds of the power of gunpowder in Europe were against the English castles in Normandy at the end of the Hundred Years War and against the Italian castles in the invasion of Charles VIII in 1494. But already by the end of the fourteenth century the impact of gunpowder was having its effect on the theory of warfare. The defence was still vertical, the utilisation of high walls being imperative because of the vast investment in existing castles, but walls were also thickened to withstand impact. Even new ones depended upon thickness for their strength. The curtain of Salses Castle in southern France was 18 metres (59ft) thick. Exposed walls were sometimes covered with timber or earth to resist the shock of cannon balls. Circular or rectangular towers tended to be replaced by pentagonal or oblique-sided ones, to deflect shot. Combustible timber projections were removed from battlements and the ditch made more of an obstacle, wider and deeper so that a breached wall would not fill it and make a bridge for the attackers. Nevertheless, the balance of power was slowly shifting back to the attacker.

Much of the changed pattern can be attributed to the northern Europeans and the French. Charles VII employed two brilliant brothers, John and Gaspar Bureau, to reform his artillery and introduce innovations. In this field the most important modification was the substitution of cast-iron for stone shot. The calibre and consequently the size and weight of guns was reduced to fire the mass-produced and more accurate cast shot. The resulting gain in penetration led to a tremendous increase in the number of guns used. The new French artillery with these advantages took the field against the English in 1449 and, for the reconquest of Normandy, was involved in sixty sieges in a period of one year. Whereas the English had taken a month in 1415 and four months in 1440 to conquer Harfleur, Charles's army recovered it in the depth of winter in only seventeen days. Often the mere sight of artillery was sufficient to cause a town to capitulate.

Trunnions were cast into the guns and made sufficiently strong for them to carry the weight and bear the shock of discharge. This meant that the guns could actually travel on their firing carriages and could be brought into action quickly. One of the features of the invasion of Italy in 1494 was the way the French guns could be used to support infantry in the initial stages of an assault, instead of following miles behind and only slowly being brought into action. Fast horses which could keep pace with the rest of the army replaced oxen to draw gun carriages. The fortress collapsed under the fury of the French guns and mortars, and the highly efficient French artillery proved its superiority at Agnadello. At the battle of Ravenna in 1512 and at Marignano three years later its employment decided the issue of the day. Probably the first writer to appreciate the full import of the new weapon was a woman, Christina da Pizzano, whose military treatise, the most complete work on the art of war since Roman times, was completed about 1410. Daughter of an Italian professor invited to France by Charles V, she must have been one of the most extraordinary women of her age. She read widely but was discerning and capable of penetrating analysis so that her work remained a valuable source of reference in western Europe throughout the fifteenth century; it was translated into English in 1488 and published in 1489.

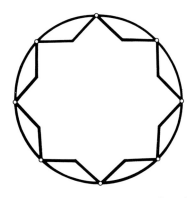

Plan of the fortifications of Sforzinda by Filarete.

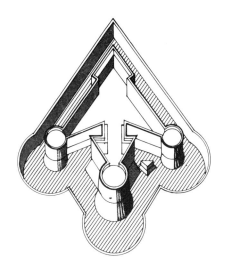

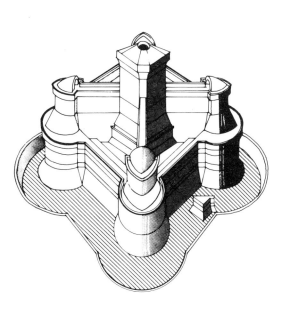

Two forts; from Francesco di Giorgio,
Trattati di Architettura.

THE EXPLOSIVE MINE

The second potent instrument was the explosive mine. It is not known when it was first used. Possibly it was employed by the brothers Bureau, but Taccola has been credited with its invention and he shows a drawing of a powder mine in his *De machinus libri X*, completed by the mid-fifteenth century. It is known that during Gonsalvo of Cordova's siege of Naples in 1495 his engineer, Peter of Navarre, exploded a mine under the walls of the Castel Nuovo much to the astonishment of the garrison. In 1501 another mine was exploded at the siege of Cephalonia.

EARLY THEORISTS

From the fourteenth century onwards the art of war and fortification became a popular subject for study. Many of the early treatises were from Germany where there was already a profound interest in firearms. Konrad Kyeser's *Bellifortis*, dedicated in 1405, traces the growth of the new technology of war. In addition to the usual siege engines handed down from Roman times and slowly perfected, Kyeser shows a wheeled artillery chariot mounting fourteen guns and protected by projecting scythes designed to cut to pieces any infantry that approached too near. Also illustrated are an armoured car to shelter sappers and soldiers and a rotating cannon consisting of six barrels which fired in turn: by the end of the century some of these machines were in use. In 1397 the Della Scala family were operating three large chariots, each of which carried 144 small mortars mounted in three tiers, a formidable weapon. Kyeser shows a wide interest in military engineering, formulating proposals for boats propelled by paddle wheels, a kind of landing craft with tailboards which could be lowered to allow the disembarkation of infantry, and telescopic bridges which could be winched out across a river by means of cables.

Guido da Vigevano's treatise, written about 1335, was a guidebook for the King of France to take with him on a crusade, a manual on hygiene and medicine, with thirteen chapters on military machines that were likely to be useful in sieges in the Holy Land. The age is full of works demonstrating methods designed to overcome the obstacle of the defended castle or town: plans for bridges that can be thrown out across ditches, vehicles that can travel like submarines along the bed of a river or ditch, boats to be navigated without vulnerable oars, and vehicles which can be self-propelled. The art of prefabrication, for rapid movement and erection, was already carried to a considerable degree of finesse.

By the mid-fifteenth century, that is even before the shattering invasion by Charles's efficient French army, the Italians were doing much of the investigation into the art of attack and defence. Many of the investigators were theorists and humanists, not practising soldiers and engineers. Tartaglia noted that 'the eye of the mind sees more deeply into general things, than does the eye of the body in particulars.' Each author drew on and plagiarised the work of his predecessors. Robert Valturio, typical of this age, was commissioned by Sigismondo Malatesta to write *De re militari libri X* which was completed about 1460. Some of its drawings were copied from earlier works. Alberti was a humanist and he admitted in his *De re aedificatoria* written about the same time that he was not a military man. Only a small part of his treatise is about defence and then only because he was interested in the design of cities. His main source was Vegetius, but Alberti expressed some thoughts of his own. He outlined the need for flank defence between towers 'so that whoever offers to approach between the towers is exposed to be taken in flank and slain; and thus the wall is defended by these towers, and the towers mutually one by another. The towers should have an open gorge at the back so that, if captured, they cannot be used against the besieged.' Alberti seems hardly to have considered the implications of attack by gunpowder except to acknowledge that the ditch is the most formidable method of defence. He thus underlined a problem which was to tax the minds of military men for generations to come: should the ditch be filled with water or should it be kept dry?

Alberti believed that the city should have a citadel, the last point of defence for its ruler and its garrison and counterpart of the medieval keep-donjon, capable of being held against subversion and treachery. The ruler must always fear treachery and for this reason the building should be 'bugged'. Pipes were to be secretly concealed in the walls so that the conversation of strangers and servants could be heard. Among other forms, Alberti advocated the star-shaped citadel which was to become an accepted solution by the

beginning of the sixteenth century. Understanding the nature of greed, he stated 'neither public bodies nor private persons can ever set bounds to their insatiable desire of getting and possessing still more and more; from which one source arises all the mischiefs of war'. On the value of fortification as a deterrent he observed 'It ought to look fierce, terrible, rugged, dangerous and unconquerable.' Perhaps this belief caused him to conclude that victories could be gained 'more by the art and skill of the architect, than by the conduct or fortune of the generals.'

Machiavelli's ideas have been much misrepresented, but because of his important diplomatic position and his clarity of thinking his *Dialogues on the Art of War* are important. In general, Machiavelli came out against dependence on fortresses and in favour of an efficient citizen's army. He advocated the value of earthworks and field fortifications to support his army. He realised and expressed the dilemma of his age: 'If the walls are made high they are too much subject to the blows of artillery; if they be made low they be most easy to scale.' He placed much reliance on ditches, but feared that those outside city walls might be filled by attackers. Therefore he advocated broad deep ditches inside the enceinte, an expedient adopted in the defence of Padua in 1509 when a continuous ditch was dug inside the rampart flanked by small casemates just as Machiavelli had recommended. But the device was normally only employed as an expedient to retrench a breach in the walls by a ditch hastily excavated immediately behind the breach, as at Mendz in 1552 and Siena three years later.

Antonio Averlino, called Il Filarete, proposed a new city for Duke Sforza of Milan, the description of which was contained in a treatise completed in 1464. The city had of course to be defended but Filarete broke little new ground, his military ideas being based firmly in the past. He gave precise instructions in the dimensions for building walls, towers and gates, but clearly his interest was more in the symbol of the ducal castle than its power to resist an assault. However its outline is interesting for, inscribed within a circle, the walls were arranged as a tenaille fortification, like the teeth of a saw, an idea reintroduced by Montalembert in the 1770s.

Emerging as the most important military engineer at the end of the fifteenth century was

The rocca at Mondavio; plan.

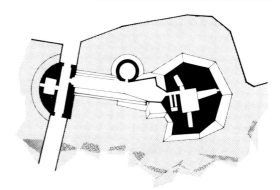

The keep and the support tower at the rocca at Mondavio.

Francesco di Giorgio, for he combined practice and theory, architecture and engineering. Between 1480 and 1486, his most fertile period, he was living and working at Urbino where he designed and built a ring of fortresses on the hilltops protecting the approaches to the city. Francesco's treatise on civil and military architecture was completed about 1480, the first major work on the art of fortification in the modern world. He was convinced that the strength of a fortress depended upon the quality of its plan rather than the thickness of its walls and he therefore became preoccupied with the trace. Like Filarete he advocated the tenaille system of serrated walls and carried his ideas into effect at the Rocca di Mondavio, at Cagli and Montefeltro, all of which were illustrated in his treatise. The outline of his forts varied, often being triangular, but most were influenced by the belief he still held in the need for a strong central tower as a point of safety in the last retreat. Francesco di Giorgio

appears to be one of the first engineers to use the caponier, a loopholed room where the defenders, protected by masonry, could fire along the floor of the ditch or indeed any other flat vulnerable surface in the fort.

The rocca at Mondavio was built between 1482 and 1492 and shows that, however advanced Francesco di Giorgio's ideas on military architecture may have been, in practice he was forced to be conservative and still stuck to the medieval concept of a high stronghold or keep as the ultimate defence in a threefold system of an entrance tower isolated by drawbridges, a support tower and a four-storey keep. There is no courtyard and every inch of space is used. The only precaution that was taken against damaging blows from cannon balls was to slope the walls in the form of an escarpment from a line two-thirds of the height up the tower. This was a device which also made scaling more difficult.

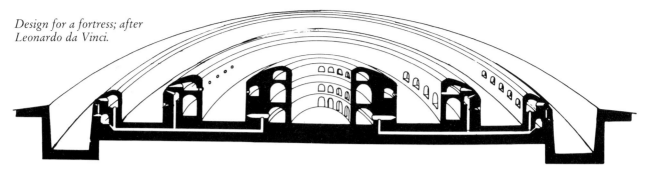

*Design for a fortress; after
Leonardo da Vinci.*

The concepts of war were changing and its prosecution becoming much more a matter of specialisation. Textbooks written for soldiers by soldiers now became a feature of the times. One of the most outstanding was by Philippe Duc de Cleves. In 1498 he wrote *Description de la forme et la manière de conduire le faict de la guerre*. As commander of the French army and governor of Genoa he was fully conversant with the tactics and strategy of his time and he showed how the professional soldier was becoming increasingly aware of the importance of geography and climate, of a need for thorough knowledge of the topography of the site for a siege, and the importance of reliable information gained through reconnaissance. As the conduct of war moved into an area of specialisation, the military engineer, versed with a thorough understanding of mathematics, came to the aid of the soldier. Thus Alberti could write that 'the besieged . . . would inform you that their greatest defence lay in the art and assistance of the architect.'

The two outstanding geniuses of the age were Leonardo da Vinci and Dürer. Outstanding because although they inherited a knowledge of the past they were able to think clearly about the conditions of the day and in particular about the profound effect on any defended position of accurate and heavy fire from cannon and mortars. Leonardo thought of himself first and foremost as a military engineer; painting and sculpture were only sidelines. About 1483 he offered his services to Duke Ludovico Maria Sforza, claiming the invention of portable bridges which were indestructible, a knowledge of how to besiege and destroy any stronghold, a method of transporting mortars which could throw stones like a storm and make smoke which could cause terror amongst the defenders, and the ability to cut mines, even under rivers and trenches, without making a noise. Concerning his knowledge of unassailable, irresistible chariots he wrote: 'And behind these, infantry would be able to follow quite unharmed and unhindered.' It is known now that much of this technology was drawn from other sources, in particular Valturio. However it is in the design of fortifications that Leonardo made his most revolutionary proposals. The characteristic of medieval fortifications had been the use of high though comparatively thin curtain walls which in addition to being vulnerable to enemy bombardment

provided inadequate platforms for the efficient utilisation of the defenders' artillery. Although, aided by the force of gravity, height was useful for dropping objects on to assault troops assembled at the foot of the walls, it had the disadvantage of causing the defenders' artillery to use plunging fire. If this did not hit on first impact, it caused the cannon ball to bounce high and its effect to be wasted. Like his fellow engineers in the fifteenth century Leonardo advocated making the defence walls lower and more sturdy to resist the enormously increased power of artillery. His machines, tanks, rapid-firing guns, the use of a type of shrapnel and breech-loading mechanism, were all part of the theory if not the practice of his day. His drawings in the *Codice Atlantico* made at the end of the fifteenth century shows the development of a ravelin not only to cover the gate, the weakest point in a curtain wall, but made sufficiently large so that the face of the ravelin is grazed by flanking fire from the two adjoining towers of the main wall. Leonardo described it thus: 'The ravelin, shield of the fortress, should be defended by the fortress, as the fortress is by it.'

Already engineers were approaching the solution of the bastion which will be discussed more fully later. Even the flanks of round towers were pierced by embrasures so that guns in the casemates could enfilade the curtain and the crown of the parapet. In 1502 Leonardo was made engineer-general to Cesare Borgia's forces in the Romagna and became concerned with the problem of minimising damage caused by projectiles hitting the curtain wall of a fortress. Exposed surfaces were made elliptical, slanting back as far as possible. Leonardo became preoccupied with the profile of the reveals of the gun embrasures, asking 'why a ball hitting a wall obliquely does not go through, as when it hits at right angles'. There followed a study of pointed projectiles using aerodynamic fins. Leonardo replaced battlements with a massive cupola elliptically shaped to deflect shot. He provided three tiers of casemates to greatly increase firepower and built-in smoke vents to clear their interiors, always a problem until the introduction of smokeless powder in the nineteenth century.

Hung on the face of his forts he used grass or hay soaked in water in order to deaden the impact of shot. Francesco di Giorgio's caponiers were by now fully developed circular ones, approached by under-

Studies of enfilading artillery fire in front of ravelin; after Leonardo da Vinci.

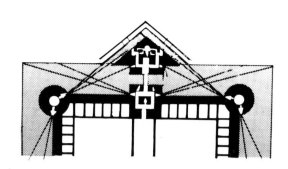

Design of a fortress showing arcs of fire; after Leonardo da Vinci.

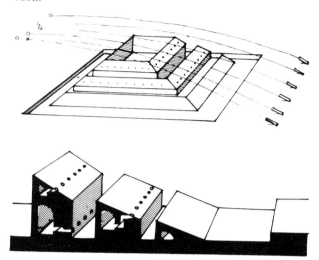

A corner of tower with cannon embrasure in a scarped wall, Salses.

ground staircases and placed at the angles of a fortress to survey and protect the vulnerable bed of the ditch. In Leonardo's final drawings he brought together many ideas in a complete synthesis of defensive techniques. A quadrilateral fortress depended upon line behind line of casemated gun positions, low with their top faces splayed towards the enemy in a continuous shallow line. Each ring of defence, separated by a ditch from the one in front, was a continuous gun platform: a fortress thus conceived was an active element in war. In this form he had achieved a balanced defensive position, each part reciprocally protected by its neighbour, with low profiles and the minimum of exposed surfaces. It was a defence in depth with detached works pushed forward mutually protectable by flanking fire.

SALSES

The Fort de Salses, built in 1498 by the Spanish engineer Ramiro Lopez to defend the approaches to Roussillon, shows that it was not only the Italians who were acutely aware of the damaging effect of artillery fire on permanent fortifications. Salses was designed in the form of a square with corner drum towers and a powerful high keep in the centre of one wall, so far a traditional concept. Like the Italians Lopez adopted the idea of steeply scarping the walls of the drum towers, in this case from about half way up their total height, a device which had been used in early medieval times to stiffen defence against battering-rams and which found renewed popularity in the roccas of

Fort de Salses near Roussillon.

fifteenth century Italy. But the significant features of Salses which foreshadowed later developments were the low-lying profile of the fort in general, its buildings sunk into a deep wide ditch, the curved upper surfaces of the curtain walls designed to deflect shot, the use of large gunports for heavy artillery to cover the ditch, and the provision of detached outworks formed like semi-circular ravelins in the ditches.

Albrecht Dürer in his *Instructions for the Fortification of Cities* carries a study of the casemate

further. In his proposals circular artillery towers would flank a city wall and have casemates low down to give grazing fire in the ditch, some 60 metres (200ft) wide. His casemate walls were hollowed out to allow the guns to run forward far enough for their muzzles to project beyond the embrasures and so keep down the smoke inside. One-metre diameter smoke flues were carefully designed to keep the internal atmosphere clear. Dürer's projects were vast in scale, involving expensive masonry, with the result that his treatise, published at Nürnberg in 1527, tended to be overlooked for several generations, his ideas being superseded by those of the Italian engineers of the sixteenth century and not revived until many generations later.

As theory was put into practice, siege warfare became gradually stabilised once more and commanders realised that the guns which had so effectively reduced a stronghold could equally well be used for its defence. Artillery duels from carefully sited gun positions, with bombardment scientifically applied, became from this time on the main feature of the siege. Niccolo Tartaglia, a mathematician from Brescia, produced in 1537 his *Nova scientia* the first important treatise on the scientific application of gunnery and the first attempt to evaluate the trajectory of shot.

THE INTRODUCTION OF THE BASTION

The greatest step forward in the techniques of defence was the introduction of the bastion. The use of towers to provide mutual defence and to flank an intervening curtain wall goes back to ancient times, but the principle had been applied in a haphazard manner. Both square and round towers left areas of their surface which could not be covered by fire from their neighbours. Engineers now discovered that by introducing triangular bastions, with batteries of guns protected and concealed in their flanks, it was possible if they were properly sited to ensure effective enfilade fire across both faces of a bastion from the flanks of its two adjoining bastions. The length of the line of defence, from the salient of the bastion to the guns in the flank, was dependent upon the effective range of those guns. No attacking troops could penetrate to the face of the bastions or their intervening curtains without passing through a barrage of fire, and it was realised that enfilade fire was far more effective than direct fire from guns firing forward which might miss assaulting infantry.

The invention of the bastion was undoubtedly Italian and it looks as though, with the early development of field fortifications by the Italians, its origins

Opposite: *Salses, showing how the profile has been lowered and adjusted to deflect artillery fire.*

Reconstruction of the rocca at Ostia by Giovanni Montiroli; after Guglielmotti.

must be sought in that province rather than in permanent stone fortifications. Field fortifications lend themselves to experiment, but with so much of the evidence destroyed it is almost impossible to attribute to any one man the invention of this or that feature in the development of fortification. Certainly earthwork bastions were used at Ravenna in 1512 and Verona in 1516, and Della Valle in his *Libro continente appertentie ad capitanii* (1524) advocates as a practical soldier the use of bastions because they are more quickly built than walls and less susceptible to artillery fire. About 1461 Michele Canale had constructed the Bastion Verde to reinforce the defence of Turin but the shape of his work has been obscured beneath later works built by the French after 1536. Francesco di Giorgio made drawings of embryonic bastions and by the time of the Sangalli's work in central Italy this had become common practice so that the claim that Sanmicheli was the first to use it on the Bastione della Maddalena at Verona in 1527 is clearly unsubstantiated. This was Vasari's claim, but it appears that this bastion was designed by Michele dei Leoni and added to by Sanmicheli after 1530. It has been suggested that Pierre d'Aubusson, superintendent of fortifications for the Knights of St John in Rhodes from 1472 and Grand Master there from 1476 to 1503, was the first to introduce the bastion in substantial form in a series of works which culminated in the Boulevard d'Auvergne in 1496, but these Knights' towers seem much closer to the four-sided pointed towers which the Romans sometimes attached to their curtain walls, and are unrelated to the systematic employment of enfilade fire in a co-ordinated defence.

The second step was to extend the defence in depth. To some extent the new bastion did this, but gradually additional works were pushed forward to reinforce the front and hold off an enemy at a distance. The covered-way became a platform outside the ditch where troops could carry out a forward defence. Tartaglia has been credited with this invention when he also advocated that the counterscarp should be made as high as possible in order to shield all the internal fortifications below the breastworks. However, a type of covered-way was probably used in the fortifications of Brescia in 1428. New structures behind the magistral line, which marked the crest of the main fortifications, also deepened the field of defence.

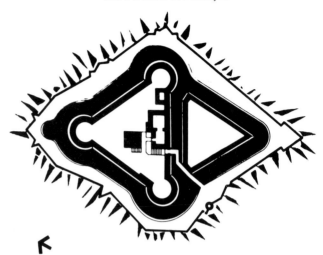

The Fortezza di Firmafede at Sarzanello.

Cavaliers, great bulky blocks, rose behind the bastions and sometimes behind the curtains, standing up like cavalrymen so that their guns had a clear view of the countryside beyond the glacis.

The Italian Wars threw up a number of competent practitioners who had gained experience in the fierce sieges of many a central Italian town. Hilltop fortresses were constructed at first with bulky round towers whose surfaces, and those of the curtains, were steeply scarped to deflect shot and to ensure that an enemy using scaling ladders would have to prop them at a dangerously oblique angle. Baccio Pontelli's work on the rocca or fort at Ostia (1483–86) belongs to this period. Ostia is important because it is probably the first example of a Renaissance building designed exclusively as a fortress and not as a palace or a residential castle. Pontelli worked with Franceso Giamberti, but was strongly influenced by Francesco di Giorgio. The appearance of the rocca was largely medieval for it had a triangular plan with three drum towers at its points. The strongest rises higher and acts like the medieval *mastio* or keep. It was surrounded by a pentagonal bastion, one of the most interesting contributions to the plan, scooped out with casemates for artillery and disposed so that its guns could at least enfilade one curtain wall and support an adjoining tower. The fort at Civitavecchia also dates from this period. It is a rather conservative fort, rectangular in shape, with four corner circular towers and a projecting seven-sided keep designed by the architect Bramante, the middle of the northern face being completed by Michelangelo.

THE WORK OF THE SANGALLI

During the first two decades of the sixteenth century there was feverish fortress-building, when theories were put into practice and, so long as results were being observed, there was little new theorising. The Sangallo family of architects and engineers had a major hand in the work in Italy which was to dominate the European scene for a century. From 1500 until the rise of the French school, itself dominated by Vauban, the Italians held the field with their new bastioned system of defence, nearly all major fortifications being carried out by them. Francesco Giamberti was the eldest of the Sangalli, designer of the forts at Sarzana and Sarzanello.

For a short while the triangular fort became popular. It had been used as far away as Scotland at Caerlaverock Castle and found several expressions in fifteenth century Italy. Its chief disadvantage was the narrowness of the fighting area at the points of the triangle. Sarzanello was originally a triangular fort with its vulnerable entrance in the middle of one curtain covered, slightly later, by a detached triangular ravelin so that the overall perimeter of the building assumed the shape of a bisected diamond. The walls of the drum towers, the curtains and the ravelin are scarped towards their base from a string course two-thirds of the way up their exterior surfaces. Although on a hilltop, the fortress has a comparatively low-lying profile and is sunk into an encircling dry ditch. The towers and the ravelin do not rise above the parapet of the curtain walls, so that the whole fortress appears flat-topped with the exception of its traditional square mastio which rises higher in the centre of the fort. Giuliano da Sangallo was responsible for many other works of military architecture including Colle Val d'Elsa (1479), Poggio Imperiale (1488) and defences at Arezzo and Pisa.

His eldest son, Giuliano da Sangallo (1445?–1516), was also an architect and a sculptor. With Baccio Pontelli (1450–92) he designed the triangular fortress at Ostia (1482–86). This is similar to designs made by Francesco di Giorgio, who was probably referring to Pontelli when he mentioned in his *trattato* that another architect had stolen some of his inventions. Giuliano was an active military engineer engaged in a number of sieges and he directed the attack on the fort at Sarzana designed by his father.

His brother, Antonio da Sangallo the elder (1455–1534), was responsible for some of the most important transitional fortresses in Italy. In 1493 he modernised Castel Sant Angelo in Rome by substituting triangular bastions for the old circular drums. At Civita Castellana (1494–97) Antonio da Sangallo designed a palace-fortress for Cesare Borgia, pentagonal in plan with two circular and three triangular bastions whose battlements lie level with the parapet of the curtain. The traditional central mastio was retained, octagonal in shape and rising higher than the rest of the fort. The design of his fort in Nepi built about 1484 is traditional, consisting of a rectangular plan with corner circular towers. In 1499 he began the defences of Livorno and between 1501 and 1502 was building his most important design, the rocca at

Below: *The Porta di Volterra at Colle Val d'Elsa.*

Bottom: *The mastio of the fortezza at Civita Castellana.*

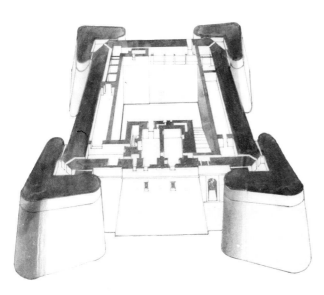

Forte del Sangallo at Nettuno.

Nettuno. This last is one of the most interesting and well-preserved forts in Italy showing the emergence of the full bastion plan. It was quite detached from the walled town, although later an outer town enceinte was added which joined a corner of the fort, so Antonio had considerable freeedom of action. He conceived the building as a perfect solution to both the practical and theoretical problems. It was square in plan, in line with the neo-platonic ideas of his time, and had four identical corner bastions whose faces were correctly aligned with the line of defence from the flank of the opposite bastion. The shoulders of the bastions were rounded to become embryonic orillons. Because of the talus of the curtain walls there was no room for batteries low down in the flank but only at parapet level. The mastio was retained and rose high above the curtain on the seafront facade.

The fort at Civitavecchia (1508–15) was

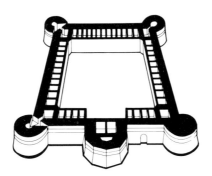

The so-called Forte Michelangelo at Civitavecchia.

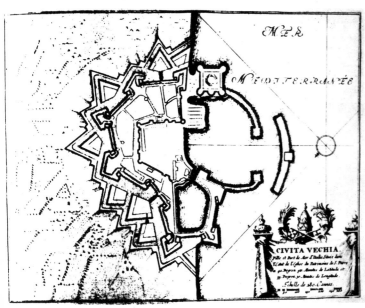

The town walls of Civitavecchia; after Fer, 1697.

retrograde for it had round towers. Its basic plan is like Nepi but with Bramante's mastio projecting beyond the curtain on the north facade. Antonio's villa-fortress of Caprarola begun in 1515 and completed by other architects is described later.

Antonio da Sangallo the younger (1483–1546), nephew of the elder Antonio, carried the Italian bastion design to its logical conclusion. He became the acknowledged expert on Italian fortifications, his great opportunity opening as a result of the shake-up of defences following the sack of Rome in 1527. The younger Sangallo designed the fully bastioned enceinte around the port of Civitavecchia. During the siege of Florence he was opposed to Michelangelo's defensive system and was later commissioned to remodel the town defences and to build the Fortezza da Basso (1534). This fort shows the full transition to the Italian bastion system. A contemporary writer, Baccile da Castilione, stated that 'the best praise that can be given to him who designed it is that it has never been used as a fort in war; but only as a symbol of power'. The angle bastion was fully established as the standard solution to the problem of the defence of towns. Vasari described it: 'the defence work enjoys a reputation all over the world and is believed to be impregnable.' One should remember that it was designed as much for internal security as external defence.

Rome's deficiencies had been cruelly demonstrated in the sack of the city, and Antonio was called during 1537 to work until his death on the vast programme for the defence of the Vatican outlined by Paul III. Machiavelli advised and Michelangelo was involved, along with numerous other engineers including Jacopo Castriotto.

Design for fortifications; after Michelangelo.

MICHELANGELO

Michelangelo (1475–1564) was engaged on two major projects of fortification. In 1529 he was procurator-general for the defence of Florence and from 1547 to 1548 was engaged on the work of rebuilding the Vatican fortifications. It is not known whether the sketches which remain were fanciful scribblings or actual projects for earthworks which he so strongly advocated. The Florentine defences, mainly outworks, are now destroyed. Surviving drawings, probably depicting temporary defences to buttress the walls of Florence and made about 1528, show a remarkable vitality and a complete change from the passive concept of defence to a dynamic aggressiveness. The forms of bastions take on an organic appearance, unrestrained by the strict geometry which is such a feature of the regular work of the Italian school. Michelangelo's drawings are difficult to decipher, but the baroque curves were primarily intended to deflect shot. The weakness of his design arose in the restricted field of fire through the limited aperture of the embrasures and the need therefore for a multitude of defensive artillery. Ackerman has brilliantly described his designs as follows: 'His bastions spring from the walls like crustacean monsters eager to crush the enemy in their claws.'

Michelangelo's contribution to the costly work of fortifying the Vatican was problematic but from Vasari it is known that he was involved in a monumental row with Antonio da Sangallo the younger. Sangallo, who had faced him at Florence, accused him of being a sculptor and a painter but not a military

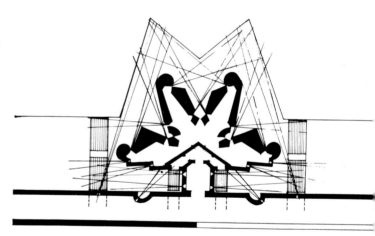

Project for the Porta al Prato at Florence; after Michelangelo.

engineer. To this he replied that he knew little of those arts, 'but of fortifications, considering the thought he had devoted to it over so long a time, and his practical experience, he believed he knew more than Sangallo and his whole family put together.'

SANMICHELI

Michele Sanmicheli (1484–1559) was the other great Italian practitioner of the first half of the sixteenth century. His opportunity came in 1530 when he was commissioned to complete the ring of fortifications which would safeguard Verona, a strategically placed city on the plain facing the route from northern Europe through the Brenner Pass. His bastions, which embraced the west and south sides of the town, were

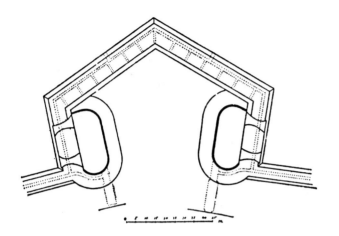

smaller than later designs, having long sections of curtain wall between them. The della Trinita Bastion, the first to be completed, was obtuse-angled in plan, giving it little working depth for the manhandling of guns. Consequently, in his later designs he tended to make the salient more acute. The shoulders of his flanks were square and the flanks themselves joined the curtains at right angles. The flank of each bastion contained a *piazza bassa*, a casemate for artillery low down to cover the ditch and enfilade the curtain.

Two of Sanmicheli's gates still stand well-preserved at Verona, although their abutments have been cut away to allow modern traffic to circulate. The

Plan of the dei Riformati Bastion at Verona by Sanmicheli.   *Porta Nuova at Verona.*

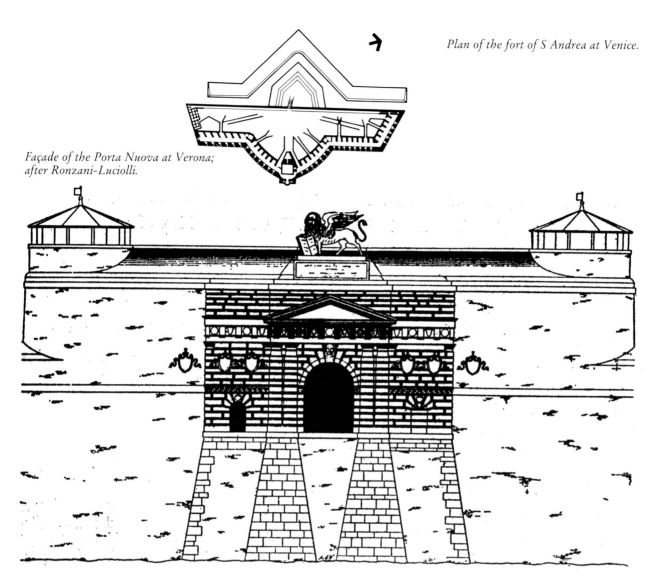

Plan of the fort of S Andrea at Venice.

Façade of the Porta Nuova at Verona; after Ronzani-Luciolli.

Porta Nuova (1533–40) lies in the middle of the curtain protected by two bastions. However the gate, in addition to its architectural embellishment and rusticated masonry intended to give it the appearance of strength, was also designed as a cavalier. Its top surface was provided with gun embrasures and strong parapets capable of making it a defensible position; it was in fact the earliest known artillery-defended gateway. By about 1550 Sanmicheli had changed his approach, for the Porta Palio, although equally impressive on the outside, was a less strong device, incapable of supporting heavy artillery on its roof and dependent upon its adjoining bastions for defence.

In 1534 Sanmicheli was requested to report on the defence of Venice, and subsequently he constructed his classic fortress at the entrance to the harbour, Sant Andrea on the Lido. This, plus a line of ancillary forts, was to protect the seaward approaches, with land fortresses in strong points such as Treviso, Padua, Vicenza and Verona ringing the landward approach.

Sanmicheli was one of the last of those artists whose work embraced a variety of disciplines. Brunelleschi, Bramante, Michelangelo, Leonardo and Benvenuto Cellini were all able to combine the practice of military architecture with other pursuits, and Sanmicheli's civil architecture is at least as important as his military undertakings. For the next generation of Italians the complexity of the subject called for specialisation and there emerged the highly skilled and independent profession of the military engineer.

THE SEMI-FORTIFIED VILLA: AN ARISTOCRATIC SYMBOL

From the time of the downfall of the Roman empire life in the country had been hazardous and it was as a result rarely populated by men of means. Only the castle or fortified town was safe from predatory raids or armed invasions. In fact the Mediterranean littoral remained susceptible to the maurauding attacks of corsairs well into the middle of the eighteenth century. However in some places conditions improved, with stable government and some relaxation from the need to maintain high standards of defensive architecture. There emerged the semi-fortified villa, conceived partly as an aristocratic symbol.

Stokesay Castle.

In Britain Stokesay Castle (1240–1305) shows how a fortified manor house could already, at the end of the thirteenth century, provide a reasonable level of comfortable accommodation. The hall is spacious, nearly 16 metres (53ft) long and some 10 metres (33ft) high, providing sufficient space for the lord's family, his guests and his servants. Set aside between the hall and the south towers is a solar, a room open to the sun's rays with a pleasant view across the wooded countryside and providing some measure of privacy and comfort for the lord and his family. Two peepholes were cut through the party walls so that he could keep an eye on guests and retainers in the hall below.

Hurstmonceux Castle (1441) is a vast brick structure built upon a square plan with bold salient octagonal towers and an impressive gateway. It was not designed to be put to the test of a siege but to symbolise the martial traditions of an arrogant ruling class. It is 'a magnificent parade of brow-beating feudal pride'. Lulworth Castle in Dorset still shows four large drum towers at the corners of a rectangular plan, but the curtain wall is adorned with richly decorated Renaissance doors and windows, no bar to a violent intruder.

Alberti, in his *della famiglia* written about

Hurstmonceux Castle.

Azay-le-Rideau.

Below: *Lulworth Castle.*

Bottom: *Langeais.*

1432, was the first to revive the idea of the villa. Quoting from Roman sources he extolled the qualities of a life in the country, not too far distant from a place of work in the city. From the time of the early Renaissance there sprung up, first in Italy and then elsewhere, buildings which retained a semblance of the fortified character of their predecessors. There is an almost imperceptible change from the castle with palatial accommodation to the palace containing an element of defence, at first functional but later only symbolic and romantic.

The French were no less proud of their chivalric background, and a group of châteaux on the Loire were built in the sixteenth century which shows the change from fortress to house. Langeais (1465–70) still presents a formidable exterior, but the garden facade is already gentler. Chaumont still retains the massive circular corner towers, its walls are machicolated and its gate is covered by a drawbridge, but both the towers and the curtain walls are pierced by commodious windows. Chambord has a quadrangular plan with massive drum towers, but the walls are pierced by large areas of glass and the skyline cluttered with delicate decoration which would topple at the first discharge of a cannon. The Bohier wing at Chenonceaux (1515–22) and Azay-le-Rideau (1518–27) are either wholly or partially surrounded by water, but although the architecture contained elements of castellated design they were never intended to withstand assault.

The lower stages of the Villa Farnese at

The Palazzo Farnese at Caprarola; after Ferrerio and Falda.

Below: *Azay-le-Rideau.*

Bottom: *Chenonceaux, showing the Bohier wing on the right.*

Caprarola were modelled on the pentagonal plan of a fortress with five angled bastions, but the superstructure, mainly designed by Vignola between 1559 and 1573, was a stately High Renaissance palace. Not so Verdala Palace in Malta (1586) designed by Gerolamo Cassar; even at this late date the building retains an element of defence, although the windows are quite large. There was a ditch and loopholes in the flanks of the small bastions for musketry defence. It was necessary for the grand master in his summer residence to take precautions against a commando-like attack by the Turks.

The Verdala Palace in Malta.

Claypotts. (Crown Copyright)

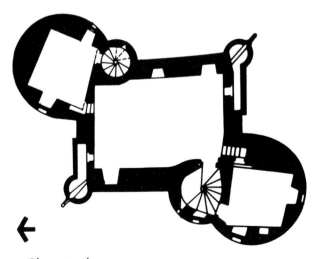

Claypotts; plan.

SCOTTISH TOWER HOUSES

Unlike the semi-fortified villa, the Scottish tower houses of the sixteenth century did not utilise defensive devices for purely symbolic reasons. These buildings were primarily houses designed for private living, safeguarded against the ever-present threat of sudden attack. They were high narrow buildings, cleverly designed so that their plans conformed to the shape of a Z or an L. Thus by staggering the towers so that overlapping fields of fire could be poured from the wide-mouthed gunports on the ground floor, an all-round ground defence could be maintained with minimum expenditure on a few handguns. As circular rooms do not provide the most convenient spaces for living accommodation, the upper rooms of these houses were cleverly turned into rectangular spaces by corbelling from the round tower. Claypotts, near Dundee, built on the Z plan between 1569 and 1588, is a splendid example of this type of house.

ENGLISH RENAISSANCE FORTS

In the mid-sixteenth century Britain once again resorted to the construction of important fortified works to defend her coast. The peaceful years of the preceding reign had helped fill the coffers so vital to Henry VIII to fit out a British field army for service in Europe. The expeditionary forces of 1513 and 1523 may have made little impact upon the European scene but they certainly provided the English king with an opportunity to make contact with European practice in the art of fortification and gave him a lifelong fascination with artillery. For many years the practice of fortification in Britain had dwindled into insignificance and the revolutionary system of the Italian engineers seemed no more than distant rumours. It is therefore understandable that when Britain came once more to re-arm her standards of fortification should be rudimentary. Henry VIII's exchequer had been buttressed from the spoils gained through the confiscation of church property, so he could undertake the most expensive scheme of coastal defence that Britain had ever witnessed. Along the south coast, at vulnerable points facing France, new forts were erected on a scale quite unprecedented. They stretched from the mouth of the Medway to the great bay at Milford Haven. Three of the most interesting examples,

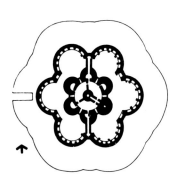

Deal Castle; aerial view and plan.

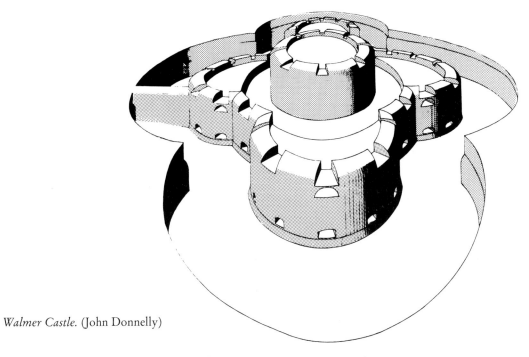

Walmer Castle. (John Donnelly)

*Plans of some of the coastal forts built by Henry VIII
showing the wide variety of plan forms and the desire for
symmetry.* (John Donnelly)

Walmer

*A contemporary cannon; a 12-pounder brass basilisk cast in
1554 and presented to Henry VIII.*

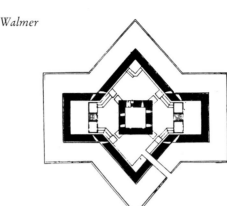

Southsea

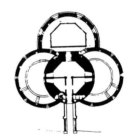

St Mawes

known as 'the castles which keep the downs', lie close
together. Deal, Walmer and Sandown were all built
between 1539 and 1540 to protect the anchorage
which lay within the Goodwin Sands. They were pure
forts rather than castles, designed as powerful artillery
platforms and were probably the work of Stephen von
Haschenperg, a German military engineer employed
by Henry between 1539 and 1543. All the forts were
centrally planned, with rounded bastions mounting
tiers of guns both in casemates and on barbette platforms. The forts invariably had a higher round central
keep and were encircled by ditches. There was nothing
elsewhere at that date quite like them.

   Certainly they were a long way from current
Italian practice, but Dürer, who was advising on the
defences at Antwerp in 1520, designed semi-circular
bastions with sloping parapets and there were other
examples in north-eastern Europe from which von
Haschenperg's ideas may have sprung. The German
engineer was sacked in 1543, officially for bad behaviour and extravagance, but perhaps because Henry
already had a shrewd idea that the engineer's knowledge was not up to date. However before he left he
had designed Sandgate, probably St Mawes and the
central fort at Pendennis, whose outer italianate bastion was added in 1598. Pendennis was started in 1539
and St Mawes in the spring of 1540. Both were
finished by 1543. Dover had a low-lying shore battery
added to its defences. The fort at Camber was constructed on a site which had in the past repeatedly
attracted French landings. There were four new forts
on the Hampshire coast, supplementary work at
Portsmouth and numerous other defences stretching
away to the west.

   Britain braced herself for an invasion likely

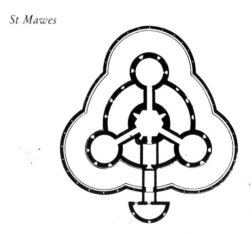

Sandgate

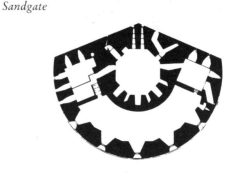

Portland

Pendennis Castle.

St Mawes.

Henry VIII's scheme for a pentagonal fort at Ambleteuse;
after Fer.

the quatrefoil-shaped bastions into pointed trefoils pushed forward, with flanks from which guns could enfilade the curtain walls. The shapes are certainly unusual although there is precedent in eastern Europe, and Francesco di Giorgio many years earlier tentatively sketched in a similar proposal for a bastion. The snag was that portions of dead ground in front of the bastions could not be covered by protective fire, and guns firing from the flanks along the face of their adjoining curtains would probably have hit the flanks of adjoining bastions. In the fortress at Ambleteuse and in the fortifications around Boulogne Rogers adopted the Italian triangular-shaped bastion as a measure of defence against enemy cannon fire. The transformation seems so sudden and so complete, in a matter of three or four years, that one must suspect the assistance of some Italian engineer. Henry VIII had a part to play, for he was a king with strong ideas who overruled Rogers' design for a triangular fort at Ambleteuse, preferring his own pentagonal scheme. At Boulogne the king added primitive cavaliers behind Rogers's bastions and inserted a radical city plan for the town, an idea which could only have come from Italy itself or from Italian designers working abroad. Rogers's lack of experience may have been crucial and could account for his eclipse as an important military engineer after Henry's death in 1547. This eclipse was not necessarily caused by the vindictiveness of his enemies. More likely he was found wanting, too set in his ways to cope with the rapid changes in the art of fortification which spread across the Channel. Neither can he escape some censure for the rapidity with which the English fortresses in France crumbled against the onslaught of the French armies in 1557. He paid the price, dying as a prisoner of war in French hands in the following year.

Sir Richard Lee, the first English architect to be knighted, had been with the army in Calais. In 1545 he was ordered to survey Tynemouth Castle where already there were Italian engineers working with the English. To Tynemouth he took two experts, Antonio da Bergamo and Giovanni Tomaso Scala. In 1557 Lee was in the Netherlands, and in January of the following year he was appointed to survey and strengthen the fortifications of the border town of Berwick-on-Tweed, which was to become his most important undertaking and the most serious British exercise in

to be mounted under the pretext of the divorce of Catherine of Aragon. An opportunity was further provided by the truce between Francis I of France and the Emperor Charles V of Spain reinforced by the Pope's bull of excommunication and the preaching of the crusade against Henry. In 1539, 1400 men were digging and building on the Downs defences and the work was rushed forward. But invasion never came and, except against isolated raids, the forts were never put to the test, perhaps fortunately for although adequate against any naval bombardment of the time most would have found it difficult to withstand a landward assault.

Work was also undertaken to strengthen the last English foothold in France. John Rogers (?1558) and Sir Richard Lee (?1513–75) were the two English military engineers engaged in the work. Contemporary drawings are valuable for illustrating the rapid transformation which took place in English fortress design between 1541 and 1546. In those years, under the pressure of war and the brilliant endeavours of a powerful king, Britain rapidly hoisted herself, in the art of fortification, from a medieval situation to a position where she could at least claim some parity with her European neighbours. Rogers' early essays at Guines Castle near Calais and in the perimeter north of the Humber near Hull are primitive expedients modelled on the forts Henry was constructing along the coasts of England. At Guines Rogers developed

Part of the Hull fortifications.

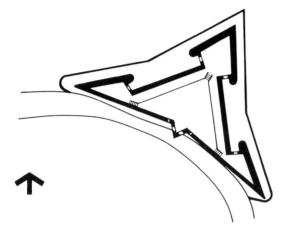

John Rogers's plan for Ambleteuse between Boulogne and Calais.

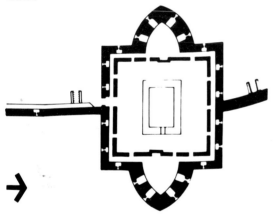

John Rogers's plan for a bastion at Guines Castle.

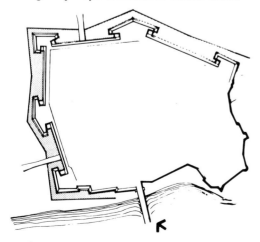

Berwick-on-Tweed; plan.

fortified town design to have survived. Lee shortened the medieval circuit of walls and threw a girdle of Elizabethan ramparts across the north and eastern faces of the city, its curtain walls and bastions modelled on the early Italian school of fortification. The work was remarkably advanced, equal to anything carried out elsewhere. This was particularly true of the Cumberland and Windmill Bastions, with their obtuse-angled plans, their flat-headed orillons and their *piazze bassi*, all of which were very close to Francesco Laparelli's work on the landfront at Valletta in Malta (1566). It is remarkable that an English engineer should have so quickly grasped the essentials of the Italian system, though it was less surprising that Elizabeth should have commissioned him, knowing her distrust of foreigners and in particular Italians. But Lee was only one of a number of men who were critically examining the new art of fortification. Paul Ive was amongst them. His book *The Practice of Fortification*, printed in 1589, was one of the earliest English books on the subject and although it drew heavily on Italian and French sources showed a penetrating mind and a man with practical experience.

Shocked by the loss of Calais in 1558, Queen Elizabeth strengthened the defences of her kingdom. Berwick was only one aspect of the work. Between 1570 and 1577 Ive was working on Castle Cornet in Guernsey where he carried out the first stage of enveloping the old medieval fortress within a protective sheath of Tudor fortifications. The second stage, built between 1593 and 1597, clothed the whole front with Italian bastions. In 1598 Ive was working at Pendennis on a similar outer screen which proved strong enough to withstand a five months' siege by Fairfax's parliamentary army in 1646, one of the stoutest resistances of the Civil War. An almost identical enceinte was constructed by Frederico Giannibelli around the medieval castle at Carisbrooke in the Isle of Wight, built mainly between 1597 and 1600.

Portsmouth was the only fully defended town in southern England. King's Bastion and the long curtain on the waterfront are part of its original fortifications dating from the fourteenth century, and Southsea Castle was built nearby in 1544 as part of Henry VIII's policy of strengthening the coast. Even in Henry's reign the town was encircled by walls on the landward side strengthened by circular towers and

Below: *Poland. The Warsaw barbican.*

Bottom: *The barbican and the Florianska Gate at Krakow.*

developed a system which was basically architectural, requiring massive permanent stone fortifications, whereas northern countries continued to rely, right up to the twentieth century, upon the construction of suitable platforms to house deterrent guns. Thus, when the Italians were moving towards a system which utilised a limited number of guns, each requiring a considerable time to reload and only capable of a limited range and striking power, the Germans and other northern races massed their guns so that they provided strong frontal fire as opposed to the Italian dependence upon enfilade.

Architecturally, the German development of the tower is a logical product of Roman and medieval thought. The barbican, a strong tower erected at the end of a bridge leading to one of the gates of a city and designed to provide a powerful outer defence, was gradually brought up to date. The solidity of medieval construction which had sufficed to deflect boulders thrown by the attacker's ballistae gave way to broad circular towers equipped with numerous casemates through which guns could fire on an attacker. Good examples remain in Germany, for instance the Spitaltor of 1572 at Rothenburg on the Tauber, but the best examples are to be found in Poland. The barbican at Krakow lies in front of the Florianska Gate and is an impressive affair of menacing turrets and medieval machicolation, modernised with the introduction of three levels of gun turrets designed to allow guns to fire over the ditch and cover the approaches. This barbican, at the end of an open bridge, was completed in 1498, but it continued to give valuable defence throughout the succeeding centuries, as in the seventeenth century its structure was joined at the neck to the Florianska Gate by a screened fortified work.

The Warsaw barbican, destroyed by the Germans in the Second Great War but recently reconstructed, shows the conservative attitude of northern designers for it was originally built as late as 1656. It is a semi-circular structure pushed out from the curtain wall with four abutting towers curved on their outer faces and crowned with crenellation, a hangover from the middle ages.

The *basteja* was the northern counterpart of the Italian bastion and its design springs from the barbican. Most have now been destroyed but it can be seen best in the drawings of Albrecht Dürer. In his

fully developed Italian triangular bastions to the north-east. But the main task of providing an effective bastion trace fell to Bernard de Gomme in the middle of the seventeenth century. De Gomme began work in 1665 to provide an integrated defensive system of bastions and ravelins and their supporting works which will be described later.

NORTHERN EUROPE

Northern countries have always had a different approach to defence. Perhaps with dependence upon more temporary building materials like timber and with a strong nomadic tradition they tended to rely more upon firepower than fixed defences. The Italians

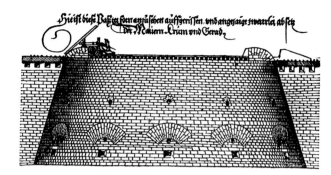

One of *Dürer's* bastejas.

An engraving of the Siege of a Fortress *by Albert Dürer.*

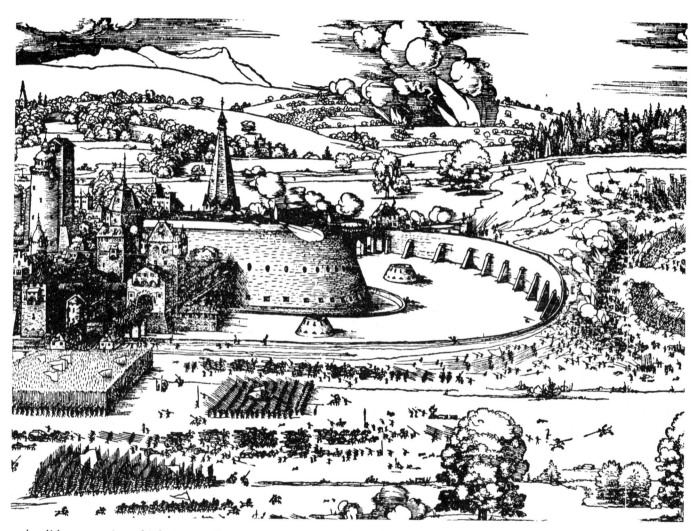

splendid perspective of *The Siege of a Fortress*, published in Nürnberg in 1527, we see all the essentials of *basteja* design. The multitude of guns, sufficient to outmatch any attacking enemy, fired both from the parapet and from the carefully constructed arched casemates, each equipped with elaborate smoke-vents, in a large curved structure, its outer walls sloping back to deflect enemy shot. The ditch is divided into two portions. The inner, adjacent to the base of the *basteja*, is filled with water, and the broad outer portion, in which stand circular *capannati* with their own gun positions to rake the ditch, projects in a broad semi-circular band to the walls of the counterscarp. The multi-gun *basteja* has an almost continuous history in

northern Europe. Renaissance examples merge into the multi-gun caponier used during the great period of German fortification construction from the middle of the eighteenth century to the end of the nineteenth, by which time it had superseded the bastion and its use had become international practice.

Renaissance examples of the *basteja* were probably incorporated into the nineteenth century defences of Ingolstadt and are shown in many sixteenth century drawings. One of the best of these is illustrated at Wroclaw (Breslau) where an aerial perspective shows a semi-circular *basteja* with casemated gun positions on two floors and space for five further guns on the roof firing through embrasures. The curtain

A basteja on the town walls at Wroclaw in Poland.

wall to which the *basteja* is attached has a curved parapet with embrasures copied from Italian engineers such as Antonio da Sangallo the younger. Also at Wroclaw, a good example of a renaissance *basteja* has been excavated and restored. It projected from the corner of the city walls, a long, low rectangular structure with a semi-circular face. It is first mentioned in documents in 1489 but was modified over the years and its gunports date from the seventeenth century. It was defended by two levels of guns, the upper level placed on the roof fired out over the countryside and a lower level had guns in the open which fired through arched embrasures. The guns were protected from in front and above by the masonry of the *basteja*. This is a system revived by General Haxo in the nineteenth century.

It would be wrong to suggest that the Germans developed only the gun platform for there are many fine examples of bastioned traces in Northern Europe. For example, the square citadel at Jülich had four corner bastions, of necessity acute-angled, a broad ditch and, beyond that, ravelins covering the curtains and counterguards covering the outer pair of bastions. The Bavarian fortress at Rothenberg (Schnaittach), built between 1729 and 1743 on a spur of rock, has a bastioned front with a large ravelin covering the central gate, surrounded by a ditch with, beyond that, a broad covered-way protected by mounds of earth called traverses, and a place of arms in the salient point. On the spur, bastions give way to a tenaille or zigzag trace to accommodate additional guns. However, it is only fair to point out that this place was designed by French engineers.

CHAPTER FOUR

The Baroque World: Defence in Depth

THE IMPACT OF THE BASTION

The 1550s saw an avalanche of publications on the theories of military architecture in Italy. Various hypotheses were tested in battle by experts who gradually developed a specialized knowledge in their field. An extraordinary consistency of style emerged which can be described as the later Italian style of fortification, probably brought about by the fact that nearly all those who wrote were practitioners whose exclusive province was military engineering. Except on rare occasions defensive systems no longer formed part of general treatises on architecture and the military engineer emerged as a professional man in his own right.

The system utilised the triangular bastion projecting beyond the main curtain-walled defence. At first bastions were very small and curtain walls very long so that guns on adjacent bastions had difficulty in flanking one another, that is providing effective enfilade fire across the face of their neighbouring bastions. The ditch, 30 to 40 metres (100–130ft) wide, had a counterscarp approximately parallel to the faces of the bastion so that this counterscarp formed a zigzag pattern on the outside of the defences. After about 1540 a covered-way, a protected passage for infantry so that they could move around screened from the fire of the attackers by higher ground, was added to the Italian system. The first recorded use of the covered-way was at Brescia in 1428. However the details of its construction are not clear and Tartaglia is often credited with the invention of this feature which was in regular use after 1540.

During the sixteenth century the Italians improved their construction and spread their ideas throughout Europe. Almost every sovereign state employed them and in Spain and the Low Countries they had ample opportunities to build and test new fortresses.

The ideal solution was constructed upon an interior polygon, although often in practice the engineers had to use their ingenuity to defend irregular sites or to modify earlier defensive systems.

The ideal front, the distance measured from the points of two bastions, was between 250 and 300 metres (275–330yds). The faces of the bastions were arranged so that they formed a prolongation of a line

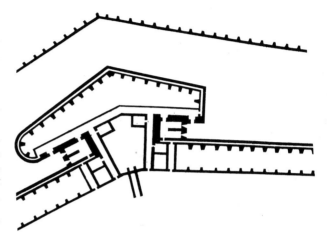

Two solutions to a typical bastion of the Italian school; after Zastrow.

drawn approximately from the gun positions in the flanks of their neighbouring bastions. These flanks projected at right angles from their curtain walls and so formed an obtuse angle with the face of the bastion. The curtain wall, which has always been the most vulnerable part of the defences was, in the early stages, covered by a semi-circular ravelin. Later in the Italian system it was covered by a triangular one, formed like a broad arrow with its faces some 60 to 75 metres (200–250ft) long, standing as an isolated outwork in the middle of the ditch. The intention was to force an enemy, before he penetrated the curtain wall of a town or fort, first to attack and capture the ravelin only to find himself still isolated in the middle of the ditch. He would next have had to direct his attack against one of the bastions only to find that this was protected on whichever side he attacked by an adjoining bastion. All this manoeuvre had to be successfully completed before an enemy could penetrate the interior.

After the covered-way had been adopted for the use of infantry on the outside of the ditch, Girolamo Cataneo proposed the re-entering place of arms. This was a space left at the re-entrant angles of the zigzag pattern made by the counterscarp of the ditch sufficient for the assembly of troops and munitions to be used against an initial attack or to be formed up for a sortie against a besieger's lines. This feature dates from 1567. Beyond the covered-way lay the glacis, sloping ground cleared of all obstacles,

Pietro Cataneo's design for an ideal city.

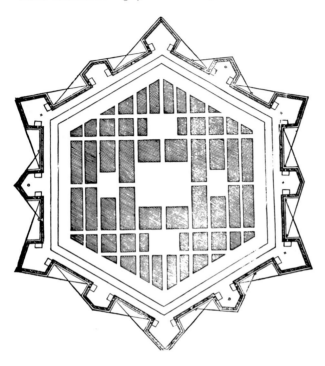

buildings and trees so that the defenders had an unobstructed view of the surrounding countryside and the attackers were forced to expose themselves to view or to use the ponderous method of mining and sapping as they slowly worked their way up to the outworks of the defended position.

LATER ITALIAN THEORISTS

Many writers described these features in this period. There is room here to refer only to a few.

Pietro Cataneo is one of the exceptions to the rule that specialisation had overtaken the writers of treatises, for he devoted one book in his *I quatro primi libri di architectura*, published in Venice in 1554, to the discussion of fortification. He clearly stated the case for the Italian system. 'In view of the new weapons such as artillery, it is much more practicable to have them [the bastions] with an angular outline instead of a circular one so that every part can be much more easily defended. Each curtain can be covered by embrasures in the bastions at the corners.' He then cited a variety of solutions to the problem, his first being a perfect square with four corner bastions like contemporary examples such as the castle at L'Aquila designed by Pedro Luis Scrivá in 1535. The art of

defence was becoming a mathematical science as the dimensions of each part under every variation of circumstance was calculated and indicated.

Giacomo Lanteri wrote two important works. His first, *Due dialoghi . . . del modo di desegnare le piante delle fortezze* came out in 1557 and two years later he published his *Due libri del modo di fare le fortificazione*. In these the art of fortification began to be fully served by the rules of geometry and took on the aspect of the science of mathematics. Engineers when writing treatises were usually concerned with the provision of permanent stone fortifications, but Lanteri was one of the first to introduce the subject of earth fortifications. He was born in Brescia and became chief engineer to Philip II of Spain.

THE PRINTED BOOK

There was a constant interchange of ideas amongst engineers in the field and in their published writings, and it is possible to trace the thread of ideas back to Roman theoreticians. Girolamo Maggi fought against the Turks and in 1564 brought out a publication incorporating Iacomo Castriotto's *Della fortificazione della città*. This work was later to influence Vauban. Maggi is always credited with the introduction of the cremaillère, but Francisco di Giorgio had used a somewhat similar though less scientifically worked out device years earlier and Scrivá had advocated it in his design for the fortress at Capua in the 1530s. The idea was to increase the permissible length of defence by indenting the curtain wall to form a series of additional flanks from which guns could fire across its face. Maggi's and Castriotto's treatise is illustrated with innumerable clear drawings, many of them in the form of aerial perspectives. Whilst working for the Venetians Maggi is reputed to have put into operation a number of his inventions including a method of setting fire to the Turkish lines of circumvallation at Famagusta, so perhaps it is not surprising that soon after his capture by them in 1571 he should have been quietly strangled in his prison at Constantinople.

Girolamo Cataneo was a Novarese engineer who was employed on the fortifications of Sabionetta by Vespasiano Gonzaga. In 1564 at Brescia he published *Opera nuoua di fortificare, offendere et difendere*, one of the most complete treatises on military architecture. This was only the first of some half a

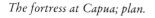

The fortress at Capua; plan.

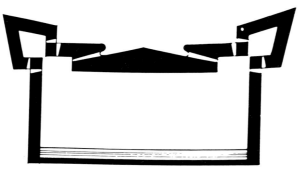

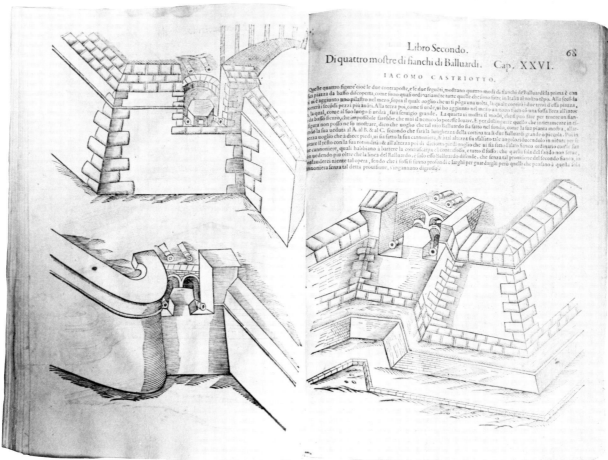

dozen long books he wrote on the subject, spreading his reputation throughout Western Europe. His works are thorough and detailed and he ranged from the broadest principles to minute details of building construction.

Captain Francesco de Marchi, an engineer from Bologna, wrote his military treatise *Architettura militare* about 1565 but it was not published until 1599. It is a most comprehensive book dealing with every sort of topic from the siting of fortresses under various conditions to the usual references to how the Greeks and Romans dealt with their problems (almost invariably added to treatises in order to give them respectability) to detailed discussions on the qualities of water. It is illustrated with a large number of clear drawings in which the author has shown the lines of fire of his defending guns and the detailed arrangements of streets and squares in a number of ideal cities

Drawing of guns firing from the flanks of bastions; after Maggi and Castriotto.

enclosed within his systems of fortification. In addition to the traditional system of Italian-bastioned fortification, de Marchi, like Castriotto about the same time, illustrated the idea of completely isolating the bastions from the enceinte so that they stood, similar to ravelins, as detached works in the ditch. This disposition had the advantage of slowing an attacker by interposing an additional ditch after he had taken possession of a bastion. In a number of examples de Marchi attached the orillon, a sort of curved shoulder, to the angle between the face and the flank of the bastion. In this way the flanks were retired or set back so that guns there were partially protected by the projecting orillon. Orillons soon became common practice in fortification.

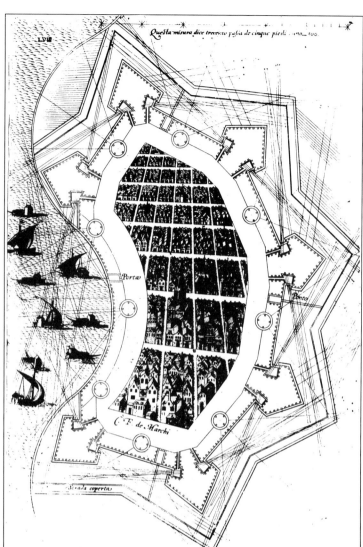

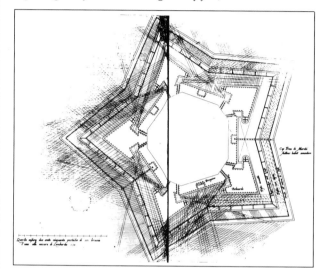

A fortified seaport; after de Marchi.

A pentagonal fortress showing arcs of fire; de Marchi.

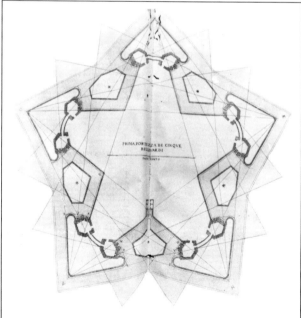

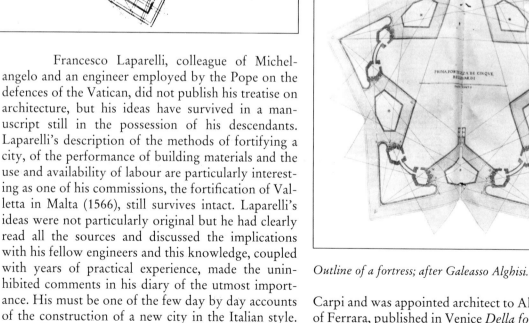

Outline of a fortress; after Galeasso Alghisi.

Francesco Laparelli, colleague of Michelangelo and an engineer employed by the Pope on the defences of the Vatican, did not publish his treatise on architecture, but his ideas have survived in a manuscript still in the possession of his descendants. Laparelli's description of the methods of fortifying a city, of the performance of building materials and the use and availability of labour are particularly interesting as one of his commissions, the fortification of Valletta in Malta (1566), still survives intact. Laparelli's ideas were not particularly original but he had clearly read all the sources and discussed the implications with his fellow engineers and this knowledge, coupled with years of practical experience, made the uninhibited comments in his diary of the utmost importance. His must be one of the few day by day accounts of the construction of a new city in the Italian style. Laparelli worked on the design for Valletta from 1565 until he set out to join the allied fleet. He wished to get into action against the Turks but died of the plague at Candia in 1570.

In that year Galasso Alghisi, who came from Carpi and was appointed architect to Alfonso II, Duke of Ferrara, published in Venice *Della fortificationi libri tre*, the most beautifully illustrated treatise of the period containing sharp, precise drawings. Book One was largely a criticism of the works of others, particularly those of Castriotto and Maggi. However his own designs were not without defects. Alghisi

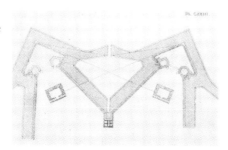

Alghisi's proposed trace for a fortress, with square cavaliers in each bastion.

Fortifications for an ideal city; after Vincenzo Scamozzi.

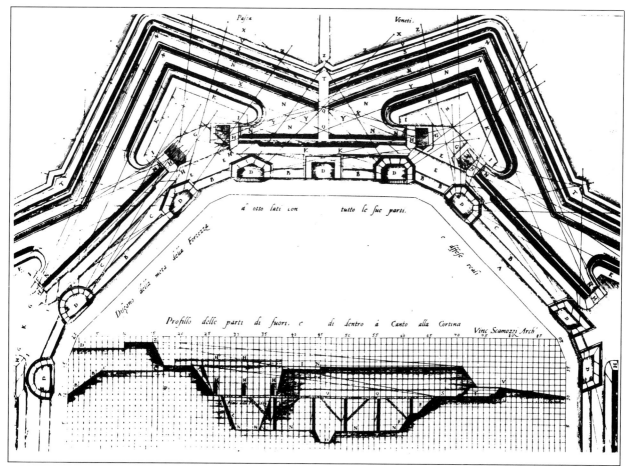

attempted to solve defensive problems by using a combination of bastions and tenailles. The tenaille is a serrated wall rather like the teeth of a saw. It was a device recommended by some German engineers but soon lost popularity in practice until it was revived in the eighteenth century by Montalembert. In Alghisi's design the trace was indented to form the tenaille, the extremities of which were capped by a bastion. In each flank of the bastion, and partly covered by orillons, he placed a hexagonal casemate for two tiers of guns, and between each pair of casemates there was a rectangular cavalier raised to survey the surrounding countryside and to provide additional firepower. The defect of the system lay in the fact that having so pulled back his curtain walls to provide the tenaille, he left very little usable space inside the fortress.

Vincenzo Scamozzi wrote the last important Italian architectural treatise to contain instructions on fortification. *L'idea dell architettura universale* was published in Venice in 1615 and the second book of the first part is devoted to military architecture. In 1593 Scamozzi had been involved in working out the design of the ideal fortified city of Palmanova for the Venetian Republic, so this theory was conditioned by practical experience. His writings are more valuable as an illustration of contemporary practice than as a source of new ideas.

It would be wrong to isolate the work of these writers without mentioning that there were many others whose books were as important and as influential as those described, men like Lorini, Belucci, Sardi and de Zanchi. Nor would it be fair to suggest that the Italians were the only ones to express their ideas on the theories of fortification during the sixteenth century. In Germany Daniele Speckle published *Architectura von Vestungen* in 1589 and was

Daniele Speckle's design for the fortifications of a city showing several tiers within each bastion.

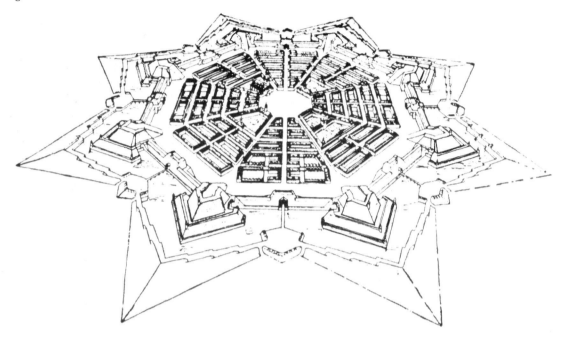

involved in the practice of his art at Ingolstadt, Ulm, Colmar and Strasbourg. He proposed several methods of fortification. He first recommended increasing the size of the bastions, which was generally done later, and providing them with triple flanks, protected by orillons, one above another for additional firepower.

He provided additional firepower on the vertical face from cavaliers which stood above the bastions and behind the middle of each short curtain. In another recommendation he furnished powerful ravelins in the ditch strengthened by flanks and a central cavalier. He also realised the importance of a covered-way as one of the most essential outworks and was probably the first engineer to design this as a cremaillère, a zigzag pattern which provided numerous faces from which the defenders could fire.

FRENCH WRITERS

French authors like Veroil de la Treille, whose *Manière de fortifier les villes et châteaux* was published in 1557, followed the Italian system. Errard de Bar-le-Duc was a more original thinker. In 1604 he published *La fortificatione reduicte en art et demonstrée*. He belonged to the corps of military engineers formed by Sully in 1602 and is really the first of the great school which was to emerge in France during the seventeenth and eighteenth centuries. Although he was not singu-

lar in realising the deficiency of some of the Italian and Spanish bastions whose salients were too acute (Laparelli had already pointed this out) he was the first who fixed, at 60 degrees, a minimum angle for the salient angles of the bastions and who adopted 265 metres (870ft) as the maximum length of the line of defence between the points of two adjoining bastions. The greatest flaw in his system was the result of making the angle between the face of the bastion and the flank a right angle, whereas the Italians always made this obtuse so that the angle between the flank and the curtain wall could be adjusted to a right angle. Bar-le-Duc's solution, although perhaps intended to protect guns in the flank, only provided a sharp angle which could be easily splintered by enemy fire. The device was far inferior to the orillon.

THE ILLUSTRATED BOOK

The printed book could spread ideas far and wide, but the illustrated book could provide as much information on one page as would otherwise require some dozen pages of printed text. People now accept the idea that a picture can often tell far more, but it must have been a revelation in the middle of the sixteenth century when illustrated books began to run in their thousands off the presses of Europe.

The methods of illustration are most important,

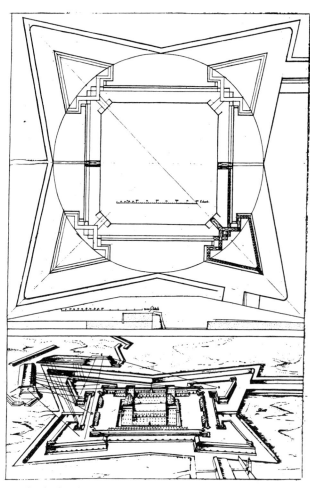

The plan and aerial perspective of a fortress illustrated in Daniele Speckle's book published in 1589.

Speckle's drawing shows a fortress seen from the air and by someone approaching it.

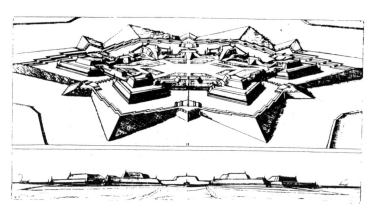

particularly the idea of combining plan, elevation and section on one sheet so that the full details of a work could be understood in any chosen scale; the use of the bird's eye view, particularly important in military architecture; the use of perspective drawings which gave a clarity to a complex idea. The first two methods appeared in Dürer's book of 1527, the first printed book on military architecture. The bird's eye view was exploited by Pietro Cataneo (1554) to show the profile and shape of his proposed forts, and by Daniele Speckle (1589) who was able to portray a fortress as seen by an enemy, as seen from the air and in its plan form. The originality of thought both in the ingenious way in which he introduces features of fortification and the way in which he depicts them, must place Speckle's book in the forefront of the early treatises on military architecture. In one plate he is able to depict the exact lines of fire of the bombarding cannon, and the sapping, bombarding and assault upon a shattered bastion. In another he shows the positions for defending artillery with perspectives of the mounted guns and intricate details of involved mechanical devices. There is a wealth of information which would otherwise have taken pages to describe.

By the second half of the sixteenth century woodblocks were being replaced by metal engravings so that the artist, using plates, could draw finer lines

and thus depict greater detail. This gave Speckle's drawings their clarity.

By the end of the seventeenth century the layout of fortresses, with all their elaborate outworks, was becoming so complicated as to make a descriptive book without illustrations a useless undertaking. The introduction of subtle curves, the interlocking of parts and the three dimensional aspects of the structure had taken on a Baroque character. The drawings of van Coehoorn show well this development. It was not confined to military architecture and found expression in the churches and palaces of the Italian Baroque; the work of men like Borromini, Guarini and Juvara. The question as to which art inspired the other is insoluble – although the professions had divided and become more specialised, military and civil attitudes to design were interwoven. Both required a complete mastery of spherical geometry; geometry is the one aspect of mathematics which can only be expressed in visual terms. If that form of architecture could be conceived in the architect's mind, it needed in preparation a knowledge of geometry and could only be communicated through graphic illustrations. Ferrerio and Falda (1655) in their cutaway three-dimensional engravings of the palaces and churches of Rome had led the way to an understanding of three-dimensional form which was to blossom into the interweaving geometrical vaults of Guarino Guarini in Turin.

VENETIAN FORTIFICATIONS

Venice was a great centre of early printing and Venetian engineers had been in the forefront in the publication of books on fortification. Men like Girolamo Cataneo, Pompeii Floriani, Girolamo Maggi,

The winged lion, symbol of the strength of Venice.

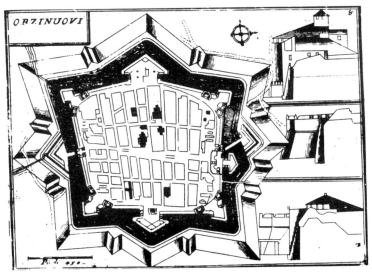

The Venetian town of Orzinuovi.

Francesco Tensini, Carlo Theti and Giovanni Battista Zanchi had all worked for the Republic and written books. As a result their fame spread and Venice played an important role in the development of the Italian basion, her engineers continuously strengthening the city's defences; the *terrafirma*, her possessions on the mainland of Italy; and her far flung overseas colonies which, due to her shortage of manpower, often could only be held with the aid of expensive fortifications, a situation which was later to face Britain in holding her maritime empire.

A highly efficient bureaucracy and expand-

ing markets, with a long cold war against the Turks which, in spite of the remark of one contemporary writer that 'big dogs seldom bite each other', broke out from time to time into open warfare, resulting in numerous sieges.

In addition to Verona, where Sanmicheli had built those early Italian bastions, the other towns of the *terrafirma* had to be strengthened by the addition of new bastion traces. Orzinuovi – where, in 1540, Michele Sanmicheli worked with his nephew in a family partnership that was to spread its practice throughout the colonies – had a formal, almost rectangular enceinte, enclosing a grid plan with seven bastions and two ravelins. Crema was fortified and so were Asolo, Legnano, Bergamo, Brescia, Peschiera and Treviso. With fine architectural flourish the gateways were decorated with columns and entablature, sculptured panels, trophies and, over the gate itself, the impressive winged lion of St Mark, insignia of the *Serenissima*, a deterrent against attack. Down the Adriatic and along the Dalmatian coast the path of fortifications flowed: Pola, Zara, Sebenico, Spalato, Curzola all received bastions or round gun-towers.

At Venice itself, on the approaches to the Lagoon where the waters swept past the Lido, Sanmicheli strengthened the fort of S Andrea, emphasising the difference in role of a coastal fort, for here the bastion solution was abandoned. In front of the earlier square tower he placed a monumental gateway, somewhat inappropriately, for it goes from nowhere to nowhere except an entrance to the fort. But on each side of the gate, long ranges of straight-faced casemated gun positions almost at water level (they do now flood at high tides), with terrepleins on top provided the maximum firepower against enemy vessels attempting to pass through the constricted waterway. To further seal the gap, in time of war a floating mortar battery could be pulled into mid-channel with booms on each side.

Three large colonial islands, liable to Turkish assault and dependent upon reinforcements were, for a while, particularly strongly held with town defences and coastal forts: Corfu, Cyprus and Crete.

Corfu guarded the entrance to the Adriatic Sea, its magnificent harbour providing adequate shelter for the largest battlefleet. The Venetians took over the island in 1203. As a result of a Turkish siege in 1536, the fortifications of the citadel, which stood on a

Venice, a model of Fort S Andrea on the Lido.

The fortifications of Corfu.

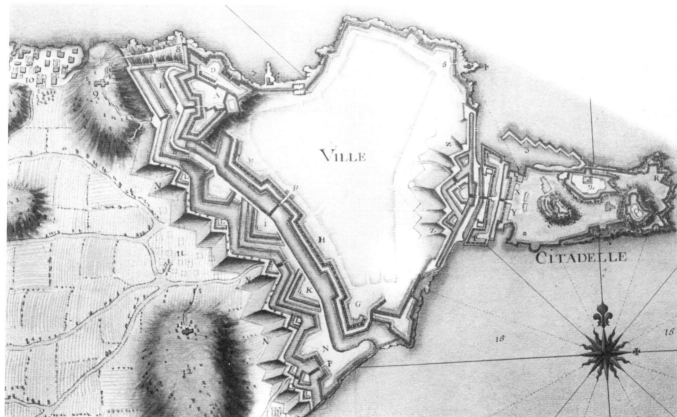

hilly promontory, were strengthened with the insertion of a wet ditch and bastions built across the neck by Sanmicheli. The town, laid out beyond a broad esplanade which acted as a glacis, was protected on its landward side by a strong front of fortification with broad bastions designed by Count von Schulemburg and with a powerful fort incorporated at the northern end. Then ravelins and counterguards were placed, in an unusual manner, beyond the wide ditch with a hornwork at the southern end. In front of these defences lay a continuous covered-way with re-entrant places of arms and a glacis. It was a formidable defensive line which was able to resist a strong Turkish investment in 1716, although their guns were able to bombard the town from higher ground to the west. When the French took over Corfu under the terms of the Treaty of Campo Formio in 1797, they placed detached forts on that high ground and fortified the island of Vido in the roadstead. As a result of the Treaty of Paris in 1815, Britain inherited Corfu and

The citadel and the landfront of Corfu as developed by the French.

A plan of the fortifications of Nicosia built by the Venetians.

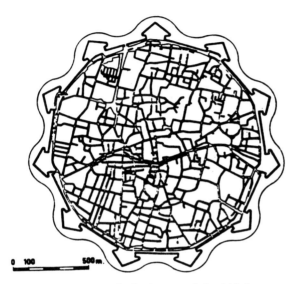

0 100   500 m.

Famagusta, Cyprus; the barbican and the Old Gate.

followed a vacillating policy of conservation and de-molition, finally slighting most of the magnificent for-tifications when she abandoned the Ionian Islands to the newly independent state of Greece in 1863. Sadly, only the citadel with Sanmicheli's bastions, and the northern fort, called Fort Neuf, remain in any reason-able state of preservation.

Venice was invested with Cyprus, the largest island in the eastern Mediterranean, in 1489 and only held on to it until 1571. In the middle of the island the Venetians rode roughshod over the buildings of the town of Nicosia, declaring its four miles of old perimeter defences indefensible, carving a new regular enceinte of eleven large standard bastions, but with no ravelins. The work was begun in 1567 to the designs of Ascanio Savorgnano. All the buildings outside the new perimeter were demolished to form a glacis and to deny the Turks useful building materials. The

Famagusta, Cyprus: the Martinengo Bastion.

pentagonal bastions had rounded orillons which covered the flanks and were protected by a broad wet ditch some 80 metres (260ft) wide which the Turks were able to drain dry when they attacked Nicosia three years later. Against their assault the capital city stood for a mere seven weeks before surrendering. Its whole garrison was slaughtered by the Turks.

The other important fortified town was Famagusta, the main port on the eastern seaboard. When the Turks attacked in 1570 its defences had been only partly modernised. The south and west fronts were covered by tall curtains walls with sloping parapets and narrow terrepleins, interspersed by semicircular towers with a strong cluster at the junction of the two walls. This consisted of a tall faceted tower called the barbican, which projected to protect the adjoining gate. In front stood a multi-gun ravelin, all making a strong though somewhat antiquated corner. The north front, a tenaille, and the north-east corner were modernised. Covering the corner stood an impressive bastion with square orillons covering broad flanks. Because the nearest semi-circular tower on the east front was too far away to give effective support, a retirade was inserted – a break in the face of the curtain halfway from the flank of the bastion, to provide additional flanking fire. With these defences Famagusta held out for ten months, long after the rest of Cyprus had fallen, but the situation was hopeless so, in 1571, the

Crete: Iraklion.

fortress surrendered. For the Turks this was some compensation for the defeat they had suffered at the great naval battle of Lepanto in that year.

Crete, the other large island in the eastern Mediterranean, was nearer to Venice, further from Constantinople and thus easier to hold. The three main coastal cities, Iraklion (Candia), Rethimon and Khana (Canea), plus three offshore islands – Suda, Grabousa (Gambusa) and Spina Lunga – were all

Crete: two of the bastions of Iraklion (Candia) with their adjacent flanks.

strongly fortified by the Venetians to hold what was, in effect, almost a slave colony.

When the Turks did attack Crete, most of the island soon fell, but Candia, encircled by its fine bastions, their powerful flanks protected by curved orillons, and reinforced from the sea, held out for twenty-two years – the longest recorded siege in history. By adopting an aggressive defence, by pushing out bold hornworks and redoubts from threatened sectors of the enceinte, a generation born under siege was able to grow up there before the city finally surrendered in 1669. Spina Lunga, with its semi-circular gun platforms, stayed in Venetian hands until 1715, but one cannot believe that the Turks tried hard to take the little island.

THE APPLICATION OF THE BASTIONED TRACE TO THE FORTIFICATION OF TOWNS

All over Europe princes and their engineers hurried to put their towns and cities into a state of defence utilising the well-tried and eminently successful system advocated by the Italians against the threat of efficient artillery fire which each year became more insistent. Though most of these fortifications have been pulled down to make way for ever-expanding suburbs, for-

tunately there are beautiful engravings by Braun and Hogenberg in *Civitates orbis terrarum* (1572–1618), by Merian in *Topographia Gallicae* (1644) and by Fer in *Les Forces de l'Europe* (1697), together with many individual drawings and paintings of the period.

Most engineers had to adopt irregular sites, but when the opportunity arose to design on a new site in flat country they invariably chose a multi-sided regular and symmetrical enceinte. The more sides that were used the greater the number of bastions and the nearer a line of bastions approached to a straight line. This permitted the construction of obtuse-angled bastions, less vulnerable to enemy bombardment and shorter, more easily defended curtain walls. Once the shape of the perimeter had been decided, a symmetrical figure with regularly spaced bastions, it was almost inevitable that the interior arrangement of the town, its streets, building blocks and squares, should follow a regular pattern. Many modern architectural historians have suggested that the origin of this regularity in Renaissance town planning was the result of an absorption of neo-platonic theories. In fact the shape of the town was dictated by the shape of the fortifications and this was the result of practical necessity.

Palmanova, lying on the flat land north of Venice, is a splendid surviving example of a fortified

Palmanova near Venice; after Braun and Hogenberg.

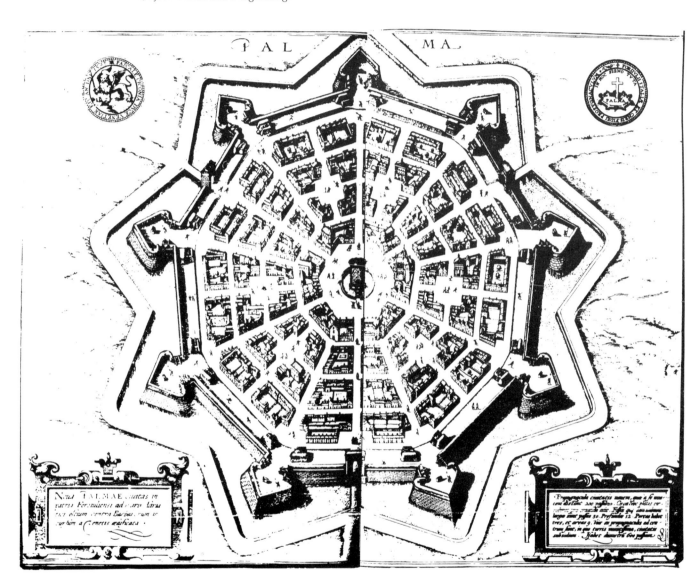

town. It was probably planned by Giulio Savorgnano in 1593. Later modified, it now consists of a nine-sided figure with angle basions from which streets run back to a square in the centre of the town. Intermediate streets run from the centre of each curtain where, in three instances, the gates are placed. Contemporary drawings tend to exaggerate the projection of the bastions. At Palmanova they are broader and more obtuse-angled than they appear in Braun and Hogenberg's engraving. Savorgnano's defensive system depended upon the bastions and their protective ditches.

Subsequently lunettes and ravelins were added beyond the main ditch to cover the points of the bastions and the curtain walls.

Valletta in Malta is probably the finest remaining example of a fortified city on a peninsula. The Knights of St John defending Malta had emerged successful from the Great Siege by the Turks in 1565 but the imminent threat of a fresh Turkish assault overshadowed the island. In these circumstances Francesco Laparelli was called in to prepare a master plan for the new city. The point of the peninsula was defended by

Below: *The landfront at Valletta.*

Bottom: *An old photograph of the landfront at Valletta
taken from the central curtain showing the ravelin and, to
the left, one of the counterguards.*

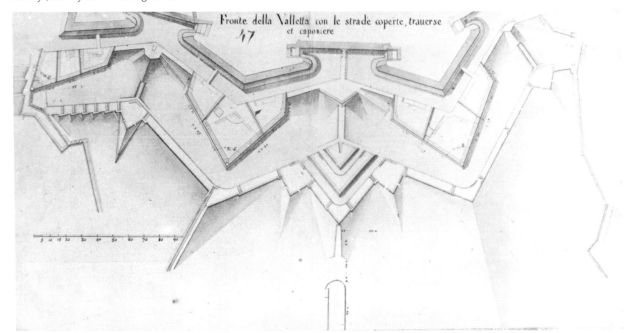

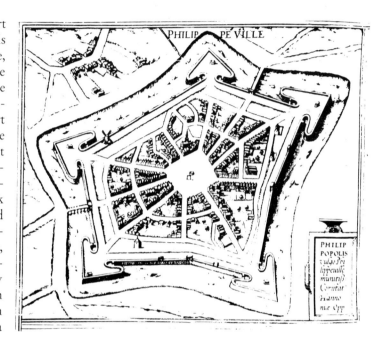

Philipville near Namur in Belgium; after Braun and Hogenberg.

the damaged fortress of St Elmo. Laparelli rebuilt Fort St Elmo on its original antiquated plan because this was the easiest and quickest thing to do and because, with the construction of the new city walls, it became no more than an advanced platform unlikely to be assaulted. If the Turks were to return, Laparelli advised the knights to construct a powerful square fort on the high ground near the neck of the peninsula. The landward front of the fort was to be constructed first and, if no time allowed, this only needed to be constructed to form the basis of the main strong landfront across the peninsula. No fresh major assault took place and the city walls were built and its streets laid out according to Laparelli's plan of 1566. The landfront of Valletta is particularly interesting because, being the strongest sector, its plan followed the principles outlined by the new school of Italian military engineers. The work is superior to Laparelli's work in Rome. Owing to the shortness of the landfront in Malta he was able to trace his curtain walls in almost a straight line, thus providing obtuse-angled bastions. He was also able to place these much closer together than had been his earlier practice in Rome where, because of the length of the enceinte, the small bastions are widely spaced. The Valletta front of 1566 is a precursor of the fully developed bastioned system of defence. Behind the bastions Laparelli placed powerful cavaliers to act as raised gun platforms dominating all the ground in front of the city. The defences stand almost as he designed them, except that orillons have been added to the rectangular flanks of his bastions and the ditch has been deepened. Low counterguards were added in front of the bastions in the mid-seventeenth century when a ravelin, now demolished, was constructed to cover the main gate.

Cities were encased wherever possible with masonry walls, but early engravings show numerous examples of the use of soil defences reinforced on their exposed vertical faces by fascines, strong wattle constructions in timber and reed to prevent the erosion of soil. Later the full advantages of earth fortifications became apparent in their ability to absorb the impact of shot without being shattered, in the lack of danger from splintering and in the ease with which a breach could be repaired.

Nearly all the main towns and cities of Europe were refortified in the second half of the six-

teenth century or at the beginning of the seventeenth century. Some, like Willemstad (1565), were new foundations. Numerous illustrated examples remain: Philipville (1555), Alkmaar (1597), Mannheim (1606), Charlesville (1608) and, in the oveseas colonies, towns like Quebec (1606).

Mannheim, lying at the confluence of the Neckar and the Rhine, is an interesting example of a fortified town. The contemporary illustrations agree on the general disposition of the fortified works but not on their details or proportions. Depending on one's point of view there was a heptagonal citadel supporting or subjugating the town whose total area was scarcely larger than that of the citadel. A bridgehead across the Rhine was protected by a hornwork, a smaller one across the Neckar by a flèche. The landfront was stiffened on the right by a detached star-shaped fort standing in front of a large hornwork, and on the left by an impressive crownwork. The point of the peninsula had a small pentagonal fort. The main enceinte consisted of Italian bastions, two of which had their flanks protected by orillons. Beyond lay a continuous ditch with its counterscarp crowned by a covered-way in which places of arms, were left in the re-entrant angles for the assembly of troops. The exposed curtain walls of the citadel were protected by

The defences of Mannheim; after Merian.

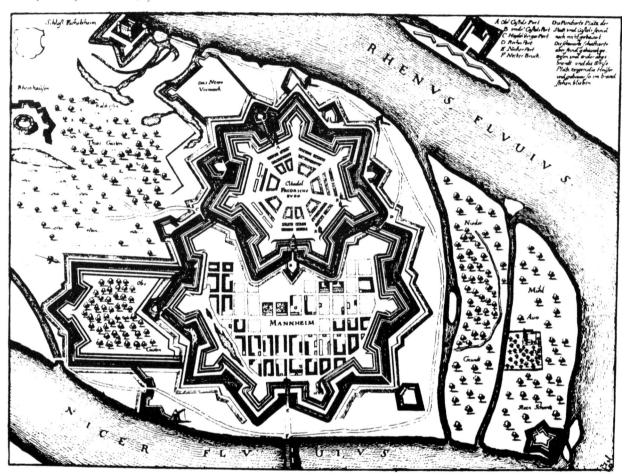

ravelins and, in two places, outworks in the form of lunettes extended the fortifications in depth.

Any wary city was proof against a *coup de main*. The major threat to its destruction lay in an organised siege when the attackers circumvallated the besieged place and proceeded either to starve it or to assault it in a systematic way. The credit for the evolution of a predetermined scientific method of approaching the walls of a fortified city must go to Vauban and his system will be described later. The main criteria were to cut trenches more or less parallel to the front of fortifications being attacked, so that besiegers could not be seen and thus flanked by artillery on the walls and bastions. These trenches were slowly pushed forward by short sections until the attackers were poised to assault a ravelin or a bastion which had to be breached before the defences of the town could be carried.

There are numerous descriptions of sieges in the seventeenth and eighteenth centuries, but none was more richly described nor more fiercely prosecuted than the great Turkish siege of Vienna in 1683. The city was girdled by an irregular polygon consisting for the most part of obtuse-angled Italian bastions supported by ravelins in the ditch, part of which was flooded. To the north lay the Danube, at this point a maze of waterways and marshy islands, its water touching the perimeter of the city. To the east was a semi-defended front with a wet ditch and beyond that a small tributary, the river Wien.

The defences were in the hands of a German military engineer called Rimpler. Having served with the Venetians at Candia in 1669 he was conversant with the Italian system. Four years later however he proposed his own system for a 'fortification with middle bastions'. No drawings were left, but in 1718

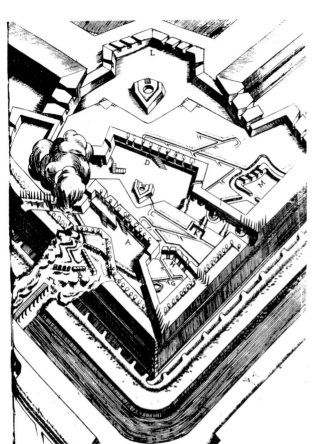

Breaching a bastion before attacking a retrenchment; after Pietro Paolo Floriani.

Below: *The Turkish assault on Vienna; after Fer.*

Leonhard Christoph Sturm published a drawing based on Rimpler's description. The system abolished curtain walls and substituted a tenaille trace, to the salient points of which were added acute-angled bastions, their faces forming an extension of supporting faussebrayes. It was an elaborate system of defence in depth with double covered-ways and several lines of ditches. Its main importance lies in the fact that its principles were adopted by Montalembert in the later eighteenth century, passing from him to become common practice among German military engineers of the midnineteenth century. Thus in the seventeenth century re-emerged a system which eventually superseded and made obsolete the Italian bastion trace. Rimpler appears to have had no opportunity to put his theory into practice, for the Vienna trace was straightforward and in line with current Italian thinking.

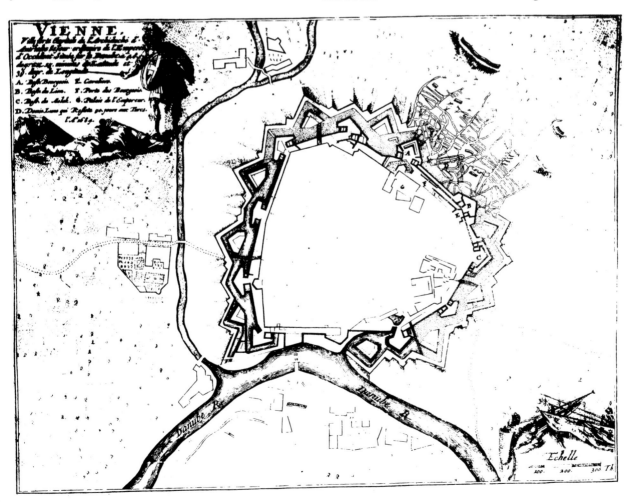

Opposite: *Castello at Bari.*

Charles V's bastion on the Fort at Barletta, 1527.

The Turks with a large force and some 250 cannon attacked through the suburbs from the south-west. In the drawings which remain their trenches appear like the maze of passages revealed in a sectioned anthill. By 17 July the city was invested and soon food ran short. The garrison, reduced from 11,000 to 4000, was in a state of extreme exhaustion. Shingles were torn from the city roofs and burnt as flares on the battlements to illuminate any Turkish activity in the ditches. The usual stories of atrocities were circulated and the Turks were accused of seizing children from their mothers' arms and roasting them before fixing them on spear points to wave aloft as an earnest of the city's fate. The line of Turkish entrenchments had begun five miles from the walls of the fortress and it slowly closed in the Burg and Lowel Bastions (marked A and B) and their intervening ravelin (marked D). There was mining and countermining and on 1 September one complete face of the ravelin erupted in smoke and flame. Pulverised continously for 22 days and assaulted on at least twelve occasions, the ravelin finally fell. Then the Burg Bastion was breached and Turkish janissaries gained a foothold. The city seemed fated when at the eleventh hour the Duke of Lorraine and John Sobieski threw a relieving force across the Danube, using prefabricated bridges which had been constructed 25 kilometres (15 miles) upstream, and fell upon the Turkish army. In terror the Turks broke off their siege and fled, their commanding general being stripped of his insignia and ritually strangled. The threat of Turkish penetration in the west was countered in what an eminent Turkish historian has called 'the most important campaign in their history'.

ISOLATED FORTS AND WATCH-TOWERS

If the main cities and towns of Europe were well guarded by elaborate systems of fortification there were many less fortunate small towns open to attack. Those near the coasts of the Mediterranean were specially vulnerable as, particularly on dark nights, ships could approach silently, to descend undetected upon an isolated stretch of shore. An early warning system was needed to signal the approach of Turkish or corsair raiders in sufficient time to allow villagers to gather in the comparative safety provided by the communal defence of a tightly packed collection of houses, and to permit cavalry forces to hurry into position to repulse the advance or, often more effective, to impede withdrawal to the coast.

In the second half of the sixteenth century

A watchtower on the coast at Gallipoli in the heel of Italy.   *Fort at Barletta; aerial section.*

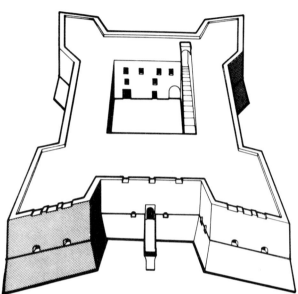

the long coastline of southern Italy began to be systematically planted with a line of coastal towers, fairly regularly spaced and supported at intervals by stronger forts. By 1569 some thirteen towers covered 120 kilometres (75 miles) of the Apulian coast supported by ten forts, all in or near towns, centred on the fort at Bari. The forts and towers were sited so that messages could be rapidly transmitted to headquarters. Other towers, spaced about 8 kilometres (5 miles) apart, covered the Gulf of Taranto and still more stretched up the Calabrian coast, along the seaboard of the Tyrrhenian Sea as far north as Rome.

Usually the towers were square, though round ones are sometimes found, and they were constructed of thick battered walls with few or no windows to illuminate the ground floor rooms. The main chamber was at first floor level, approached by ladder or drawbridge from a high stone staircase. The roof, strongly constructed to support cannon, was capped by machicolation, corbelled from the main walls and providing some defence for the base of the tower. The soldiers' accommodation was sufficiently isolated from attack so that in normal conditions an enemy would by-pass a tower rather than waste time on its bombardment, the essence of their raids being speed and surprise. It should also be remembered that ships of the period were not designed to fire broadsides. Usually frail galleys susceptible to fire from the shore, they invariably gave any coastal defences a wide berth.

In Malta an elaborate warning system was constructed by the Knights of St John. Towers were built there in medieval times but the systematic plan for the distribution of inter-communicating watchtowers did not originate until after the Great Siege of 1565. During the first half of the seventeenth century the Knights of St John constructed towers at all likely landing points. These towers were remarkably uniform in design, consisting of two rooms one above the other and space on the roof for two cannons which, during the day, were used for signalling the approach

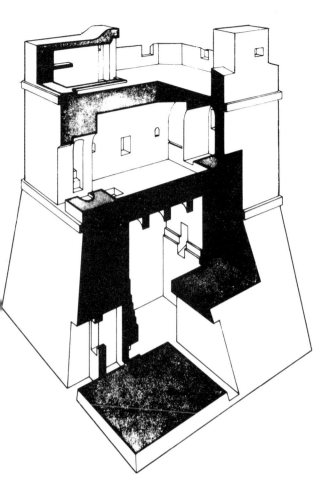

A Maltese coastal watchtower.

Below: The Wignacourt Tower at St Paul's Bay in Malta.

Bottom: Fort St Lucian in Malta.

of corsairs as well as to deter their landing. At night signal bonfires could be lit on the roof. Each tower was square and had a strongly scarped base culminating in a bold string course and a parapet with embrasures. The towers were designed for a garrison of four.

The most vulnerable areas were defended by forts, the earliest being the Wignacourt Tower built on St Paul's Bay in 1610. Fort St Lucian soon followed, with Fort St Thomas in 1614 and the fort on the island of Comino two years later. These buildings are strange. On first sight they give the impression of being square forts built on a full-bastioned trace, such as would have been expected after the visit to the island of such eminent Italian military engineers as Lanci, Serbelloni and Laparelli. However, on close inspection it can be seen that the forts are square blocks with immensely thick battered walls. The corners of each fort were stiffened by towers whose walls rose vertically so that, although their bases touched the face of the curtains, their tops projected considerably in front of them, giving the impression of being bastions. This is particularly so in cases like Fort St Lucian where the towers in plan resemble true bastions, their faces being aligned with their neighbours' flanks. This is a device which Antonio da Sangallo carried out at the Fort at Nettuno a hundred years earlier when he was attempting to evolve the true bastioned trace. It is incredible that the Knights' knowledge of the theory

Fort St Thomas in Malta.

Opposite: *The Cottonera Lines in Malta.*

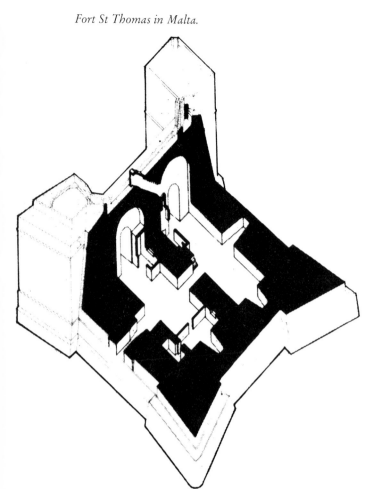

An early seventeenth century cannon of the Knights of St John

Gregory near Zejtun and incorporated high up within the thickness of the transept walls a narrow passage with two small windows sited directly on to the towers of these forts. From earliest times churches have been used as places of refuge and as stores for military equipment and ammunition, but it is interesting to find an example of a church being extended specifically for the purpose of fitting into an overall defence plan.

ITALIAN MILITARY ENGINEERS IN THE SEVENTEENTH CENTURY

During the first half of the seventeenth century the Italians continued to dominate the scene and only gradually towards mid-century was their pre-eminent position taken over by the French. As a result of this, Italian engineers began to turn to France for their ideas and the work of the French school, fully established by Vauban, held the stage almost unchallenged until the middle of the eighteenth century.

In the seventeenth century Malta remained a fruitful place of employment for the Italians. As the range and effectiveness of artillery improved, the depth of defences had to be increased to prevent the bombardment of the vital parts of a city, like the arsenal, the dockyard or the headquarters; and to blunt any assault so that a point of exhaustion might be reached before the final lines of defence were broken through. The Knights of Malta now found that they needed a second enceinte well beyond Laparelli's landfront of Valletta and a series of encircling bastions outside the sixteenth century defences of the harbours and the towns which bordered them. They first commissioned Pietro Paolo Floriani, a notable Italian engineer who had seen many battles and planned many fortresses and was the author of one of the most influential treatises of the period, *Difesa et offesa delle piazze* (Macerata 1630). Floriani submitted his first project in October 1635 and against considerable opposition his proposals were accepted and the Floriana Lines were built. They consisted of a triple centre bastion supported by demi-bastions and a fortified wall which ran back along both coasts of the promontory

of fortification should have been so rudimentary as to allow them to sanction these designs by local military engineers. There were no embrasures except at the tops of the towers and enfilade fire was an impossibility.

The forts at St Lucian and St Thomas were low-lying, near to the sea, and could thus not signal directly to the headquarters at Valletta. An intermediate signalling station had therefore to be selected and constructed. In 1614 the knights added two transepts and a dome to the fifteenth century church of St

Opposite: *The Floriana lines in Malta showing the hornwork and crownwork on the left: the lines shown projecting beyond the glacis are countermines.*

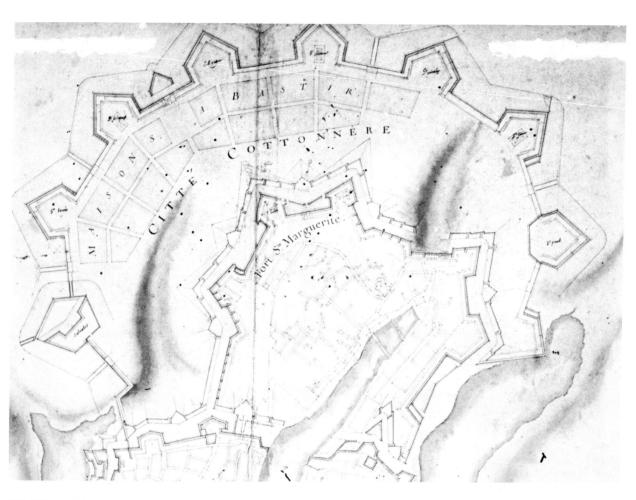

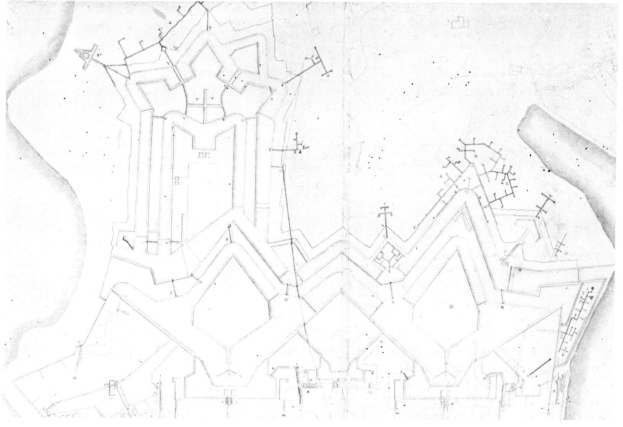

Romano Carrapecchia's Zabber Gate in the Cottonera Lines, 1675.

to join the main defences of Valletta. The work of aggrandisement went on. Vincenzo Masculano da Firenzuola began a ring of fortifications on the hills of Santa Margherita and the Mandra in 1638 to strengthen the landward approach to the Three Cities which lie across the Grand Harbour from Valletta. Antonio Maurizio Valperga arrived in 1670, constructed a fausse-braye and a new ditch in front of Floriani's bastions and ravelins and pushed out a noble horn-work, protected by a crownwork and a lunette, to act as a powerful outwork along the south-western edge of the lines. His client, the Grand Master Nicolas Cotoner, possessed of grandiose ideas, was not content with this, so Valperga then planned one of the most ambitious schemes in Europe. The Cottonera Lines, begun in 1670, stretch in a great arc to girdle the towns on the south-eastern seaboard of the Grand Harbour. At great expense eight bastions were built, but most of the vital outworks had to be omitted as the work drained the coffers of the Knights and over-

stretched the ability of their troops to man and defend the lines. Finally built in durable stone, the gateways embellished with rich architectural trappings, the seventeenth century defences of Malta stand almost intact. Not overgrown by vegetation, nor concealed by suburban sprawl, they present to this day the finest examples of their type in Europe.

THE PARTS OF A FORTRESS

It could be said that, by the middle of the seventeenth century, the bastion trace had reached its full development, bearing in mind the range and power of any artillery then available to besiege it. Admittedly it was to continue to be used with modifications and additions, particularly to the outworks, for almost two centuries, but this was its classic period. Therefore, it would be advisable at this point to describe the various parts of the system and the way in which they functioned.

To begin, the military engineer would prepare plans of the trace usually starting from the tip or salient point of two bastions which he joined by a dotted line on paper. This distance between two bastions was called a front of fortification. Then using

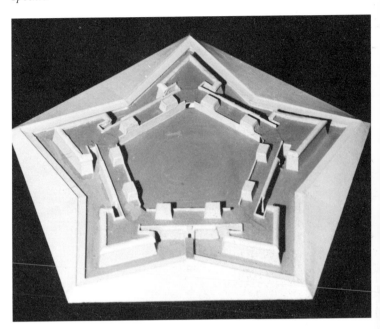

A model of a fort showing bastions and cavaliers; after Speckle.

geometry and working from the outer edge inwards, he drew all the parts of his plan, the faces of the bastions running back to the flanks onto which he joined the curtain. If he was converting an existing place he might have to start with the line of the curtain wall and work outwards. In many of the sixteenth century designs the flanks would be recessed and perhaps stacked at several levels, the guns firing over each other much to the discomfort of the gunners, those below subject to blast and those above wreathed in thick acrid smoke. At that period the recessed flanks would be protected by orillons, ears that projected to screen the guns in the flank from enemy bombardment, but allowing them to enfilade the face of the opposite bastion. The engineer would know that the greater the number of bastions, the greater the cost of the fortress, but also the more obtuse the flanked angle or the salient of each bastion would be. With a triangular work the salients were very acute, could be knocked off by enemy bombardment and left little space for guns to be mounted there. Site conditions usually dictated the number of fronts, thus the number of bastions which could be used, and the engineer tried to create a balance. All things being equal, the pentagon was the best form allowing plenty of space within the enceinte and providing well shaped bastions.

By the middle of the seventeenth century orillons were less often used and the angle at which the flanks joined the face of the bastions at the shoulder, and joined the curtain – the 'angle of the curtain' – became important. The solution adopted depended on the number of bastions used and the preference of each engineer. For example, Errard de Bar-le-Duc placed his flanks at right angles to each bastion at the shoulder. De Ville and usually the Italians and Dutch made their flanks at right angles to the curtain wall, thus flanking both curtain and opposite face. Pagan and Vauban usually designed their flanks to lie at right angles to the line of defence, the line which ran from the salient of the adjoining bastion, along its face and thus, in those cases, to the junction of the flank with the curtain. As cannons were replaced by muskets for close defence from the flanks, this method of laying them out was favoured because musketeers tended to fire straight forward often without aiming. Cannons in the flanks could be disabled by bombardment; musketeers could be replaced more easily and switched

faster to any threatened flank, but because of the shorter effective range of muskets, the bastions had to be placed closer together.

When the plans and sections were completed they were sent for approval, sometimes accompanied by large models which laymen appreciated and found easier to understand. It should be remembered that the section, or profile, of the work was as important as the trace or plan, to prevent the defences being overlooked and commanded.

Then began the building of the fortress. The plans were usually laid out on a table in the middle of the site, lined up with the positions where each bastions would be built. The engineer would then sight 'capitals', the lines which ran out from the centre to the salient point of each bastion. Using chains to mark off distances and stakes pushed into the ground, gradually the whole trace would be pegged out. Only then could building work begin. A foundation would be dug following the line of the ramparts and enclosing the enceinte. There, in a permanent fortress, they would start to build the revetment, a rampart wall of stone or brick which would rise about 10 metres (30ft) from the wall of the ditch. In good ground conditions the bottom course of the foundations would be constructed of large flat stones tilted inwards to take the thrust of the wall above. When the ground was less

A fort with its ditch defended by caponiers; after Francesco di Giorgio.

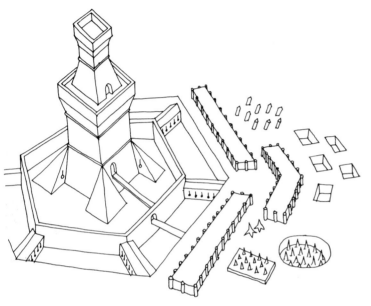

stable they might have to start with a framed-up timber raft, or on marshy ground, with timber piles driven deep. Sometimes a mesh of tree branches was embedded in the earth. On wet sites, where the water table was high, it was difficult because trenches tended to fill with water quickly, so stretches of foundations had to be built immediately the excavations were cut in that sector. Usually, as the revetment was built up, the ditch was excavated and the *déblai*, or spoil from it, was placed up behind the revetment and well tamped. This soil, piled behind the ramparts, was called the *rémblai*, and the engineer tried to design the section through his fortress so that the amount of *déblai* dug from the ditch matched the amount of *rémblai* needed behind the ramparts: it was expensive to have to bring additional earth from elsewhere.

Sometimes, and particularly in the advanced works and outworks, a demi-revetment was built, only half the height of the rampart, and earth, sloping back, was heaped on top. This was cheaper than building a full revetment and the masonry was better protected from bombardment.

To strengthen the revetments, counterforts, or interior buttresses, tapered and sometimes arched, ran back into the ramparts. Near the top of the revetment wall they placed a cordon, a projecting curved stone moulding which kept scaling ladders off the face

of the fortifications. Above that they sometimes placed a tablet and then a sloping parapet often pierced by embrasures which, splayed out towards the front, were lined with brick or stone and open above. Guns which fired over the parapet were said to fire *en barbette*.

Behind the parapet, which was about 5.5 metres (18ft) thick, they constructed a firing step so that infantry could fire over the top of the parapet. Behind the step and on top of the *rémblai* they built the *terreplein*, some 13 metres (44ft) wide upon which to mount the guns, to allow them to recoil and be reloaded, and to leave enough space for ammunition carts to pass behind. Ramps, gently sloped, led up to the terreplein from the ground level of the fortress and a wide space, the esplanade (called in Italian the *pomerio*), was left outside the building line to allow quick and easy communication to all fronts of the fortress.

On the terreplein, and usually within the bastions, cavaliers could be constructed – raised gun platforms which increased their range and, if there were high ground outside the fortifications, might match height for height. Cavaliers were vulnerable to bombardment but the debris from them did not fill the ditches and did not make a bridge of rubble onto which an attacker might climb.

At the foot of the revetment or rampart wall, there was sometimes a berm, also called a *chemin des rondes* (a roundway) – a passage for infantry covered by a continuous mound in front called a *fausse-braye*. This feature was probably first suggested in the sixteenth century by Francesco di Georgio. Both features were unpopular, because troops could be showered by debris from above, and were gradually phased out.

The ditch could be wet and broad, or dry and much narrower. Sometimes a dry ditch could be flooded through sluices from a nearby river, a torrent of water being able to wash away any temporary bridge constructed by the attackers in their attempt to cross the ditch. Where water was available, the traditional barrier in medieval architecture had been a moat, but it had its disadvantages such as those which also applied when the area was inundated or flooded around a fortress. Stagnant water could bring disease, often a greater killer than the cannon, and, at the very least, set up 'noxious vapours'. A crafty enemy could

An ornate gatework by Wilhelm Dilich, 1640.

sometimes drain the moat or inundation leaving the besieged 'high and dry'. In winter the water might freeze and form a safe platform of approach, so on frosty nights the garrison's first duty was to break up the ice and stack it in jagged array in front of the ramparts. For a small garrison a wet ditch was useful. Not only could it hold fish, it could also protect against a surprise attack. In a siege it hampered the use of battering rams and prevented mining. Dutch engineers, both in Holland and in England, often used a double wet ditch. But for large fortresses conducting an active aggressive defence, a dry ditch was best. There part of the garrison could assemble prior to making a sortie which might destroy the enemy's artillery and break up his advanced trenches. Psychologically, sorties sometimes turned the tide of war. The dry ditch had to be wide enough to hold a sizable raiding party and make bridging and filling difficult, but not so wide as to allow an enemy to breach the base of the ramparts with his cannon fire. The ditch might also be used as a refuge for the fleeing inhabitants of the countryside and for cattle.

Most ditches were placed outside the ramparts, but Machiavelli favoured putting them behind the walls so that they could not be filled and bridged by an enemy.

Often in the middle of the dry ditch there was a deep cut, sometimes 'V' shaped, called a *cunette* or *cuvette*, to carry off flood water, to act as a further barrier and to discourage mining, although equally it made the digging of countermines by the garrison more difficult. Sometimes at vulnerable places in front of the flanks engineers like Laparelli and the English writer, Robert Corneweyle (1559) advocated the excavation of pits some 6 metres (20ft) deep.

In the case of dry ditches it was necessary to be able to turn them into killing grounds to destroy those so foolhardy as to have descended there. Vauban was to use *tenailles*, long low works placed in front of the curtain wall, running from bastion flank to flank like sections of *fausse-braye*, and sometimes having their ends turned out to form demi-bastions where guns could also cover their faces. However, the primary reason for building tenailles was to place an outer shield to protect the base of the curtain ramparts from bombardment – to take the brunt of the attack. Another solution was to build free-standing pillboxes on the floor of the ditch. These were called by the Italians, *caponnati*, and one still survives in the middle of the ditch at Carmona near Seville, built between 1471 and 1474. Dürer was the first to illustrate them in a printed book in 1527 – little conical structures bristling with guns which would have been linked back to the fortress through an underground passage; but this was a dangerous device because, if captured, it could be rushed by an intrepid party of the attackers who might gain sudden access to the interior of the fortress. Soldiers in the *caponnati* must have felt very exposed and it can hardly have been a popular outpost, but several of the Italian theorists show them in their books – Zanchi (1560), de Marchi (1599) and the Englishman, Corneyweyle (1559), but they soon went out of use.

The caponier was a more popular device. Similar in concept, it consisted of a small pyramidal-roofed structure attached to and projecting from the rampart walls, often at the salient point so that guns in it could fire down each adjoining face. Towards the end of the fifteenth century Francesco di Giorgio drew numerous examples in his treatise and many early ones were built, particularly in France. At Craignethan Castle in Scotland an early caponier with a pointed roof was constructed right across the ditch, into which faced three oblong gunloops little above ground level, the two outer ones being set obliquely to increase their field of fire. In 1533 a large, three-storey caponier was built out from the ramparts at Ulm and, eleven years later, four were constructed from the central keep to the interior faces of the outer walls at Southsea Castle. In 1630 Pietro Paolo Floriani showed them in his book, protected by triple rows of stakes to prevent them being rushed. After that there were few examples built until, towards the end of the eighteenth century, Montalembert revived the idea on a grand scale, proposing vast multi-gun caponiers in front of his envelope; these were soon copied by British engineers on many occasions, in particular on the Maker Height at Plymouth (1787), in the same year at Gibraltar, at Vido Island on Corfu in 1824, at Old Fort Henry, Kingston, Ontario in 1829 and by the Americans in coastal defences like Fort Schuyler in New York Harbour (1833). Really big ones followed on the continent of Europe, employed particularly by the Germans and Prussians, and their use became standard practice, largely surplanting the bastion for flank defence in the second half of the nineteenth century.

The third method of defending the ditch was by using counterscarp galleries. These were casemates dug under the outer wall of the ditch with guns firing back, in reverse, along the ditches to be protected.

Counterscarp galleries were unpopular with the garrison who felt isolated in them even though they had an underground escape route and a line of communication back to the fortress. They first appear in print in 1559 in Corneyweyle's book. Then other theorists show them – Simon Stevin in 1594, de Marchi in 1599. Towards the end of the seventeenth century there was a new burst of interest, largely through influence of Menno van Coehoorn who illustrated them in 1685 and 1702. The English copied his loopholed galleries (there was an English translation of his book in 1705) and built them at Landguard Fort, Harwich in 1717, at Castle St Philip on Minorca before 1735 where they ran as continuous galleries in the counterscarps of the redoubts, on Anholt Island and at Fort Townsend, Newfoundland in 1812. They also used them at Vido Island in 1824, at Kingston, Ontario in 1829 and at Halifax, Nova Scotia in 1832. For a while counterscarp galleries were popular, also being built by the Bavarians and the Prussians.

Additional works were also placed in the ditch, or sometimes beyond it, like ravelins to protect curtain walls, tenellons and demi-lunes to protect flanks and salients of bastions. Ravelins, triangular works sometimes with flanks, could be strengthened by the insertion of redoubts within their walls, and could be joined to the fortress by a *caponnière*, often used by Vauban, a corridor flanked by loopholed walls which covered its passage from enemy sight. It must be remembered that, in military architecture, the word 'covered' does not mean built over or roofed, but rather that a work is screened from enemy view and protected from direct fire.

The outer wall of the ditch – either vertical or sloped, revetted with brick or masonry or left in natural earth, all solutions that would effect its incline – was called the counterscarp. On top was placed the covered-way, approached by steep steps from the ditch, a broad flat area along which infantry could pass freely. The idea of protecting this outer line beyond the ditch is said to have been invented by Nicolò Tartaglia (1500–1557), but it is probably much older than that. By the mid-sixteenth century it was common practice. In front there was a *banquette*, or firing step, so that infantrymen could fire out onto the countryside and all the ground beyond sloped away in carefully faced pleats of land called the *glacis*, upon which

Section through a drawbridge and fortified gateway by Dilich.

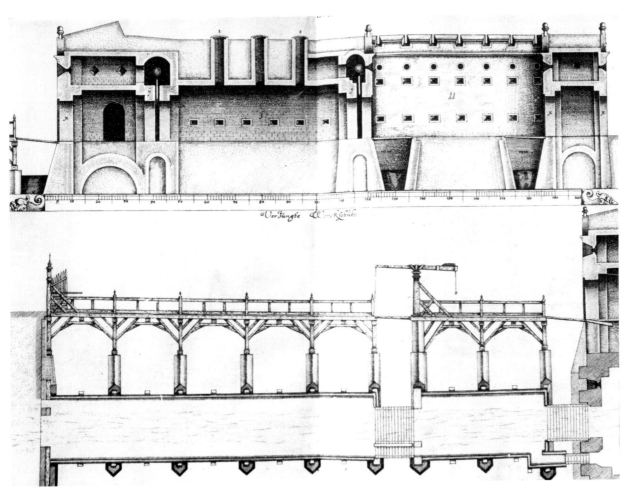

an attacking force would be exposed to full view and subjected to withering fire.

The line of the counterscarp and thus of the covered-way would lie parallel to the faces of the bastions and, in the salient point, there would be set a place of arms, the curve of the counterscarp allowing ample space for the assembly of troops prior to launching a sortie. Large places of arms could hold up to a thousand infantrymen. Pietro Cataneo is said to have invented the re-entrant place of arms in 1574.

Normally traverses, earth piled up in heaps, were spaced along the covered-way to protect its troops from enfilade fire. Passages, called *crochets*, ran around them and later the outer edge of the covered-way was sometimes serrated, *en cremaillère*, to provide a succession of flanking positions. Traverses must

be early in origin. They were certainly proposed by Tartaglia, but they did not really become essential until some 150 years later, after Vauban invented ricochet fire, a method of bouncing his shot which, without the protection of traverses, could be lobbed to disable one gun after another mounted on the faces of the bastions or upon the curtain wall.

Early on, the top of the sloping glacis would be criss-crossed with a palisade, but after Gabriel de Naudé moved this back to the banquette to protect it from destruction by the attackers' gunfire, this became general practice.

Beyond the foot of the glacis lay the zone of servitude, open swept countryside where civil building was restricted or forbidden.

Finally, as time went by, outworks were

Portrait of Vauban.

added to hold off an enemy with even more powerful guns, at arm's length.

A variety of ambitious devices, the most popular called the hornwork, were added, projecting from vulnerable curtains and occasionally from bastions out towards the besieger. Some were built well before any assault, like the great crowned hornwork at Floriana in Malta; others, like those at Candia, were pushed out during a siege. Basically, they consisted of long, parallel, or nearly parallel sides where many guns could flank the adjoining works, and a head, consisting in a hornwork of two demi-bastions, and, in a crownwork, with the addition of one or more bastions in the centre. The head, as in Malta, could be doubled up and ravelins added to cover the short stretches of curtain wall. Lille, under siege, had many thrown up to add to its protection.

Further out still, detached redoubts and forts could be placed to interlock with supporting fire or to cover vulnerable avenues of approach – valleys, roads, railway lines. Eventually these were to become in the nineteenth century, and starting at Paris, complete rings of detached forts which encircled nearly all the capital cities and large urban conglomerations of Europe.

In conclusion it would be well to mention the citadel, that fortress within a fortress. Often placed at one end of a fortified town it supported the other fortifications and, being self-contained and completely military, acted as a final fall-back position from which to continue the defence. But often there is a more sinister intent, a citadel built to overawe its town, to subjugate its inhabitants by an occupying force and discourage them from surrendering their city at a premature stage in a siege. Thus a citadel was often a hated place, an object of terror and dictatorship to the inhabitants of the town. There are many examples as at Florence and Siena built for this purpose, but the best is probably the earliest classical example, the pentagonal citadel built for the Spanish by an Italian engineer, Pacciotto of Urbino in 1567 at Antwerp. One of the finest remaining examples was built by Vauban at Lille.

VAUBAN

By the mid-seventeenth century the balance in the capabilities of attack and defence reached a climax. No other age saw the erection of such elaborate fortifications on so vast a scale, and on no earlier occasion were they so surely doomed. Much of the credit for both situations must go to Vauban. This is why he is important.

Sébastien le Prestre de Vauban was born in Burgundy on 15 May 1633. Before his eighteenth birthday he had joined the army to rise, in 1703, to the rank of Marshal of France. During his long life as a military engineer he worked on more than 160 fortresses and directed 40 sieges, all of which were successful. In the first five years of his army service he was wounded on five occasions. At the age of seventy, after returning from his last siege, he wrote *Traité de l'attaque des places*. It was a secret document not intended for publication, but produced for the use of the Duke of Burgundy, grandson of Louis XIV. In the preface Vauban wrote 'May it please you to keep it to yourself, and let no one else have it. . .'. Nearly three

Below: *Vauban's First Method; after John Muller 1746.*

Bottom: *Vauban's Third Method; after John Muller, 1746.*

years later, and shortly before he died, he wrote *Traité de la défence des places*. In his behaviour and his writing there constantly appeared his maxim 'never do uncovered and by force what can be done by industry'.

Vauban's name is usually associated with three systems of defence. In fact he did not lay these down; they were deduced by his pupils and followers from the fortresses that Vauban had designed, for he had written 'the art of fortifying does not consist in rules and systems, but solely in good sense and experience'.

Vauban's first system, which he used in more than thirty places he fortified, does not vary greatly from the traditional pattern then evolving in the hands of French and Italian military engineers. It consisted of a front of about 330 metres with generous bastions and large flanks making obtuse angles with both faces of the bastions and the curtain walls. The curtains were protected by low tenailles joined by a caponier to a ravelin lying farther out in the ditch. Beyond lay the covered-way, interspersed by traverses to protect his troops, and places of arms in the salient and re-entrant angles. Vauban's caponier was merely a protected bombproof passage joining the tenaille to the ravelin. Only in the nineteenth century did caponiers and counterscarp galleries usurp the ditch-flanking functions of the bastions. Caponiers gradually assumed colossal proportions at places like Posen (1828) and Dover Castle, becoming many-tiered multi-gun keeps. Vauban's second system was the result of his practical progress in siegecraft which induced him to modify the trace of his fortresses. Discovering that whenever a bastion was captured the loss of the town followed, he transformed his bastions into counterguards separated by a ditch from the curtain wall, which was strengthened at the corners by two-storey polygonal towers, stoutly constructed to contain cannon enclosed within bombproof casemates and firing through embrasures. Vauban's third system was his most complex and was only used once, at Neuf-Brisach. It consisted of a front of considerable depth, with cavaliers on the bastions, counterguards and tenailles, a ravelin with its own counterguard and large re-entrant places of arms. It was expensive and was not employed after Vauban's time, but fortunately there remains an almost complete example of this work preserved at Neuf-Brisach.

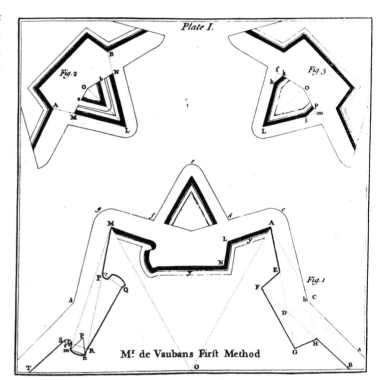

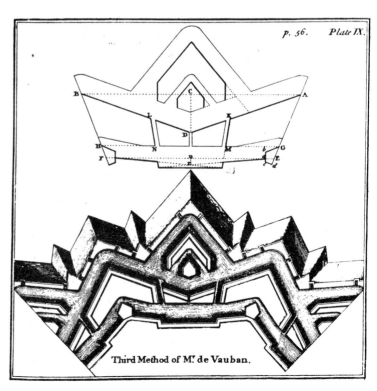

Right: *Vauban's curtain and bastion on the Colmar front.*

Below: *Model of the new town of Neuf-Brisach* (Neuf-Brisach Museum)

Bottom: *The Colmar Gate at Neuf-Brisach.*

Under the terms of the Treaty of Ryswick France lost Brisach and the ground on the right bank of the Rhine. Louis XIV, realising that his flank was exposed, commissioned Vauban to design a new fortress within French territory. In 1698 Vauban submitted three projects, of which one was chosen, and the place was put in a state of defence by 1706. It was originally designed to contain only military personnel, but the octagonal space within the bastions was converted into a grid-iron town with a large central square.

This scant description does not do justice to the elaborate scientific nature of Vauban's constructions, but as his fame rested upon them, practically every military engineer of note who followed described his systems in considerable detail. They became the imperative solution for the French school of engineers.

Vauban's fame rests unjustly on his military architecture, for it was he who swung the balance in favour of the attack, establishing its superiority over defence for nearly two hundred years. Before Vauban's time the attack on fortresses had been unsystematic. The lack of method was evident in the Turkish assault on Vienna in 1683. In a memorandum written in 1704 he decried the haphazard and unsystematic character of attack. 'When we succeed,' he wrote, 'it is rather owing to the weakness of the enemy than to our own merit.' He probably remembered the sight of English grenadiers marching across a half-mile

The inner gate at Longwy by Vauban.

of open ground with drums beating and colours flying in the assault on Namur in 1695. 'I never saw anything like it, or even approaching it; for the magnitude of the blunder, I mean, not for the grandeur of the action, for I find that too senseless to admire it.' His system of attack was based on the use of parallels which he first used effectively at the siege of Maestricht (1673). Starting about 600 metres (650yds) out from the fortress to be attacked, and working at night, he detailed small detachments of men, 25 and an officer, to open up

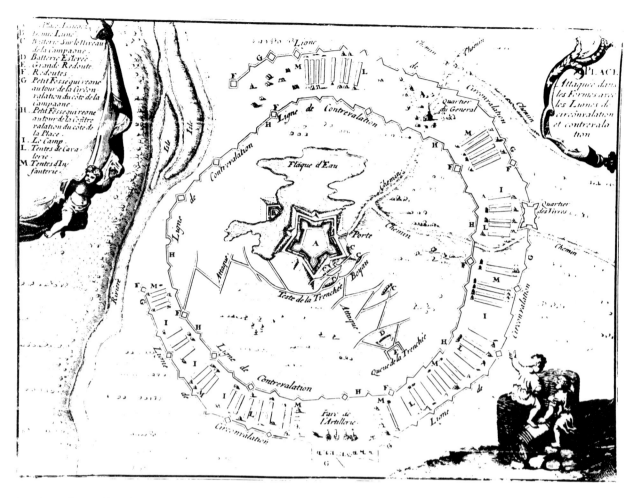

Attack on the ravelin of a fortress showing the position of the besieger's batteries and his parallels and saps.

trenches running parallel to the front he wished to attack. On the second night he constructed batteries whose guns were intended to keep the defenders quiet. Then began zigzag approaches, each approach concealed from the besieged; by the fourth night the approaches had reached halfway, when a second parallel trench was constructed. More zigzags followed and by the ninth or tenth night the third parallel was cut at the foot of the glacis. The artillery next opened up a breach in the ravelin and then in the bastion. The crowning of the covered-way was the most dangerous task (at Philipsburgh in 1676 it had cost the lives of 1200 men) and the work was best done systematically. The attackers then descended into the ditch, taking cover behind the rubbish which had been brought down in the breach of the ravelin and the bastion. In ordinary circumstances the assault on the fortress would commence at dawn on the twentieth day of the investment.

Not many sieges can have progressed with this clockwork precision, but the vindication of Vauban's system of attack is surely the complete success of all the sieges which he himself directed.

Colonel John Jones, of the Corps of Engineers, summed up Vauban's contribution.

By the middle of the sixteenth and the commencement of the seventeenth century, works were so well covered and so skilfully disposed, that the defence of towns obtained a momentary superiority over the rude efforts of the attack as then practised – for example the Dutch against Philip II and III. Unhappily, however, for this pre-eminence, Louis XIV appeared personally on the scene, and brought to the attack of fortress a preparation in ordnance, ammunition and materials, so vast and costly, as even at this day to excite astonishment; and thus supported, the genius of one man, Vauban, perfected in the first offensive campaign of that Monarch, a covered mode of attack, by a combination of Labour and Science, which rendered easy, by the steady advance of a few well-trained brave men, the reduction of places capable of defying for ever the open violence of multitudes. These increased means of attack caused the art of concealment to be further studied, till at length, in well constructed fortresses, not a single wall remained exposed to view, and the sap and the mine became as indispensably necessary as the gun and the mortar to the success of a besieger.

LILLE

Lille in northern France is a typical example of a town influenced both by Vauban's methods of attack and defence. When it was besieged in 1708 the town was defended by thirteen large bastions and four half-bastions with most of the curtain walls covered by ravelins standing in a broad wet ditch. Beyond the most vulnerable points stood four large hornworks, much used at that time, their curtains in turn covered by ravelins – defensive screens pushed well out into the countryside, a good part of which had been inundated with flood water. At the south end of the town a bastion position was occupied by a strong pentagonal fort defended by its own outworks. On the north-west edge of the town stood Vauban's magnificent regular pentagonal citadel, a geometrical form of sheer beauty, but with each line in plan and profile laid down to provide a maximum defensive capability. The

pentagon, with its elaborate outworks and ditches, was isolated from the town by a broad esplanade, and the total area of its defences occupied a space about one-third of the area of the inhabited town.

VAUBAN'S FOLLOWERS

Vauban's methods were perpetuated, with minor modifications, by numerous French engineers, the most noteworthy being Louis de Cormontaigne whose assault went in on the twenty-second day of the siege. Cormontaigne's *Architecture Militaire* was published as a secret document in 1714, but the information was soon stolen and an unauthorised edition came out abroad in 1741, followed by others. Although he was not a very original thinker, two of his ideas merit attention. He revived a notion popularised by the Italians that a straight line of defence is most easily held, because broad obtuse-angled bastions could be covered by ravelins and could thus not be enfiladed by enemy fire. He therefore recommended a

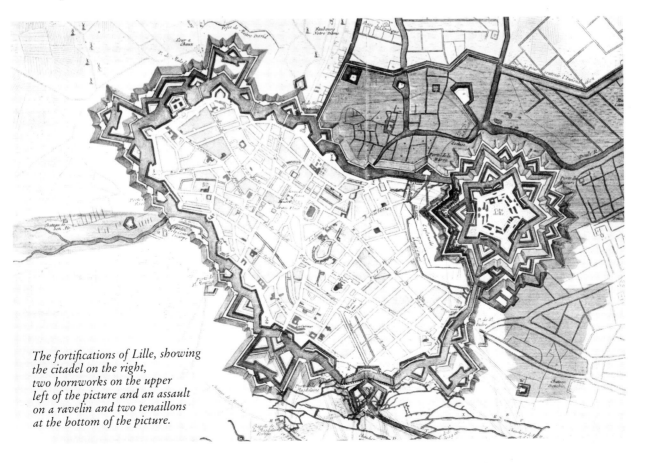

The fortifications of Lille, showing the citadel on the right, two hornworks on the upper left of the picture and an assault on a ravelin and two tenaillons at the bottom of the picture.

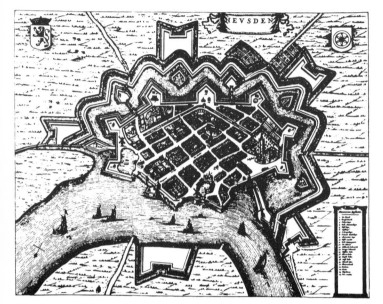

scale was that once the strength of a fortress was known few commanders would feel in honour bound to resist an attack beyond the time predicted for its success.

The work of these men is splendidly preserved in a series of large scale models which are still housed in Les Invalides in Paris. These depict the most important fortified cities built along the Franco-Belgian frontiers from the seventeenth to the nineteenth centuries, and one shows in great detail the devastation wrought on the citadel at Antwerp in the protracted siege of 1830–32.

THE DUTCH SCHOOL

The Dutch were fortunate in living in an area of low-lying ground most of which could be easily flooded by the rivers that traversed it or by the sea. This gave the inhabitants an advantage which they quickly seized in the wars of independence when meagre garrisons held at bay the full highly-organised force of the Spanish imperial army. The Dutch school of military engineering began to rise to a position of importance in the middle years of the sixteenth century. The defences of Alkmaar date from 1573–75, Elburg from 1580, and Jacob Kemps fortified Heusden in 1581, the defences of which have now been painstakingly restored to their original state. Adam Freitag published his *New and Enlarged Military Architecture* in Leyden in 1631.

Naarden is an old Dutch town, walled from the middle ages, several times captured and its defences rebuilt. In 1673 William III ordered a reconstruction with fortifications based on the New Dutch System. The architect was Adrian Dortsman and the military engineer Willem Paen. Naarden's defences were again brought up to date during the Franco-Prussian War when mortar casemates were constructed. Because of its strategic position, the fortifications were kept in operation until quite recently and this accounts for their remarkable state of preservation. The seventeenth century bastioned trace and the water defences also remain intact and the town is a magnificent example of its period.

Centuries of war threw up many able Dutch military engineers, but the most important was undoubtedly Menno, Baron van Coehoorn. His strength was often pitted against Vauban for whom he was a worthy rival. The two men held almost diametrically

large triangular fortress with a strong citadel placed at one salient angle, arguing that the enemy would then be forced to attack one of the remaining two angle bastions. Defence could be concentrated here and the bastions covered by a narrow projecting hornwork. Cormontaigne also worked out his 'scale of comparison'. This was a device whereby the strength of a fortress, and thus the number of days it could be expected to hold out, was calculated against a hypothetical attack, assuming that the besieger followed the general rules of the game. The disadvantage of this

Below: *Naarden in Holland; aerial view.* (KLM Aerocarto)

Bottom: *Naarden, the flank of a bastion.*

Naarden, the curved flank of a bastion according to the New Dutch System.

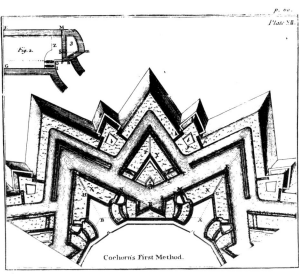

Coehoorn's First Method; after John Muller.

opposed attitudes to attack and defence. Where Vauban was cautious, slow and thorough, Coehoorn sacrificed everything to surprise, speed and a murderous artillery bombardment. His particular passion was for the deployment of numerous small mortars of a type which still carry his name.

An early writer compared the two men:
Vauban, employing no more guns than were necessary, using all his influence to restrain his troops, not allowing them to advance, except under cover, and bringing them in this way to the foot of each work, had made it his study and pride to spare them; and had done this without slacking the siege. Coehoorn, accumulating ordnance, sending the troops across the open to make assaults at a distance, and sacrificing everything to his eagerness to shorten the siege and to scare and frighten the defenders, had economised neither money nor men, nor in fact time.

The critic was in fact a Frenchman, but he underestimated Coehoorn whose career was remarkably successful. One of his fortresses, Namur, was captured by Vauban who refortified it. Three years later Coehoorn recaptured it. He was appointed a corps commander in the Duke of Marlborough's army and fortified numerous cities, some with complete success.

In 1685 he published his three systems of fortification for Dutch sites where water was readily available to flood the ditches and the surrounding

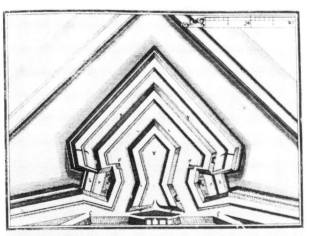

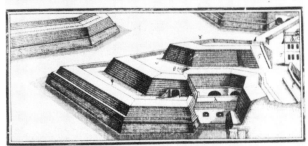

The type of bastion adopted by Coehoorn as illustrated in Dilich's Peribologia, *1640.*

Plan of Bergen-op-Zoom, showing the Fort d'Eau on the left; after John T Jones.

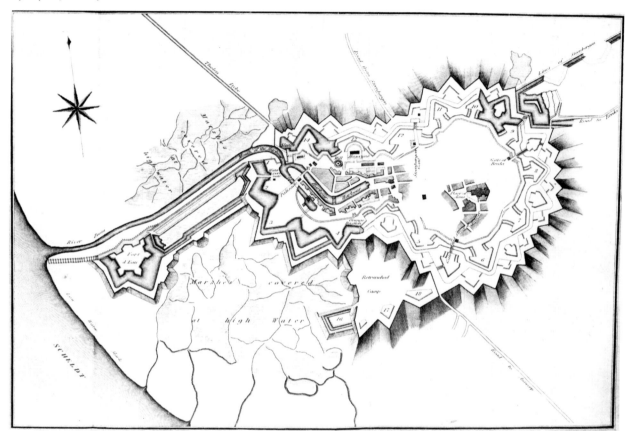

countryside. In plan his first method looked remarkably like Vauban's but the similarity was superficial. Coehoorn's bastions were more complex (marked A and B). In front (XG-XH) lay a dry ditch before the outer face of the bastion was reached. A bonnet (E-F) hung above the salient angle of the bastion and was joined to the inner bastion by a low bombproof caponier. The flanks of the bastions were large and deep with space and embrasures for adequate artillery defence, and the orillons became strong towers containing magazines. The orillons were constructed in the form of hollow counterforts consisting of several membranes in that, if the enemy's guns broke through one skin of masonry, he was faced with the necessity of destroying the next, and so on. Deep counterforts, not filled with earth, had a great advantage. If they collapsed under bombardment the minimum of rubble slid down into the ditch providing scant cover for the besieger's assault troops. All Coehoorn's systems had elaborate outworks to expose the enemy everywhere

Coehoorn's Third System; after John Muller.

Montalembert's multi-gun tower and caponier; after Lendy.

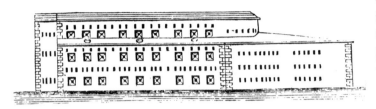

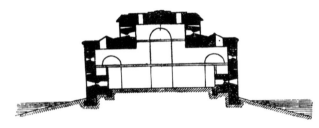

to cross fire, and these works were succoured by means of boats. Wet ditches were always a problem for although they deterred an attack, except in the depth of winter, they made it very difficult for the defenders to withdraw from an untenable position. A last-ditch stand in the outworks was not normally required in the defence of a fortress whose defences were designed to absorb the blows of the attack by means of a succession of defensive rings. Defending troops had to retire from the outworks in any boats that were available and undamaged, carrying with them their wounded; alternatively they were forced to swim for their lives.

Coehoorn's second and third systems, although carefully worked out, were never applied, for the defensive rings required such a vast amount of land that the area remaining within the fortification would have been almost too small to accommodate and arm a garrison sufficient for their defence. Coehoorn in 1688 fortified Bergen-op-Zoom and made it one of the strongest Dutch fortresses, secured on the west by the estuary of the Scheldt and on the east by the Lines of Steenbergen. The defences proved their worth 125 years later when, occupied by a small French garrison of about 2500 men, the town was surprised in a night assault by British troops under the command of Sir Thomas Graham. The British corps consisted of about 10,000 men. Aided by winter conditions, for the dykes refused to function adequately and flood the surrounding ground, parties of the British broke into the place, but the defenders, thinly supporting the out-

works (Fort d'Eau had only 60 men in it), used the fortifications as a natural deterrent and concentrated their small force to counter-attack any threatened position. By these means the attackers were cut off, killed or captured.

FRENCH ENGINEERS IN THE EIGHTEENTH CENTURY

Throughout the eighteenth century the French school of military engineers was held in great repute and was employed in numerous commissions beyond the frontier. Two names stand out: Montalembert, their most controversial figure, and Carnot.

Marc René, Marquis de Montalembert, was born in 1714. When eighteen years old he joined the army and was present at many of the sieges of the Seven Years' War. Brought up in an age when Vauban had perfected the art of attack, Montalembert turned his attention to the needs of the defence in an attempt to redress the balance. Whereas most of the French engineers were prepared to stick with absurd obstinacy to the traditions of fortification evolved by Vauban and his contemporaries, Montalembert searched desperately for other means of defence. Understandably his ideas faced opposition from his fellow engineers and his progress on the ladder of promotion was prejudiced by his forthright opinions. Like many innovators, his life could have passed unnoticed and his recommendations consigned to oblivion were it not for the fact that his suggestions were accepted with alacrity by the rising power of Prussia and transmitted to the German states during a period of feverish rearmament in the nineteenth century. In 1761 Montalembert was appointed governor of the Ile d'Oleron and put out to graze. The last 38 years of his life were spent writing the eleven thick volumes of his *Fortification Perpendiculaire*. He objected strongly to the bastion trace, pointing out that curtain walls were quite useless. These had always been recognised as the weak points, the most negative element in the defence, requiring all the other works to cover them. The ability of guns on the bastions to pour enfilade fire across the front from their faces and flanks had been an advantage when the range of cannon was short. When a greater concentration of more accurate weapons became available, cross fire did not make full use of the effective range of which the weapons were

Polygonal fortification according to Montalembert.

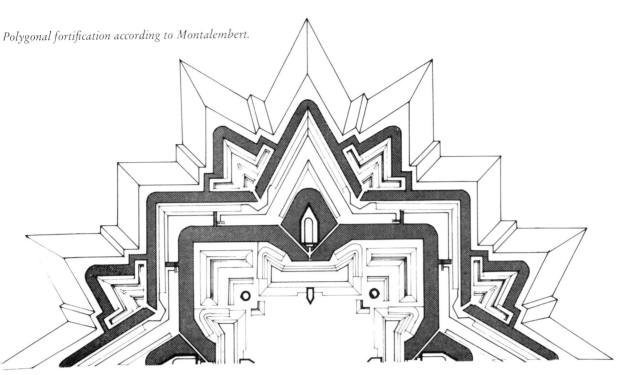

capable. Montalembert therefore substituted a tenaille trace. The idea had been advocated years earlier. Both Italian and German engineers had suggested its use in the sixteenth century but it had never really become popular. However its revival seems to have been due to Heinrich von Landsberg (1670–1746) who in 1712 was probably the first engineer to point out the defensive qualities of the tenaille trace in *Nouveaux plans et projets de fortification, pour défendre et attaquer les places.*

The tenaille trace consisted of a series of triangular redans, abutting each other at right angles to form a continuous saw-edged front. Beyond the tenaille trace lay two lines of counterguards and behind it stood strong, two-storey circular towers, each containing 24 guns capable of firing out across the countryside. The system therefore had four distinct enceintes which, for their subjugation required four successive breaches. It was introduced in 1776 and is normally referred to as 'perpendicular fortification'. In the following year Montalembert produced his 'polygonal fortification' which contained immensely strong caponiers, three storeys high, armed with 27 guns in casemates and numerous infantry loopholes. The caponier, intended up to the time of Vauban as a secure means of communication between two defensive works, thus became a strongpoint in its own right.

It was these two last features, the multi-gun tower and the multi-gun caponier, which were taken up and developed with such enthusiasm by the Germans and the Austrians. The gun, protected by a bombproof casemate, its embrasures covered by solid shutters and designed for the minimum usable aperture, was the foundation of Montalembert's defensive system.

Casemates were not new; they had been advocated by Dürer and other early engineers but they had fallen out of favour with the development of the bastion. However with the development of ricochet fire, said to have been first used effectively by Vauban at Philipsburgh in 1688, the need was felt for more adequate protection of guns and crews. Fortunately the new gun carriages required a much smaller complement of men. However, because their size was reduced, guns could be placed closer together to increase the concentration of fire and so became an even more attractive target for retaliation.

Carnot sensed the frustration felt by the aged general whose recommendations had not found favour in France. In a letter he advised Montalembert to 'look to posterity to render you the justice that is due to you'.

Lazare-Nicolas Carnot rose to importance as a result of the French Revolution. From being a captain of engineers he became a colleague of Robespierre and in 1800 Secretary of War to Napoleon Bonaparte, at whose request he wrote *De la défense des places fortes* in 1810. Carnot excelled as an organiser, but possessed sufficient foresight to accept innovation. In 1783 he had been working on captive balloons which, ten years later, were first used as a means of reconnaissance. He attacked the conservative attitude of the French Corps of Engineers and, drawing heavily on Montalembert, advocated the construction of a string of tough fortresses to guard the frontier.

Carnot's eminence was shortlived. Napoleon disregarded his advice (not to risk his all in one battle) and after Waterloo Carnot was forced to flee from France. He raised three main points in his treatise, each subsequently open to criticism. He advocated vertical fire from mortars in retrenched casemates,

Below: *Fort Manoel in Malta.*

Bottom: *Fort St Louis at Toulon.*

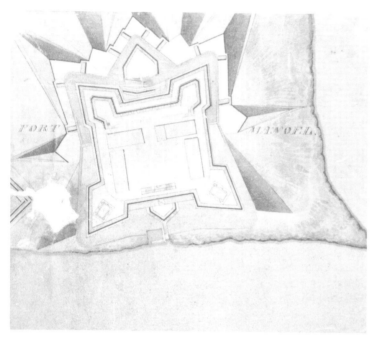

hidden from the enemy and yet capable of lobbing their shells over the work which protected them. Secondly, he realised that with the introduction of ricochet fire the covered-way had largely lost its value and would not protect his troops. He therefore recommended countersloping glacis, clear ground which sloped up from the ditch towards the open country. An attacking enemy would be caught in full view on his open gentle inclination. Thirdly he recommended the use of detached walls, a device adopted by the Austrians at Verona where the scarp walls were not tied back to the earthen rampart, but stood free. The walls were pierced by several tiers of loopholes through which infantry could fire muskets or grenades at the attackers exposed on the countersloping glacis.

FRENCH DESIGNERS IN MALTA

In practice the French engineers clung to their traditional concepts, but their reputation was still high and they were invited by the Knights of Malta to carry out

Battery at Comino near Malta; aerial section.

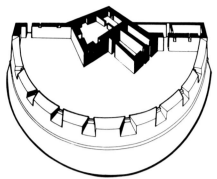

Fort Tigné; from an old photograph.

most of their eighteenth century projects of fortification. Fort Manoel is a typical example of their work. It was designed by the French engineers de Tigné and Gion de Mondion who arrived on the island early in 1715. The fort was square with four corner bastions, the cheapest solution for providing anything like a reasonable space for an adequate garrison within the walls of the enceinte. The curtain of the landfront was protected by a tenaille and a ravelin in the dry ditch, the adjacent curtains by lunettes connected by caponiers, and there were the usual Vauban devices such as traverses, a wide covered-way and adequate places of arms on the landward front. Fort Manoel is a fine example of a pattern of no great originality repeated elsewhere on innumerable occasions.

In the middle years of the eighteenth century the Knights began to stiffen their defences, along the coasts of Malta by building, at vulnerable points, infantry lines and a number of semi-circular batteries of a type evolved by the French at the end of the previous century. Fort St Louis (1692–97) at Toulon is a typical prototype.

The Maltese batteries all followed this pattern. Built on the seashore, they had a semi-circular front of between four and eight gun positions firing through embrasures in the parapet, and the garrison

was accommodated in two rooms at the back of the fort, the walls lined with loopholes for muskets. The middle of the landfront was protected by a redan similarly loopholed.

The last important fort built by the Knights before they were thrown off the island by Napoleon's troops was Fort Tigné. Begun in 1792, this coast defence fort was designed by A S de Tousard. An unusual work, it consisted of a quadrangular enceinte with embrasures for cannon, a wide ditch with loopholed galleries in the angles of the ditch to provide for its defence, and a maze of countermines laid beyond these galleries to be exploded in the event of an assault. In one corner of the quadrangle stood an isolated tower, two storeys high and 18 metres (60ft) in diameter, approached by a drawbridge and intended as a defensible keep, a last defence in the event of a siege.

COLONIAL FORTS

The maritime nations of the west penetrated along the coasts of Africa and Asia and into the hinterland of South America, establishing commercial bases which had in time to be defended against the greed of others. So European ideas on fortification spread across the world and little forts sprang up on distant shores, simplified models of those in use at home. The

Fort Raleigh; plan.

The square Castillo de San Marcos in Florida.

Fort at Puerto Rico; plan.

Portuguese were among the earliest to build colonial forts. By the end of the fifteenth century they were beginning to fortify the West African coast. A century later they built Fort Jesus at Mombasa designed by João Batista Cairato. It was a square fort with bastions, some of whose flanks were covered by orillons. It was a sort of caricature of Italian practice, had strange cavaliers raised in the salient angles of two bastions and an entrance gate formed in the flank of a third. Macao on the China coast was strongly fortified after the unsuccessful Dutch attack in 1622. The Monte Fort, a typical square work with four corner bastions, was a simplified version of Fort Manoel built a century later. An almost identical fort, the Castillo de San Marcos, was erected by the Spaniards on the

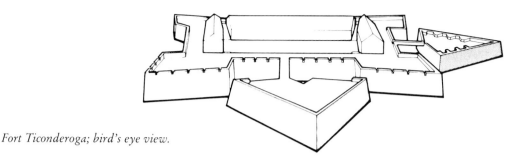

Fort Ticonderoga; bird's eye view.

coast of Florida in 1672, and is now splendidly preserved by the United States National Park Service.

      The British also built their forts, at first small
and somewhat primitive like Fort Raleigh (1585) on
Roanoke Island in the new land called Virginia. Its
plan is strange, perhaps illustrating the primitive
knowledge of fortification held by English sailors and
early colonists. It consisted of a diamond overlying a
square, with one corner of the diamond converted into
rudimentary heart-shaped bastion of a type that
Rogers had used at Boulogne and another point cut
short to form the entrance to the fort. Stranger still is
Ralph Lane's fort at Puerto Rico built in the same
year. There are similarities, for this fort also consisted
of a diamond overlying a square, but at Puerto Rico
one salient angle was converted into a spur, a device
used consistently by English colonial fort builders on
the west coast of Africa, and the opposite salient was
omitted, to be replaced by two re-entrant arches in the
middle of which lay the entrance.

      By the eighteenth century British engineers,
if not recommending valid innovations, were at least
building in an accepted European manner. Fort
Anomabu on the Gold Coast, begun in 1756, consisted of a square with corner bastions following a well-
established tradition.

THE STRUGGLE FOR CANADA

In the struggle between the French and the English for
the domination of North America, Fort Niagara, on
the shores of Lake Ontario, played a vital role because
most of the Western fur trade passed that way. From
early in the eighteenth century, and largely for political reasons, the French engineers had often restricted
their endeavours to the construction of machicolated
redoubts which looked much like fortified houses surrounded by palisades, rather than providing regular
forts. But the French defences at Niagara, begun in
1726 and designed by Gaspard-Joseph Chaussegros de
Léry, where the river entered Lake Ontario, consisted
of a square bastioned earthwork fort, plus, across the
peninsula, a defensive line which was not built. Within
the fort they built a stone house with machicolated
dormers on the roof, a building which still stands. De
Léry's towers are forerunners of the French *tours-
modèles*, the standardised designs approved nearly a
century later by Napoleon. In 1755, the French, under

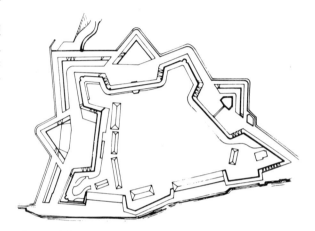

The citadel at Quebec; plan.

Captain Pierre Pouchot, began new fortifications
across the peninsula in the form of a hornwork in the
style of Vauban, with a central ravelin, *caponière*,
places of arms and a covered-way. The British captured the fort during the war of 1759, after a memorable siege.

      Elsewhere the French were busy consolidat-
ing their settlements. On the rivers which run between
New York and Montreal they built, in 1755, Fort
Ticonderoga, a square bastioned structure with triangular works called demi-lunes placed in front of the
north and west curtain, a ditch, a rudimentary
covered-way and the semblance of a glacis. The fort
was originally constructed of logs backed by earthen
ramparts but was later reconstructed in stone. At
Louisbourg, commanding the Cabot Strait, the French
built their main stronghold on the North American
continent, a port with its landfront protected by a
fully bastioned front. Montreal was also defended and
Quebec had four large bastions and two demi-bastions
running across the Heights of Abraham. Within this
enceinte lay a second line of partly constructed defences, with broad obtuse-angled bastions and, at the
core of the city dominating the Heights, stood the
star-shaped fort of St Louis which was later converted
into a British strongpoint. No wonder Major-General
Wolfe hestitated to commit his troops to a frontal
attack on so strong a fortification, and instead chose to
mount one of the most brilliant amphibious operations in history, scaling the precipitous cliffs and

Fort William at Calcutta.

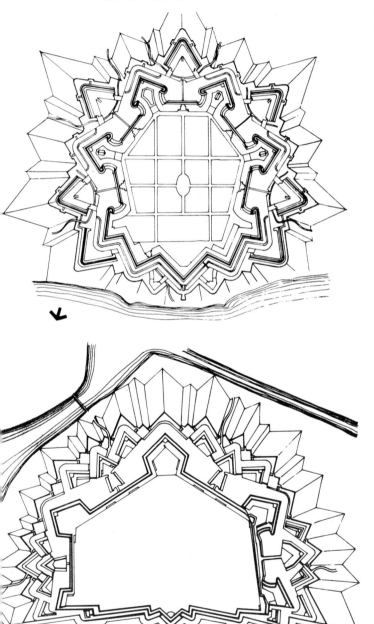

Fort St George at Madras.

attacking at a point the French considered to be inaccessible, to earn that famous tribute from the king: 'Mad is he?' asked George II, 'I wish to heaven he would bite some of my other generals!' In 1818 Lt-Col E W Durnford submitted his plan for enlarging Fort St Louis and converting it into the citadel of Quebec making it in its day the most formidable fortress in North America. New bastions were built, strengthened on two sides by counterguards, and three ravelins were constructed in front of the curtain walls.

INDIA

In India the British strengthened their defences in the eighteenth century. Clive's two preoccupations after recapturing Calcutta in 1757 were to provide an army strong enough to defend the East India Company's possessions and to build a fortress sufficiently capacious to hold that army. The old fort was quite inadequate, so John Brohier was instructed to prepare plans for the new Fort William on a virgin site by the river. The designs were executed in two months, and the trace followed in its broad outlines the work of Cormontaigne and the French school of engineers. Brohier struggled with the problem of inadequate labour handling unfamiliar materials in a building enterprise that was without precedent. He became involved in the corruption which was a part of Indian life and was arrested for fraud in 1760. A succession of engineers struggled in an attempt to redress the situation. Work dragged on till 1774 and it took a further seven years to fully arm the fort, which became the first substantial fortress in British India.

At Madras on the Coromandel coast Patrick Ross began a complete reconstruction of Fort St George in 1770, laying out a trace in the form of a large semi-octagon, its back facing the sea.

FORTS IN BRITAIN

The British were slowly forging an engineer corps capable of holding its own with its European counterparts, but several generations were to pass before it could assume some position of eminence, and then mainly in the field of coastal defence.

The Civil War of 1642 found Britain with less than a handful of towns protected by permanent fortifications. The realisation of this deficiency threw the country into a frenzy as citadels and earthworks

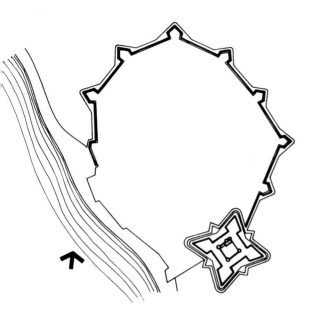

De Gomme's plan for Liverpool.

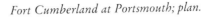

Fort Cumberland at Portsmouth; plan.

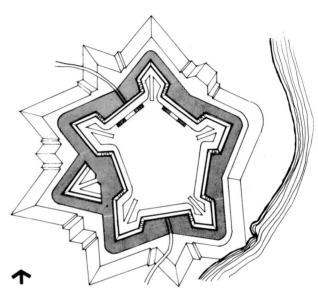

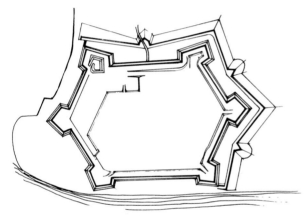

The citadel at Ayr in Scotland.

were hastily constructed to resist attack. For Liverpool Sir Bernard de Gomme produced a plan in 1644 for enclosing the medieval castle within a quadrangular-bastioned trace from which would extend a curtain wall punctuated by seven bastions in an arc to be terminated on the banks of the river Mersey by two demi-bastions. In 1652, with the declaration of a commonwealth between England and Scotland, construction began on four Scottish citadels, Ayr, Inverness, Leith and St Johnston. They were designed in a grandiose style by British standards to impose a protectorate upon a largely hostile population. At Ayr the citadel formed an elongated hexagon with earthen ramparts, a wet ditch which could be drained by a cunette, a covered-way with small places of arms in the shallow re-entrant angles and a glacis. The work was designed by Hans Ewald Tessin.

De Gomme was a Dutch engineer who had served with the royalists in the Civil War. Understandably his opportunity came with the restoration of the monarchy when Charles II made him engineer-in-chief to undertake, in 1665, a major programme of refortification for Portsmouth. Working on the original enceinte he remodelled the bastions and added four large ravelins to a wider moat. As one might expect from a Dutch engineer, water was to play a vital part in his defensive systems. The work of reconstruction took over twenty years to complete and rather ironically was largely carried out by Dutch prisoners

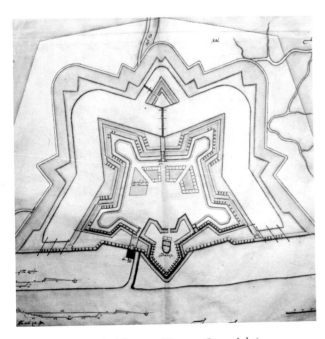

Tilbury Fort on the Thames. (Crown Copyright)

An embrasure covering the ditch at Fort Cumberland.

and re-entrant angles. As one would expect, the river frontage was most strongly armed with its parapets pierced by numerous embrasures.

Except for the Scottish troubles Britain in the eighteenth century felt fairly secure from foreign invasion and saw no cause to emulate her neighbours in the construction of vastly expensive fortifications around her cities and coastline. Her powerful fleet had by then become the first line of defence. With the exception of the stiffening of the Portsmouth defences by the construction of Fort Cumberland, a regular pentagonal work, in 1786, the sole outlet for British military engineers on home soil lay in the north of Scotland. Fort Augustus was built between 1729 and 1742, designed in the form of a square-bastioned fort by John Romer. In order to end once and for all the threat of Jacobite uprisings the British government embarked upon a policy of fortress-building in the highlands. Part of the work consisted of reconstructing forts that had been slighted in the uprising of 1745–46 and part in the erection of new works. The most imposing of the new structures was Fort George at the entrance to the Moray Firth which leads up to Inverness. This fort still remains in its entirety, splendidly preserved. Fort George was designed in 1747 by William Skinner on a narrow spur of land projecting into the sea so that, like Valletta some 200 years earlier, the main task for the engineer lay in providing a strong landfront across the neck of the peninsula with adequate direct fire out to sea from the point. The landfront consists of two full bastions lying behind a broad ditch. From their salient angles, batardeaux extend to the covered-way to control the water level in the ditch. The entrance, marked by a monumental gate and approached by a timber bridge, is covered by a bold ravelin supported by two lunettes which stand in the re-entrant places of arms. Sallyports give access to places of arms situated on the foreshore and the long sides of the fort are punctuated by broad bastions and terminated by smaller demi-bastions. Around the ramparts runs a broad terreplein, linking the bastions and the curtain walls and approached from the parade ground by gentle ramps up which artillery pieces could be manhandled. The guns fired through embrasures in the parapets and the flanks of the bastions provided positions for enfilading the adjoining faces. At the angles of the bastions echaugettes, or round

of war. This design made Portsmouth the strongest fortress in Britain, a position of eminence it was to retain with modifications up to the abandonment of permanent fortifications at the end of the Second World War. In 1673 de Gomme designed a regular pentagonal citadel at Dublin, its trace modelled on the New Dutch System. His best-preserved work is at Tilbury where in 1670 he constructed a regular pentagonal fort dependent upon broad water defences formed by a double ditch and surrounding marshy meadows. In Dutch style, sluices regulated the level of the water in the moat. The government had been badly frightened by the devastating Dutch naval raid up the Medway in 1667. The Thames' sole protection was the little round-fronted blockhouse constructed by Henry VIII and later incorporated as a cavalier into one of de Gomme's bastions. The new fort was designed to prevent any repetition of the affair. De Gomme's drawing shows a fausse-braye within the inner moat, a ravelin interrupting the system of drawbridges on the landward side and covering the main gate, and a broad covered-way with places of arms at both the salient

Fort Augustus at Inverness; plan.

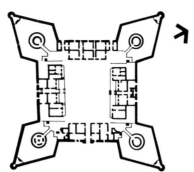

Fort George at Inverness.

sentry boxes, are corbelled out to survey the surrounding terrain and from them a passage leads through the earthwork of the parapet to the terreplein. If the fort shows no great originality it is at least a competent design, beautifully detailed and excellently constructed. William Skinner knew his job. By 1769 Fort George was complete, the last major fortification to be constructed in Britain for nearly a century, if one excepts the work on the Western Heights at Dover, begun in 1803 in the face of a threatened French invasion, and designed to transform the hill into an entrenched camp for 5000–6000 men.

CHAPTER FIVE
The Return of the Tower

There have been towers built throughout history, some to provide a refuge from attack, a sort of keep of last security. And some have been built to act as lookouts, to give warning of impending danger of a raid. But towards the end of the eighteenth century they began to proliferate once more and to assume a new aggressiveness.

Basically there are three types of towers, each with its own function, although these functions have, from time to time, overlapped, sometimes a tower being used for one, two or all three purposes.

First of all they could be used as a safe keep, or a final fall-back position if all the other fortifications fell, and this was the function of most of the earlier towers before the introduction of effective missile defence. There are numerous examples throughout Europe and, during the medieval period; for example, fine detached keeps were built at Aigues Mortes, Coucy and Flint castles. However, the keep was often not favoured by the military command for it was thought that soldiers might vacate their positions too readily and seek shelter in the keep.

Secondly, there were towers designed as lookouts to watch a stretch of coast and give warning of an impending raid or invasion. Their elevated position gave the observer a better field of view and their stone or brick walls gave him some protection so that a landing party would tend to by-pass such a tower rather than subject it to assault or siege, a process which would delay their advance inland.

A large number of these towers were built on the orders of the Viceroy of Naples in 1563 along the southern coasts of Italy. Placed close enough so that each could see its neighbours, they formed an almost continuous line from Apulia, round the heel and the toe of Italy and up the coast of Calabria, and eventually along the seaboard of the Tyrrhenian Sea as far north as Rome, with more built on Sicily and Sardinia. They did not follow a standard design – some were square in plan with deep machicolation; others, such as those built by the Aragonese, were tall round towers. They were constructed of thick battered walls with few or no windows to illuminate the ground floors. The main chamber was at first floor level, approached by ladder or drawbridge from a high stone staircase. The roof, strongly constructed to support cannon, was capped with deep machicolation, corbelled from the main walls and this provided some defence for the base of the tower. Signalling towers were built along the Mediterranean coast of Spain and, in fact, wherever the Turks threatened attack and money could be found to counter this threat.

In Malta an elaborate warning system was constructed by the Knights of St John. Towers had been built there in medieval times but the systematic plan for the distribution of intercommunicating watch towers did not originate until after the great siege of 1565. During the first half of the seventeenth century the Knights of St John constructed towers at all likely landing points. The Grand Master, Alof de Wignacourt, ordered a number of coastal towers to be built at vulnerable points on the coast capable of signalling news of impending attack to each other and to the headquarters by flag or gunfire during the day and by fires at night. A further five were ordered to be built by the Grand Master Lascaris in 1647. These towers followed a standard design, consisting of two rooms, one above the other, and space on the roof for two cannons (thus also being examples of the third type of tower) which, during the day were used for signalling the approach of corsairs as well as to deter their landing. Each tower was square and had a strong scarped base culminating in a broad string course and a parapet with embrasures. The towers were designed for a garrison of four.

The third type of defensive tower was built to deter an attack, being strong enough to resist bombardment and capable of attacking an enemy's ships or their landing parties with guns in casemates or on the roof. With the introduction of gunpowder and the increased efficiency of cannon in the fifteenth century it became feasible to build strong gun platforms of this type. It should also be remembered that ships of the period were not designed to fire broadsides. Usually frail galleys, vulnerable to attack from the shore, they invariably gave the coastal defences a wide berth.

Multi-storey gun towers had been built at Roumeli Hisar and other sites on the Bosphorus, and at Modon on the Peloponnesus of Greece there was a fine three-tiered tower built about 1480. By that time they were scattered widely and not just for coast defence. For example, at Prague five years later they built the round Powder Tower with four floors of guns firing in casemates, its roof being covered by 5.4 metres (18ft) of soil to make it bombproof. The Kaiserturm at Kufstein, built between 1518 and 1522, was a round tower, its interior vaults springing from a central column like that adopted on the later Martello towers, and with three floors of guns covering all the ground around.

Between 1480 and 1520 the Knights of St John had built Fort Agius Nicolas at the entrance to their harbour at Rhodes. It was really a three-tiered tower with a multitude of guns facing out over the water and it was only one of a number of multi-gun towers built soon on the coasts of the eastern Mediterranean which possibly influenced the building of coastal gun towers by the English king, Henry VIII.

THE ENGLISH COAST TOWERS OF THE SIXTEENTH CENTURY

The formation of a holy alliance against England and the threat of imminent invasion caused Henry VIII to initiate an important and extensive project for the defence of the coasts. Along the south coast of England, Henry rapidly constructed a number of interesting forts, each with radiating gun positions on several tiers and with a central safe keep. He also built a number of blockhouses, circular gun towers, sometimes concentric like the one designed by John Rogers at Ambleteuse in the English zone of Northern France in 1546. The blockhouses had guns on their roofs firing through embrasures, protected in the Italian fashion by curved battlements. One is shown in a painting, its guns engaging an enemy off Portsmouth. The idea could have come from almost anywhere in Europe. For instance, there is one almost identical illustrated by Pieter Breughal the elder in his painting of 'The Tower of Babel' of 1563, but the most likely source of inspiration is Italian. The Venetians had built them and two are illustrated guarding the Bay of Lepanto in a painting of the battle of 1571, and Gabriel Busca shows an identical one to the English example at Portsmouth in his *Instrutione de'bombardieri* of 1598, illustrating contemporary Italian practice.

THE GROWTH OF THE GUN TOWER

Soon the multi-gun defensible tower, capable of both taking on an enemy and providing a secure place of retreat was common. Witness the great four-storey

A tower on Jersey.

gun tower which projects boldly from the Festung Marienberg. It was probably built by Balthaser Neumann between 1675 and 1683. Also important are the strong gun towers built by the Swedish military engineer Erick Dahlberg for the defence of Göteborg shortly after 1687. Fort Kronan was a strong square tower with its corners chamfered and with two internal floors for guns firing out in all directions through splayed embrasures. His Fort Lejon was round and had three floors of guns beneath a conical roof, its base being protected by large triangular caponiers which projected to give, in plan, a star-shape to the ground floor. But amongst the most impressive examples were

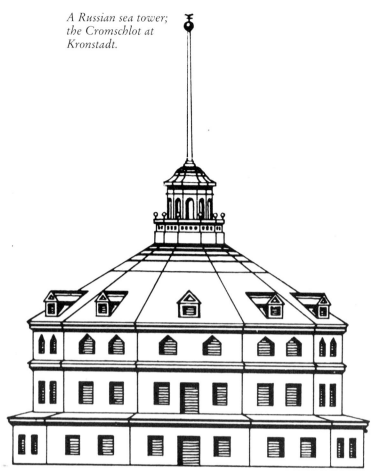

A Russian sea tower; the Cromschlot at Kronstadt.

those built by the Russians in the sea at Kronstadt to defend the approaches to their capital at St Petersburg. In 1704 they built the Cromschlot, a facetted tower rising and built back in four tiers, capable of being armed with a large number of guns. This was the sort of multi-gun solution that was to be advocated by Montalembert in his *La Fortification Perpendiculaire* of 1776–84 and his project of 1780 for the defence of Cherbourg with detached round towers.

In 1757, Maurice, Count de Saxe, had suggested surrounding a town that required defending by a ring of detached circular towers spaced some 450 metres (500yds) apart. These, he said, would be superior to redoubts. He designed them to look rather like upturned flower pots, about 8 metres (25ft) high, the front half, facing the enemy, built solid and the rear half containing rooms within the thick semi-circular walls. On the roof would be mounted guns. The idea was later to influence British engineers.

THE DEVELOPMENT OF THE KEEP

Although there are isolated examples of round towers being built or used within forts – especially in France as, for example, that illustrated by de Ville in 1639 – in the late seventeenth century Vauban once more popularized the use of the keep, this time as a tower of refuge for his coast batteries. Fine examples exist at the Fort du Chapus of 1690–92 and the coastal tower at

Camaret, built between 1694 and 1695. In both these cases the tower forms both a keep and a defensive position for muskets to cover the gorge and the ditch at the rear against any possible land assault. In 1685, Vauban designed a round tower on four floors with steeply battered walls and bold machicolation at Belle Ile. It stood, like the earlier Venetian examples, in the middle of a round battery of guns firing through embrasures out to sea. In 1764 a great detached central keep was built in the form of a four-leafed clover for the core of the great Prussian fortress at Silberberg (Srebrna Gora) in Silesia. In 1792 D'Arcon was advocating and using the strong circular keep as a fall-back position in his lunettes, vulnerable outworks protecting fortresses like Mont Dauphin. In the same year, the French military engineer, Stephen de Tousard, built Fort Tigné in Malta. This was a coastal work, designed in the form of a lozenge protected by counterscarp galleries and with a powerful round keep at the end of the central traverse and on the point of the least vulnerable corner of the lozenge. The keep had cannon on the roof and two floors for musketry defence firing through loopholes. It was a design that greatly impressed the British Army when they and the Maltese captured the place in 1798.

THE BRITISH USE OF GUN TOWERS

In 1778, when France allied herself to the American colonists in revolt, it seemed certain that France would invade Britain and might capture the Channel Islands. As a result of this threat it was proposed to build thirty round coastal towers to protect Jersey, some 9–12 metres (30–40ft) high, considerably taller and thinner than the later Martello towers, and spaced some 450 metres (500yds) apart. Twenty-one were built. Almost immediately there followed a proposal to build fifteen towers on Guernsey. The design of the towers on the two islands differed; those on Jersey had four bold boxes with machicolation projecting from their parapets and were wider, some 10 metres (34ft) in diameter with the walls at the base 2.4 metres (8ft) thick. Those on Guernsey had thinner walls – only 1.2 metres (4ft) thick – and no machicolation but a shallow sloping parapet. The Governor of Jersey, General Henry Seymour Conway, obtained authorisation from the Board of Ordnance. In his letter to the Secretary of State, in which he made a case for the

Malta: Fort Tigné.

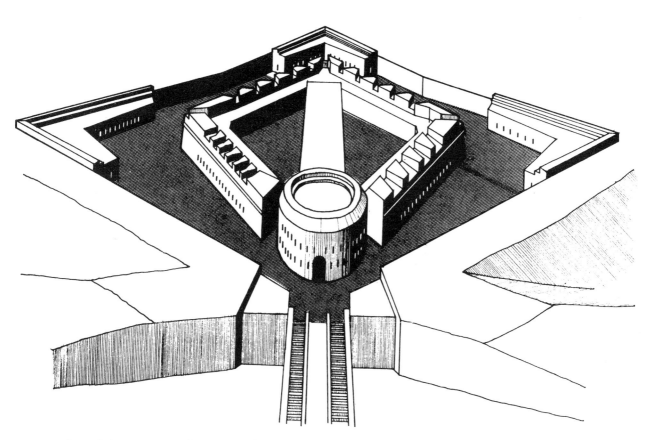

construction of these towers, Conway explained that they were based on the theories of Count Maurice de Saxe who had proposed them as outer, isolated defences for fortified towns.

Many of the Channel Island towers were built to support batteries. Sometimes they lay in the centre of a circular battery or wall, sometimes, as at Fort Saumarez, there was a three-gun battery in front, attached by the corner of a square battlement. At Mount Crevelt a semi-circular battery, which stood in front of the round tower, was joined by connecting walls in 1810. Thus there was often an interdependence between guns at ground level and those on the roofs of towers.

It is said that an incident at Mortella Point in Corsica in 1794 caused the British to adopt a policy of defending their home and colonial coasts by means of strong gun towers and thus to adopt the name 'Martello tower'. In the year previous, HMS *Lowestoft* had bombarded an armed circular tower which had surrendered after two hours. The tower was soon recaptured by the French but, in February 1794, it was again attacked by the Navy, this time by HMS *Fortitude* (74 guns) and HMS *Juno* (32 guns). Much to the surprise of the sailors, the British ships were repulsed with serious losses and it had to be left to the army to besiege the tower. Even then it took two hours of heavy and continous bombardment to subdue this

tower into surrender, even though it contained a garrison of only 38 men firing two 18-pounder and one 6-pounder smooth-bore cannon. The British were impressed, particularly John Jervis, George Elphinstone, David Dundas, Abraham D'Aubant, Thomas Nepean and John Moore, all of whom were present on Corsica and were to be instrumental, in one way or another, in influencing the later British policy on the construction of coastal gun towers. Admiral Sir John Jervis sent a model of the tower to London, writing, 'I hope to see such works erected . . . on every part of the Coast likely for an enemy to make a descent on.'

The Cape of South Africa was captured from the Dutch in 1795 and it was realised immediately that defences were needed to repel a possible counterattack. The new British governor was Vice-Admiral Elphinstone so one is not surprised to read that he proposed and began the construction of two round coastal towers to defend the harbour at Simonstown. Craig's Tower, not until later to be called a Martello tower, was built in 1796 and had a semi-circular battery ranged in front of it. In its rear, the tower protected the main reserve naval magazine in the colony. The tower had vertical walls built of stone and a central circular column to support the timber floors and the gun platform on the roof. It thus appeared more drum-like than the later towers in Britain. These comprised two floors and a roof platform. From the first

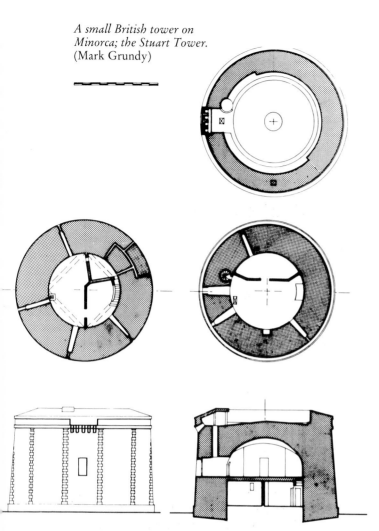

A small British tower on Minorca; the Stuart Tower. (Mark Grundy)

floor, three large embrasures opened towards the countryside.

The next towers to be built were against the French in Canada, at the naval base of Halifax where three were put up between 1796 and 1798. These were more impressive than the ones in South Africa and each had a hollow shaft in the middle to be used for a hoist, but which must have been weaker than a solid pillar.

The Mediterranean island of Minorca was to see the most extensive use of these gun towers where the British had installed themselves to watch French naval activity out of Toulon and provide an army base for operations in Malta and Egypt. The general commanding the forces on the island was Lt-General Sir Charles Stuart who had been on Corsica during the British campaign.

The French had captured Minorca in 1756 and held it until 1762. Their action in securing the coast was very different from that later adopted by the British. The French built a series of coastal earthwork redoubts and entrenchments close to beaches which might be used for landings. When the British

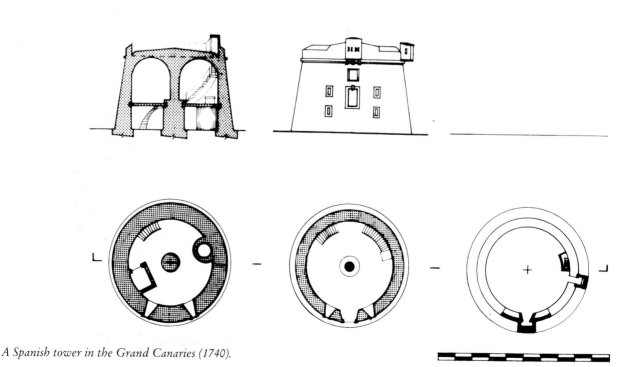

A Spanish tower in the Grand Canaries (1740).

The British Alcaufar Tower on Minorca. (Mark Grundy)

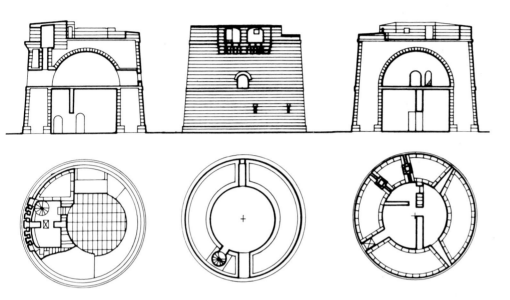

reoccupied the island in 1798, their first priority was to secure the ports and anchorages at Mahon, Cuidadela and Fornells by building a series of round gun towers, the main concentration being placed around Port Mahon, the fleet anchorage. Basically there were two types, large and smaller, described by Lt-Col Pasley in his book in 1822 for he was there supervising the building of some of them. Although the idea of building gun towers may have come from the one on Corsica, the design certainly did not. The Minorcan towers are modelled on Spanish design and have much in common with, for instance, the tower at Gando, in the Grand Canaries built by Spanish engineers about 1740, or, more likely, from the two Spanish towers built on Minorca about 1781. They all looked like inverted flower pots with the doorway at first floor level protected by machicolation above. Like the later Martello towers, the Gando tower had a central pillar supporting a bombproof vaulted roof – the two Minorca towers, like the British ones there, did not. They nearly all had provision for hot-shot furnaces.

The British proposed a scheme of fifteen towers on Minorca, incorporating the two Spanish ones and the Spanish octagonal tower of St Nicholas with its semi-circular battery, built in 1690 on the coast beyond Cuidadela. The British towers were designed by Captain Robert D'Arcy and seven were completed within a year. The most unusual one was at Santandria. Circular in plan, it was topped by a continuous ring of machicolation, and the tower was sunk into a broad ditch with vertical counterscarp walls and a single counterscarp gallery approached by an underground tunnel. It also had low musketry galleries in the tower to cover the floor of the ditch.

In spite of historical precedent, the British were not, in the early years of the nineteenth century, firmly committed to building round towers. There

An unusual British design; a square tower at Trincomalee in Ceylon (1806). (Kevin Ingram)

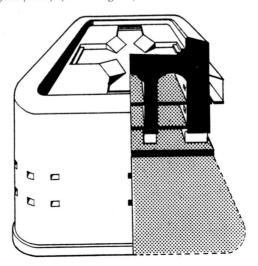

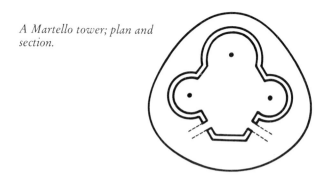

A Martello tower; plan and section.

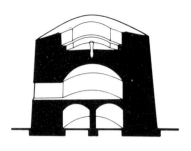

Martello tower at Dymchurch in Kent.

were strong arguments in favour of square towers, of the type used by the French early in the eighteenth century and known as the *tour réduit*, and developed by Napoleon Bonaparte as the *tour modèle*. The square plan was rejected by the British mainly on the grounds of cost and because, on experiment, it was found that shot glanced off circular towers causing less damage than that hitting flat surfaces squarely. However, they did build at least one, in 1806 in the hills above the port of Trincomalee. It was of solid construction in two storeys with the corners of the square plan chamfered off. About that time, though possibly a few years earlier, they also built a large round tower on a hill above the port at Hambantota, also in Ceylon. It was designed by Captain Gowper

and consisted of a drum with vertical walls some 7.6 metres (25ft) high and 12 metres (40ft) in diameter. It had broad loopholes alternating on two floors and the doorway was on the first floor approached by a flight of timber steps.

THE MARTELLO TOWERS IN ENGLAND

In 1798 it was clear that the main threat lay nearer home and that the invasion of England was a serious possibility. Since 1801, the French had concentrated at Boulogne the Army of England and had got ready two thousand vessels to transport it across the Channel. By 1803 it was obvious that the French were making preparations and had every intention of attacking Britain. This threat was to lead to the building of what were called the 'towers of sea batteries' or 'sea towers' and which were eventually called the Martello towers, and to turn southern England into an armed camp.

The initial proposals put forward by Ford were for square towers, but this idea was abandoned in favour of round ones. The towers were to be placed about 550 metres (600yds) apart so that their guns could cross, and some, though not all, were to be built to strengthen batteries. Unlike the *tours modèles*, many were to stand as isolated works to protect any part of the coast vulnerable to enemy landings. They were also to guard the marsh sluices.

The line of Martello towers proposed by the Defence Committee of 1804 was to stretch from Eastbourne to Dover with a gap at Dungeness Point, and then up the east coast from Clacton to Aldeburgh. In that year Lt-General Robert Morse, the Inspector General of Fortifications, sanctioned the building of 103 Martello towers, the Royal Military Canal which would act as a retrenchment some 48 kilometres (30 miles) long, and two redoubt-forts. These were round independent forts mounting some eleven guns and holding a garrison of about 350 men.

Unlike the French *tours modèles* which were standardized down to the smallest detail and divided into five distinct types to cope with every situation, the British Martello towers, although basically standardized, varied considerably from place to place, and those on the east coast were larger – cam-shaped or ovoid – thicker on the seaward side and containing two staircases in the thickness of the walls. Right up to

Model of a Martello tower on the east coast of England.
(G Gribble).

the Second World War, British engineers have always seemed reluctant to accept standardized solutions, preferring to adopt a somewhat makeshift policy.

Built of brick, for which millions were required in a short space of time, and clad in hard stucco, the Martello towers looked like upturned flower pots. Most of those on the south coast were placed in dry ditches and were not attached to batteries in the French manner. Slightly elliptical in shape, they had a base diameter which varied from about 14 to 15 metres (46–50ft), at ground level between 12 and 13.5 metres (40–44ft), and at parapet levels from 11 to 12 metres (36–40ft). By using an ellipse, the walls were made thicker at the front to face enemy bombardment, being about 4 metres (13ft) at the base, diminishing to 2.7 metres (9ft) at the top, with a thickness of about 2 metres (7ft) at the rear, diminishing to 1.5 metres (5ft) at the top. Many of the towers have now gone, collapsed into the sea or been demolished, so it is impossible to check on the variations in size and shape, but even Pasley, who was involved in their construction, admitted that they varied from place to place.

There were two storeys, the lower one containing magazines, stores and a water tank, the upper one accommodation for the garrison, lit by loopholes and carefully ventilated by winding air holes usually carried up towards the top of the tower. The door was at first floor level, approached by a ladder or by a draw-bridge. There was a ladder and a trap door, or sometimes a staircase, leading to the gun platform on the roof. Some had a furnace for hot shot. Again they varied internally, although most had a central pillar, either supporting the springing of the brick arches which supported the first floor, or supporting an annular arch which was semi-circular, elliptical, parabolic or segmental, and upon which rested the platform and the pivots of the guns on the roof. Lendy was to write that 'the small Martello is circular, with a diameter of about thirty feet [9 metres] and a height of at least twenty-four feet [7.3 metres] to resist escalade', but most seem to have been about 10 metres (33ft) high and some up to 12 metres (40ft). The extraordinary variations in the dimensions given by many contemporary authors, some of whom were actually involved in the design and construction of the towers, leads one to the conclusion that, in the executed solutions, the engineers were far from adopting a standard design.

Those on the east coast of England were started in 1805 and not completed until 1812. General Morse suggested that forty should be built, but in the event only twenty-nine were completed including the larger one at Aldeburgh in Suffolk, on the northern end of the line, built to a quite different design being quatrefoil in plan.

Captain, later General, Sir William Whitmore designed and built the Martello towers that studded the coasts of Essex and Suffolk. He had his problems for many of the towers were erected on marsh land reclaimed from the sea. He was to write,

these towers caused me anxiety in as much as the soil was of the consistency of butter and when a great weight was given to one side in the progress of building over another the mass of masonry had a tendency to incline on that side. In one of these towers, first one side sunk and then the opposite, which we got down by merely opening the surface of the soil where the soft mud rose and overflowed. By this process one of the towers was, after sinking bodily ten feet [3 metres] finished to its full height and remained erect.

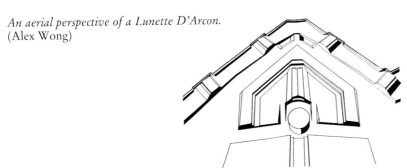

An aerial perspective of a Lunette D'Arcon.
(Alex Wong)

THE MARTELLO TOWERS IN IRELAND

A rebellion against English rule broke out in Ireland in 1798 but it was put down savagely. As a result, when the French landed there a few months later they were not supported by the Irish population who had been cowed into submission. The invasion was a failure, but Ireland had always been thought of as the weak link. To protect some of its coastline, particularly in the south and around Dublin Bay, it was decided to build many Martello towers and these were begun a year earlier than those constructed on the south coast of England. The Irish towers were simpler in design, without the elliptical plan so that the walls were the same thickness all round. In fact they were much closer to some of those British towers that had been erected on Minorca than to the English examples – plain round buildings in dressed stone usually with a machicolated gallery over the doorway.

THE FRENCH TOWERS

The French were as important in the development of the gun tower, having been largely responsible for its revival in the first place. Vauban had designed towers as last retreats and in order to defend his coastal batteries from an attack from the rear. There are also examples of French engineers enwrapping medieval circular towers within fully bastioned forts, as at Fort Carré in Antibes where a round tower built by Henry II about 1550 was later enclosed within a square bastioned fort.

The most influential early attempt to integrate a round keep with a well designed redoubt was the work of General Jean-Claude Eléonore Lemichaud D'Arcon who, in 1792, published a paper in which he described a lunette he had designed. It consisted of a regular pentagonal fortlet with a triangular ditch following the line of the outer faces, protected by casemated counterscarp galleries at the salient point. In the middle of the gorge stood a circular keep tower covered by a pitched roof and defended through musketry loopholes. It was to be used for a last stand by the garrison and it communicated with the main fort by means of a covered caponier which acted as a traverse. The Lunette D'Arcon was important because it was accepted by the military authorities and a number of examples were built at Metz and Mont Dauphin. More important, Carnot's brother, when he was made director of the archives of the fortifications, ordered a model to be made in 1797 for the instruction of army officers, so the design became well known amongst French engineers. It formed the basis for the French design of Fort Tigné in Malta, begun in 1792.

Montalembert was important because of the suggestions he made for the construction of strong artillery towers containing casemates for heavy guns, able to fire across the countryside or to be used in close defence across a ditch. His round gun towers would have been much larger and more powerfully armed than the towers subsequently built by the French and the British, and he was to inspire German engineers who would later build such towers in places like Silesia.

The French *tours modèles* are even more influential even though few were built. The prototype had been built in 1800 by French engineers west of Alexandria during the French occupation of Egypt. It was a square tower built to hold a garrison of twenty-five men, with cannon on the roof, the parapets and the first floor walls pierced by musketry loopholes and the base protected by four projecting machicolated drop-boxes. The tower stood in a square ditch surrounded by a glacis whose slope lined in with the loopholes on the parapet.

In 1811 Napoleon, wishing to remedy the disorder into which the coast defences had fallen, gave orders that, in future, guardhouses, powder magazines and small service buildings for coast defence, along with other small works of fortification not necessarily on the coast, should be housed in bombproof loopholed towers which could be used as keeps in the interior or the gorges of batteries or forts. Everything was standardised down to the last detail and five standard designs for the *tours modèles*, plus a standard design for a battery – the *tour réduit* – were produced varying in size from the large tower, called No 1, which was 8 metres (27ft) high from the bottom of the ditch to the top of the parapet, to tower No 5, which was small, single-storey and roofed with a pitched roof. Designed later, they differed in two respects from the English Martello towers. First, they were designed to be used in conjunction with other

Below: *A Prussian Montalembert tower at Kozle, now in Poland (1805).*

Below: *Prussian Montalembert tower at Kozle; section through the tower showing the artillery casemates and the smoke vents.*

works of fortification and not to be free-standing. Second, they were square in plan. The document from the Minister of War mentions that several plans of towers were drawn up by the General Committee of Fortifications and that Napoleon selected the best which were represented in the five model-towers described and illustrated. The Ministry pointed out that bomb-proof towers were expensive and could not be built on every site where it was necessary that a tower should be constructed. In fact, because of the state of the war very few were built. Six were projected in 1812 for the defence of the naval station at Toulon and several were designed to cover Brest. Some were built near La Rochelle and on the island of Oléron, at least two in

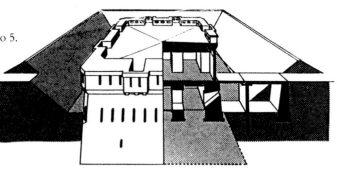

A drawing of a tour modéle No 5.
(Richard Roberts)

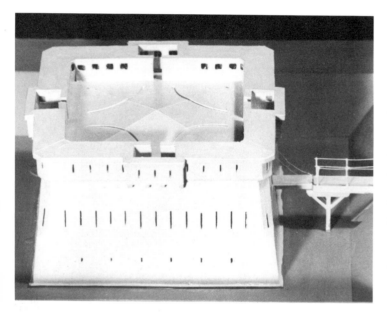

A model of one of the larger French tour modéles. (James Rutherford)

the Netherlands and some were designed for the Adriatic coasts.

Although they were intended primarily for coast defence, placed in conjunction with coastal batteries, the *tours modèles* were occasionally used to form a line of defence, the towers being evenly spaced out and joined by a continuous entrenchment as, for example, at Quelern and on the Ile de France (Mauritius) where the towers had a land role, supporting existing lines of fortification.

The French towers continued to be used for many years. The Commission on Fortifications of

1841 recommended the grouping of all buildings used for coast defence in one single building type which would also serve as a keep. This was to be modelled on the *tours modèles* of 1811. The new works were classified as first class redoubts with towers for 60, 40 and 20 men respectively, second class keeps without artillery (a defence against muskets and strong enough to resist a *coup de main*), and coast batteries where the traditional semi-circular trace gave way to a rectilinear one which could be broken back in straight lines.

In spite of the adoption of rifled artillery by the western navies, the French continued to use the masonry works and towers following the model of 1841 and, indeed, not much different from that of 1811, using earthwork cover and traverses to protect them.

THE MARTELLO TOWERS OVERSEAS

Soon the Martello tower began to proliferate, particularly in the overseas colonial possessions of Britain. In 1808, Ralph Bruyères built four unusual Martello towers on the Heights of Abraham in front of Quebec, unusual because they were used as detached works, mutually supported against a land attack, whereas others had hitherto been designed almost entirely for coast defence. In fact, Captain, later General Sir Charles William Pasley, who had been involved in the design of the early Martellos and was later the director of a course on military engineering, stressed in 1822 that Martello towers were not recommended for inland fortresses or positions for, although their curved walls might deflect the inaccurate fire from ships' guns, they could not withstand the

A section through one of the tours modèles.

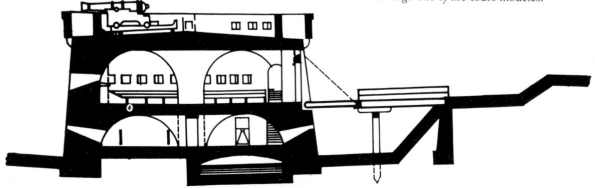

An unusual British tower at Curzola on the Adriatic coast.

bombardment of land batteries. The Quebec towers were spaced out evenly in a straight line across the Heights and in front of the middle one Bruyères intended to build a bastion-shaped redoubt with its ditch defended by caponiers at the shoulder angles. E W Durnford proposed adding redoubts to each Martello on the Heights. This line of land Martellos was unusual for the English to build and far closer to a system occasionally used by the French with their *tours modèles*.

Captain George Whitmore, who had planned and built the Martello towers on the east coast of England was posted to Malta in 1811 where he prepared a project for a tower and dependent batteries to secure the anchorage at the nearby island of Lampedusa.

Also in 1811, Captain William Hoste won a narrow naval victory at the Battle of Lissa in the middle of the Adriatic, but his ships had to seek shelter to undertake repairs in the harbour of the nearby island. Writing to London he said, 'I think a Martello tower built on the eminence of the head of the harbour to secure it from a *coup de main*, with a garrison of three hundred to four hundred men would, whilst you possess naval superiority, keep it quite secure from any attack from the opposite coasts of Dalmatia or Apulia.' Once more the Navy came out in favour of Martellos. In September of that year, Captain Bennett, RE surveyed the island of Lissa (Vis) and reported that it should be fortified with batteries. In addition to other fortifications, the British built Bentinck Tower, a three-storey circular tower and, shortly afterwards, Fort Wellington, another round tower pierced by loopholes, but with thinner walls strengthened by two cross walls from a central pillar which supported the vaulting in a manner similar to that used on the English Martello towers. Nearer the mainland, the British captured the island of Curzola (Kortula) in 1813 and held it until July 1815. During that time they built a circular gun tower on the hill above the fortified town and its harbour. The tower, called Fort Wellington, had steeply sloping walls pierced by two alternating bands of large loopholes and a further band near the top, just below the cordon, of much thinner ones. Its sloping shape and its rings of loopholes made it different from the normal English Martello towers.

Anholt Island, off the coast of Denmark, was captured in May 1809. In 1812, Captain G G Lewis

A British proposal for building a tower and a battery on Anholt Island (1812).

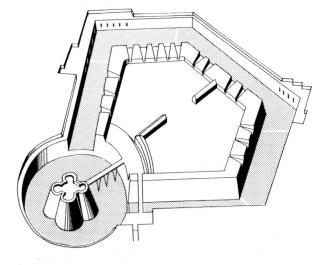

Canada: a Martello tower at Fort Frederick, Kingston, Ontario (1846).

proposed a number of fortifications including a tower for four guns built in the form of a four-leafed clover with walls that curved out towards the base, making them much thicker there. There were casemates on the first floor and a vaulted interior but no central pillar. The tower formed a keep for a polygonal battery but was separated from it by a ditch and vertical counterscarp walls.

Nearly everywhere the British sought to defend their possessions with new or existing gun towers. In 1813, Captain Dickens, RE was called upon to report on the possibility of strengthening the coastal lookout towers on Malta, but, in that instance, nothing came of the proposal. In fact, in 1828, Captain Harry Jones reported that 'the towers, in general, were not constructed to receive heavy artillery – in fact, many are not capable of it and must only be considered in the light of watch-towers – and not as Martello towers which, from their construction and as used in England were intended to hold out for a certain time.' Four years later the army abandoned fifteen of the Maltese towers.

A Martello tower was built in 1822 at Ferry Point on St George's Island in Bermuda and another in 1830, designed by Lieutenant Brandreth, on Ascension Island.

The most impressive programme of Martello tower building was in Canada. In addition to the three early towers built between 1796 and 1798 at Halifax naval base and the four at Quebec built in 1808, two more were built at Halifax between 1811 and 1814, one at St Johns, Newfoundland and the last four spectacular towers were planned at Kingston on Lake Ontario in 1828, but not built until 1845–51. There, four towers were built in a semi-circular cordon covering the entrance to Kingston Harbour and the start of the Rideau Canal. They were large and somewhat similar to the east coast towers in England, but were covered with timber conical snow roofs which could be removed in time of war, and some were protected by bulbous caponiers projecting from their bases. The central pillar was placed eccentrically so that the wall at the front was thicker than the wall at the rear. The gun platforms on the roof were formed in a trefoil pattern to take the pivot mountings of three guns. Fort Frederick tower had a diameter of 18 metres (60ft) and a height of 13.7 metres (45ft) within its ditch, and a wall thickness of between 2.7 and 4.57 metres (9–15ft). It was thus much bigger than the Martello towers on the south coast of England.

THE CONTINUATION OF MARTELLO BUILDING

The popularity of Martellos seemed undiminished. In 1812, as a result of America joining in the war, two Martello towers were built on the Orkney Islands to protect the convoys being assembled to cross the Atlantic. In 1834, five were built on the island of Jersey to supplement the earlier ones. In 1845, Lewis was still advocating a variety of tower designs based on the Martellos in an article he wrote for the *Professional Papers of the Royal Engineers*. So popular had become the name that six so-called Martello towers were built in America, although they differed considerably in design and shape.

To guard the naval dockyard at Pembroke, British engineers built two gun towers between 1848 and 1851, tall blocks rising from the sea, one for a single gun and the other mounting three guns on its roof. Both had tall arched recesses containing machicolation somewhat similar to that used on the towers at Genoa some thirty years earlier.

Finally, a large oval tower, the Brehon

Below: *The north-east tower defending Pembroke dockyard (1848–51).*

Bottom: *Fort Boyard off the Ile d'Oleron (1804–59).*

Tower, was built between 1854 and 1856 on a rock in the sea halfway between Guernsey and Herm, rather like the large oval French sea fort built earlier at Fort Boyard near Oléron, and a forerunner of those to be built in the sea to guard the approaches to Portsmouth.

OTHER GUN TOWER PROJECTS ON THE CONTINENT

In 1814, the British general, Lord William Cavendish Bentinck, having been in command in Sicily, led a successful expedition against French-held Genoa. Immediately he began to reconstruct the fortifications abandoned by the French. Hopes that Genoa might become a free city were dashed at the Treaty of Paris when the place was annexed by the royal house of Savoy (Piedmont). Engineers faithful to the Savoyard cause were appointed, including Major d'Andreis who had been trained in Vienna. Andreis had enlisted in the British army and, in 1816, joined the Piedmontese and began, about 1820, to build a series of round gun towers placed outside the fortified walls which climbed up the mountainside behind the port of Genoa. Possibly inspired by British, French and Austrian ideas, this was, nevertheless, a novel concept of using towers as a forward screen for a fortified line. The towers were round, with scarped walls pierced by a ring of loopholes fairly low down and given the appearance of verticality by a boldly projecting machicolation between which rose sixteen tall arched shafts from just below the cordon line. This gave the towers an almost medieval appearance. In addition to making them look very elegant, this also meant that the whole of the round base and the lower loopholes could be covered from the roof.

The most novel and controversial works lay at Linz in Austria, a town which was fortified by Prince Maximillian with thirty-two round towers, work on which commenced in 1830. Each tower was sunk into the ground and surrounded by a narrow ditch. The excavated material was used to form a glacis in front of each tower, the projection of whose surface lined up with the crest of the parapet. There were three floors, including the basement, and embrasures covered the ditch. The gate at first floor level was approached by a drawbridge. The most significant features were on the roof. Here eleven guns, mounted

*Genoa: one of the towers built to stiffen the fortified walls
behind the city (c1820).*

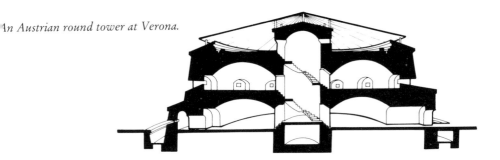

An Austrian round tower at Verona.

on newly modelled carriages so that they could be placed together, could be laid so that their fire grazed the glacis in front. The guns were devised to enable all to be brought to bear on any given point at any time, their carriages being easily swung round on the inner circle of the tower. This was a great advance on earlier towers, such as those proposed by Montalembert where the lines of fire were governed by the angles of the embrasures and, in the event of a frontal attack, guns round the remaining three-quarters of the circle were forced to stand idle. It should be understood that the towers at Linz were designed to protect a military camp and to cover an army which would in turn support them. This germ of an idea developed into the entrenched camp of the late nineteenth century. Critics argued both for and against these circular towers but they soon fell out of favour and most people, including the inhabitants of Linz, tended to refer to them as follies.

North of the Austrian-controlled city of Verona lay a high spur with precipitous cliffs. Its approaches were guarded by the strongly fortified city, and on this ridge Franz von Scholl placed five circular forts modelled on those at Linz. They were later considered liable to be breached by enemy bombardment, but this would seem unlikely unless the enemy guns were well concealed, as the circular forts on their elevated position had a fine view in all directions and were capable of pouring devastating fire on either side of the spur, whereas guns lower down had little chance of retaliating. Everywhere the masonry is precise and tight fitting. It has resisted time and the obvious indifference of the Veronese. The towers, surrounded by a narrow vertically-walled ditch, had two internal floors with casemates for guns, and guns on the roof plat-

form, covered by a shallow pitched conical roof. In the centre of each tower there was a large hollow drum of masonry supporting the vaulting and containing the circular staircases which led to the platform on the roof.

The Russians, too, were building round gun towers at Bomarsund on the Åland Islands in the northern waters of the Baltic Sea. In 1829 Russian engineers prepared a scale model of the defences for the new naval station which would be ice-free for most of the year. Serious building began in 1832. The defences consisted of a multi-gun fort, semi-circular in shape, joined to five detached gun towers by a defensible wall and a military road nearly a kilometre (⅝ mile) in length. In addition there was a strong circular gun tower placed at each side of the entrance to the harbour with a proposal for smaller towers on a breakwater and a screen of seven, which were never built, out in the country opposite the main fort. In the summer of 1854 the defences were attacked by a combined

Plan and section of a Maximilian tower at Linz.

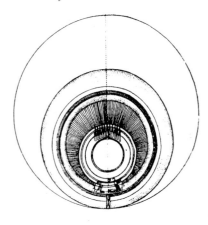

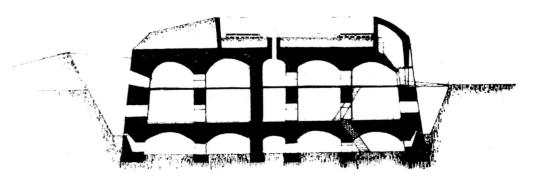

The entrance to a round tower at Verona.

Opposite: *Penrhyn Castle.*

Anglo-French force, bombarded by the fleet and besieged by an army of 10,000 men. The forts fell, but whether the victory was due primarily to naval bombardment, or to army assault, or more likely to a combination of the two, has never been satisfactorily decided.

Perhaps the forts built in the sea in the 1860s to guard the naval stations at Portsmouth and Plymouth, for they were really round armoured gun towers, were the last of the line of a development that goes right back in history. Only time will tell.

CHAPTER SIX

The Nineteenth Century: Escalation

THE ROMANTIC IMAGE

The early nineteenth century is an age of contradictions. It attempts to reconcile the flights of fantasy of the early gothic revival with the stark reality of industrial revolution, the heroics of Balaclava with the mur-

derous slogging at Inkerman and Sebastopol, and the image of a chivalrous past with the hard practicality of survival under conditions of modern war. It was an age when beer barons, slate magnates and extravagant monarchs built fortified residences for the fun of the game. The mock-castle imparted or implied the

Redoubts on the Lines of Torres Vedras; after Jones.

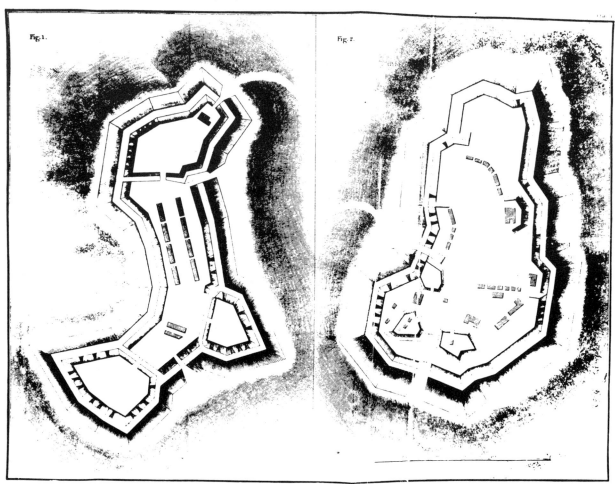

semblance of an aristocratic background for an occupant all too often feeling a little uncertain in a newly created position of wealth or power. It has been shown how the Marquis of Bute reconstructed Castell Coch with painstaking authenticity in 1875, and how Napoleon III had commissioned Viollet-le-Duc to carry out what amounted to the rebuilding of Pierrefonds Castle in 1858. Most of the British clients seem to have gone for the Norman style which pushed their respectability back to the very beginning of the middle ages. One of the best examples is Penrhyn Castle, designed by Thomas Hopper in 1827 in a perfect romantic landscape, its great keep modelled on Rochester. The building cost Lord Penrhyn half a million pounds. These romantic castles were part of a new enthusiasm for the medieval world which found expression in

Walter Scott's novel *Ivanhoe*. The most extravagant demonstration in this world of make-believe was the fairy castle commissioned by Ludwig II of Bavaria. After seeing Louis Napoleon's work at Pierrefonds, Ludwig resolved to emulate him in an even more extravagant and fanciful manner. Neuschwanstein was begun in 1869 to the designs of Eduard Riedel, but subsequently developed by others. It has been aptly described as 'one of the most fascinating toys in the world'.

THE LINES OF TORRES VEDRAS

The opening of the new century found Europe in the grip of war and Britain involved for the first time for nearly a hundred years in the preparation and deployment of an army on a continental scale. In the Peninsula

The attack on Burgos; after Jones.

Wellington's army withdrew to the prepared Lines of Torres Vedras, thrown up in 1810 to cover the roads to Lisbon. To their astonishment the French were checked and left exposed to starve on inhospitable slopes through a fierce winter, whilst the British army sat snugly recuperating behind the security of the lines. Their construction had been planned by Colonel Fletcher as one of the most ambitious secret projects of the war. The works, which are normally classed as field fortifications, were sited with great care to take full advantage of the rocky front which stretched for a length of 25 kilometres (9.5 miles) from the Tagus to the Atlantic and guarded the passes through which the roads ran to the capital. The main front consisted of 59 redoubts mounting 232 guns and armed with a garrison of 17,500 men. In advance of this stood further redoubts forming valuable outposts. Lisbon lay 19 kilometres to the rear. Five months after commencement the works were handed over to Captain John T Jones who later became one of the most important writers on English fortifications and whose descriptions of the sieges of the Napoleonic Wars are invaluable. Wellington fell back through heavy rain and swollen rivers, withdrawing his 22,000 infantry and 3000 cavalry with a similar number of Portuguese to the security of the lines where he exploded the myth that any army which holds its ground must surely be beaten. From this position he turned withdrawal into victory so that Jones was able to write: 'It is not, perhaps, too much to add, that this failure before Lisbon gave a fatal blow to the general belief of French invincibility, and taught oppressed Europe to resist and become free.'

The redoubts varied in size and shape according to their position of importance and the ground upon which each was sited. They show a remarkable adaptability on the part of the British engineers who were perhaps less inhibited by a conservative education than their French counterparts.

The defence of Lisbon demonstrated four points. It showed that in certain circumstances defence, after a century of reverses, could once more prove successful. It illustrated the usefulness of secrecy. It pointed to the value of the irregular disposition of fortifications to suit ground conditions. It also proved to be the forerunner of the idea of using isolated forts, supported by a field army, to bar an enemy's advance. Although these defences have been called the Lines of Torres Vedras, they were in reality embryonic barrier-forts, a system which was to find its fullest expression in the Maginot Line.

Throughout the Peninsular War the British were sadly short of sappers and miners, and those they had were expended at a prodigal rate. In the following years the British army was forced to besiege a number of Spanish towns garrisoned by the French behind regular fronts of fortification stiffened with formidable outworks. Credit for the success of many of the assaults must go to the expenditure of life which Wellington, fighting against time, was prepared to accept. Badajoz, Ciudad Rodrigo and Burgos were all

An early nineteenth century 32-pounder naval gun at Deal Castle.

This is another thorough book on the subject and it includes an historical study of the development of fortification, probably the earliest example in English. Meanwhile in 1849 James Fergusson had published *An Essay on a Proposed New System of Fortifications*. He was an architect and somewhat diffident at expressing himself on military matters, but his book covers more than its title suggests, and is particularly interesting because it contains a summary of the ideas and recommendations of many of his contemporary European engineers. Although he may have been a dilettante in military matters, his opinions were nevertheless sufficiently respected by the experts for him to be invited to be a member of a royal commission on defence.

The most thorough, competent and all-embracing early book on fortification in the English language was written by Captain A F Lendy: *Treatise on Fortifications; or, Lectures delivered to Officers reading for the Staff*, published in 1862. It shows that by mid-century British engineers were not only conversant with contemporary developments throughout Europe but were beginning to feel sufficiently confident to put forward recommendations in the field of coastal defence. These theories were the first really outstanding British contributions to the science of fortification since the construction of the Edwardian castles in Wales late in the thirteenth century.

besieged, the first on three occasions. According to Jones as many men were lost before Badajoz as would have been sufficient for ten sieges undertaken with science and careful labour. His experience in battle made his observations on the attack of fortresses highly pertinent.

BRITISH THEORISTS

Other British engineers were forging a workable knowledge of the science of fortification. C W Pasley's *Course of Elementary Fortification* is one of the first of a long line of reliable textbooks intended for the training of the professional engineer, books which towards the end of the century became the standard manuals of field and permanent fortification. Pasley opened with a short history of the Corps of Engineers and its predecessors and then, having defined terms, for the art and science of fortification was rapidly evolving its own specialised semantics within the English language, he went on to describe the geometrical methods involved in the setting out of fortresses, leaning heavily on the practice of Vauban. His book is the first fully comprehensive English work. Lieutenant Henry Yule (1820–89) of the Bengal Engineers, later to be knighted and best known for his glossary of Anglo-Indian words, produced in 1851 his *Fortification for Officers of the Army and Students of Military History*.

EUROPE REFORTIFIED: THE BELGIAN BARRIER

The years which followed the downfall of Napoleon and the settlement of the Congress of Vienna saw the establishment reasserting itself and the restoration of authority. After the battle of Waterloo (1815) many of the fortified towns in northern France and Belgium were found to be in a sorry state. Some had been battered into destruction, others had largely fallen down through neglect or been demolished.

To prevent a recurrence of a French invasion of Europe, Britain began what was probably her most ambitious programme of fortification building in her whole history, and that on foreign soil. Just a month after the battle, Lord Liverpool was writing to Castlereagh, 'We shall never be forgiven if we leave France without securing a sufficient frontier for the protection of the adjoining countries.' It was assumed it would take between five and seven years to complete a

Festung Ehrenbreitstein at Koblenz: rear façade of the curtain.

barrier at a cost of some £5 million. The cost would be shared between Britain and the Netherlands, and a share imposed upon France. The Duke of Wellington proposed that a commission of Royal Engineer officers should be sent out to restore the ruined fortresses and build 'such new posts as were pointed out in a report'. Although large, it was a conservative undertaking, mainly following traditional systems of fortification – what we today would call a vast conservation scheme. To help the allied engineers there were fine French drawings and splendid large scale models preserved in Les Invalides in Paris.

Ironically, as soon as the practical work was complete the whole political situation changed.

The fortifications of the Netherlands, those enormous bulwarks, raised with so much cost and labour as a means to strengthen the government and set the French at defiance, suddenly passed, without any sufficient cause, into rebel hands. The Dutch rule and English influence alike vanished from the land, French interests took their place, and, in a few months, these fortresses, and the county they cover,

became a barrier directly opposed to the views and intentions of the powers which gave them existence.

GERMAN FORTIFICATIONS

The kingdom of Prussia formed the eastern and northern barrier to any expansionist threats from France, and the Germans were determined to entrench themselves with the utmost rapidity and the maximum vigour. After Vauban's demonstration of the superiority of attack over defence and Napoleon's rapid advances through Europe, a long cool look at the potentialities of defence was needed if the *status quo* was to be maintained against the ever-present threat of national and social revolution.

The strategic implications of a state of war were first contemplated in modern terms by Karl von Clausewitz, who in 1815 became chief of a Prussian army corps and later Gneisenau's chief of staff. His most important writings are contained in *Vom Krieg*, part of which is devoted to a consideration of the strategic value of fortresses. In the past, wars had been limited by funds and the seasons. Now Clausewitz

The rear of a caponier at Ehrenbreitstein and plan.

foresaw that huge standing armies would mow down opposition and fortresses would become no more than knots holding together a strategic web. Conscription had enabled France to raise a standing army of 732,000 in 1796.

There is no space to enumerate the eleven conditions Clausewitz specified as the functional reasons for the establishment of fortresses; briefly, he pointed to their use as a secure depot for the vast arsenal and stores required by a modern army and their function as a tactical point of connection to secure the flank of any army in the field.

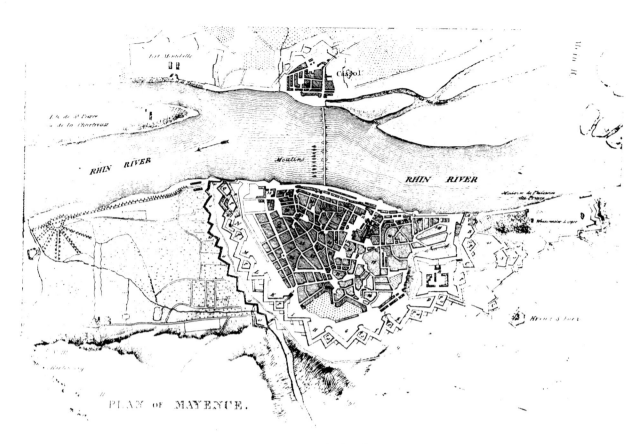

The fortifications of Mainz, 1838.

KOBLENZ

Feverish activity ensued in the towns which bordered the Rhine and the Danube. Koblenz was one of the first to prepare itself for an attack. It lay on the junction of the Rhine and the Moselle, with a population of about 12,000 and a garrison of about 11,000. Its main fortress had been destroyed by the French in 1799 and now its perimeter was enclosed behind a much larger enceinte, and the craggy, immensely strong fortress of Ehrenbreitstein was reconstructed to form the 'Gibraltar of the Rhine'. A new landfront was built on the hilltop above the river, consisting of a ravelin with a three-storey caponier designed as a strongly armoured outwork on the eastern flank. To the west the ground fell steeply to the river bank and needed no elaborate fortifications to make it invulnerable, but on the spur to the south another series of outworks dropped to a lower level culminating in Fort Helfenstein. Across the north front 40–50 guns could be brought to bear on any besieging artillery which came within range. The defensive guns were dug into casemates 12 metres (40ft) deep and fired through tunnel-shaped embrasures.

      Ehrenbreitstein, rebuilt between 1817 and 1828, was supported by other forts which ringed the town, of which Fort Alexander, modelled on the work of Montalembert, was the most notable. The fort was designed by General von Aster. The contemporary defences of many of the other German towns, like

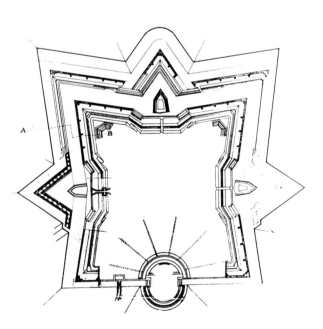

Fort Alexander at Koblenz.

Cologne, Rastatt and Mainz, have now been demolished to make way for urban development. Mainz on the Rhine was a great army camp for 13,000 troops and about this time a new enceinte was thrown around the city by the Austrian general Scholl. It consisted of a tenaille front zig-zagging in an arch across the river

A gun embrasure in the Ludwigstor at Germersheim, 1840.

Plan of Germersheim.

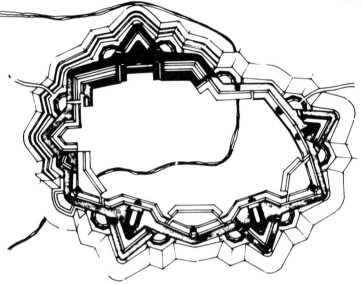

an irregular polygon shaped like a detached bastion with strong caponiers placed in front and rear to cover its ditches. The plan of 1838 shows the approximate positions of the proposed adjoining forts which were to link up with the Hartenberg on the left to form an outer screen of detached forts some 500 metres (550yds) in advance of the continuous town walls.

GERMERSHEIM

Farther up river lies Germersheim, its early nineteenth century fortifications almost intact. There the pattern was the same: an inner enceinte of Prussian fortifications depending for their strength upon massive multi-gun caponiers and an outer ring of detached forts. The defensive scheme was designed by Ritter von Schmauss and built in the 1840s. It was beautifully carried out in a combination of precise brickwork and rusticated masonry, the gates richly carved and ornamented.

from bank to bank, with outlying forts, all built in the 1830s and designed to prevent a *coup de main*. Forts like Kreuz Schanze already showed the pattern which was to dictate the layout of so many of their successors throughout Europe. Fort Kreuz Schanze was

Side elevation of the Ludwigstor showing gun embrasures.

Details of the Ludwigstor.

Below: *Rear elevation of the gate.*

Bottom: *The Ludwigstor gate.*

Opposite: *Gun embrasures at Ingolstadt.*

Plan of Ingolstadt.

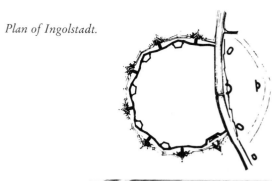

Ingolstadt: ravelin at the south end of the enceinte.

Entrance to the south wall of the town.

INGOLSTADT

The defences of Ingolstadt on the Rhine are even more extensive and impressive. The town is surrounded by parkland in which its fortifications still stand preserved. Ingolstadt was originally fortified by Daniele Speckle in 1575 and a contemporary model of the defences by Jakob Sandtner survives in the National Museum of Bavaria at Munich. It depicts a walled town buttressed with regularly spaced drum towers, some of which remain. At the south and west corners stood mighty semi-circular bastions of steeply battered form so that they resembled truncated pyramids, their parapets pierced by embrasures. The new defences were designed by General Streider and built between 1828 and 1845. Undoubtedly Speckle influenced the new works. The town was surrounded by a line pierced at intervals by powerful U-shaped defensible barracks, their wings crowned with gun platforms and their fronts originally covered with counterguards. Between each pair of barracks stood a powerful caponier with its attendant works. At the junction with the Danube there was a large semi-circular-headed ravelin which seemed to follow the shape of Speckle's earlier bastion. The enceinte was surrounded by a wet ditch. On the the side of the river a great oval casemated work with projecting wings was the Réduit Tilly (1820) which formed a bridgehead supported on each side and in front by forts also oval and casemated. In the country beyond lay a series of detached works consisting of an inner ring of lunettes and small works and an outer ring of ten forts.

The arch of a gateway through one of the keep cavaliers.

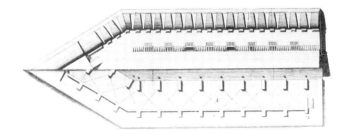

Left and opposite: *The plan and section of one of Montalembert's proposed multi-gun caponiers.*

ULM

Standing on the northern bank of the Danube, Ulm has always been a strongly fortified town. After the Napoleonic Wars and between 1842 and 1859 it was refortified as a federal fortress of Württemberg by the Prussian engineer, Major Karl Moritz von Prittwitz. The bridgehead on the other side of the river belonged to Bavaria and was fortified by Theodor Ritter von Hildebrant in a quite different style. The fortress of Ulm was enclosed within an inner line of walls and massive drum tower gates, almost romantic in style – a

symbolic deterrent. There was an outer girdle of detached forts, originally fourteen in number and in the space between the two defensive systems lay an enclosed camp for an army of 100,000 men.

The inner line and the citadel were modelled on the New German System derived originally from Montalembert's Polygonal System. It consisted of a number of self-supporting works, called *kornwerke*, capable of all-round defence. Although they are sometimes referred to as bastions, in the strict sense they are

Ulm: the Blaubeurer Tor, a gateway in the city walls.

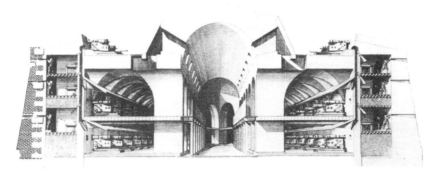

not, being more like forts connected by lines of fortification. The job of flanking the ditch was taken over by casemated batteries in large, curved caponiers which projected into the ditch itself. Between these caponiers the ramparts are long and straight, one on the citadel being 600 metres (650yds) long. Beyond the ditch lay covered-way and glacis under which were dug countermine galleries running, in places, for a distance of 40 metres (44yds). The outer forts, built in the 1850s, were polygonal. Fort Soflinger Turm had five outer faces and a re-entrant gorge containing barracks in a keep slightly over a semi-circle in shape. In contrast, Fort Unterer Eselsberg was almost square with its two outer faces protected by a Carnot wall with embrasures through which infantry could fire. The earth ramparts rose from a gentle slope. In the salient

The light shaft in the keep of the Wilhelmsburg, the citadel of Ulm, designed so narrow to keep out the shells from enemy howitzers or mortars.

Ulm: the Bastion Kienlesberg (Werk X), a multi-gun caponier.

point there was a double caponier, shaped in the form of 'cats' ears', behind which sheltered a mortar battery, and the opposite corner contained barracks in an almost semi-circular keep whose ends terminated in projecting caponiers.

As the years passed the fortress of Ulm was strengthened and expanded. After 1877, traverses were added to counter the threat from rifled projectiles and, between 1881 and 1887, more advanced forts were built. In both Ulm and Neu-Ulm on the other side of the river there remain some of the finest examples of nineteenth century military architecture in Germany.

Franzenfeste; after Geographie Militaire.

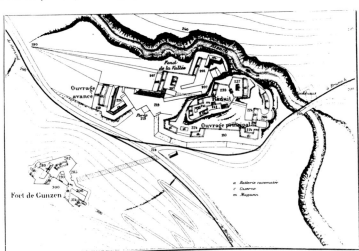

AUSTRIAN FORTIFICATIONS

Austria under the rule of Metternich, the most conservative of the re-established states, set about putting its defences in order. Guarding Vienna from the west, Linz and Salzburg were to be refortified and, to prevent any penetration from Italy through the Tyrol, the famous 'quadrilateral' was formed, its sides resting on the rivers Mincio and Adige flanked by powerful fortresses at Peschiera and Mantua. Its base camp was formed by the fortified city of Verona. Farther up through the passes in the Alps lay isolated forts with the immensely powerful Franzenfeste, barring the approach to the Brenner Pass.

The novel and controversial works at Linz, which was fortified by Prince Maximilian, have already been described (see page 153).

The fortifications of Verona were modernised by the Austrians in a series of beautifully executed commissions between 1830 and 1866. Before 1830 the Austrians had considered the Holy Alliance sufficient guarantee of their security, but the first of the liberal revolutions in France in that year caused them to reconsider the security of their possessions in Italy. The work on Verona was begun by the general of the Austrian engineers, Franz von Scholl, and completed by his successor Colonel Tunkler. The initial project consisted of redesigning Sanmicheli's bastioned trace to the south and west of the fortifications north of the river which culminated in the castle of S Felice. Most of the original Renaissance trace had been destroyed in 1801 leaving only the Bastions of di Spagna and S Francesco intact. Perhaps out of respect for the great Italian architect these were retained with only minor modifications, but all the other bastions were rebuilt using accurately cut polygonal tufa. This type of construction characterises much of the Austrian engineers' work. The new bastions were built with detached walls and countersloping glacis as recommended by Carnot, having the advantage that musketeers could stand in the space between the walls and the ramparts to cover the ditch and the glacis. The salient angles of the bastions were crowned with small bastionettes to enfilade their faces. But von Scholl's trace must be considered as of secondary importance to his outer ring of detached forts built between 1832 and 1843. This heralded the concept of the entrenched

Interior of the Forte S Caterina at Verona.

camp, consisting in this case of outer forts capable of supporting each other behind which lay a continuous enceinte acting as an additional line of security for a mobile army of 120,000 men. The forts varied in shape, but many were polygonal, their four outer faces lined with casemates and their gorges left open, protected only by muskets. In its centre each had a strong circular keep.

North of the city lies a high spur with precipitous cliffs. Its approaches were guarded by the city, with the castle of S Felice on the right flank and three detached forts on the left. This ridge was reinforced by Scholl (see page 155) with five circular

Opposite: *The town gate at Peschiera on Lake Garda.*

Below: *An Austrian fort in the hills above Torbole.*

Austrian defences on the Bastione S Spirito at Verona.

Bottom: *Gun embrasures guard the valley.*

forts modelled on those at Linz. The Austrian defences are vast, and Verona would certainly have been a tough nut to crack by the middle of the nineteenth century.

The Austrians were primarily interested in the possibility of an attack from the south-west. Wherever there is a well-placed hillock in the outer Alto Adige one finds a castle or a small fortress. Fran-

zenfeste, now called Fortezza, straddles the valley looking south towards Italy, enclosing the defile of the Brixen Klause. Lying on the great post road from Verona to Innsbruck, it consisted of two distinct works joined by an underground passage and placed within musket shot of each other. The lower one, the main fort, was built on a granite rock in the centre of the valley, where the river, taking a sharp bend, forms a

An Austrian bastion at Peschiera.

natural ditch 60 metres (200ft) deep. The fortress was almost impregnable, holding a garrison of 1200 men with three months' supply of food and water and ample additional resources in the form of reinforcements and running water at its back.

POLAND

Poland is undoubtedly one of the best places to study nineteenth century fortresses for there three great armies met. The most powerful forces in Europe, the Prussians, the Austrians and the Russians faced each other, dug in and built strong permanent defences. In 1794 Poland was divided into three states, its national

A multi-gun circular caponier attached by the Austrians to the walls of the Castle of Wawel at Krakow.

independence devoured. Each of the nations which occupied its territory demonstrated their own national characteristics in the field of military architecture.

The power of Prussia stretched in a big sweep from Kalingrad (Königsberg) on the Baltic Sea to the borders of Galicia in the south-west. In the north she built powerful fortified towns, extending the medieval and renaissance defences into a new complexity at Königsberg, Gdansk (Danzig), Torun, Poznan (Posen), Szczecin (Stettin), and south-west of the River Oder built a line of fortified towns that blocked the approaches to Germany across the lowlands of Silesia. Glogow (Glogau), Wroclaw (Breslau), Swidnica (Schweidnitz), Silberberg (Srebrna Gora), Klodsko (Glatz), Nysa (Niesse) and Kozle were all put into a state of defence west of the Oder.

The Russian defences lay at Warsaw, Modlin and Deblin, holding the line of the River Vistula, at Lomza and at Briest (Brest Litovsk), with a powerful base-camp at Vilna.

The Austrians held Krakow (Crakow), Przemysl, Juraslaw, Lwow (Lemberg) and Halicz (Halice). These were the great fortresses of Europe to which must be added the Russian defences of Leningrad (St Petersburg), Kronstadt, Sveaborg and the Åland Islands which are mentioned elsewhere.

PRUSSIA IN POLAND

There were two great periods of Prussian fortification. The Old Prussian System was dominated by the work of the military engineer Gerhard Cornelius Walrave. A Dutchman, born in 1692, he grew up to absorb the French system of Vauban, but his work developed in a different direction. The main characteristic was the reintroduction of the tenaille trace, a scissors form of defence and an idea that dates back to the fifteenth century but which had been largely ousted by the Italian bastion system. In front of the main tenaille line Walrave placed forts in a continuous pattern, acting like ravelins, or individually sited on dangerous lines of approach. For example, at Swidnica he bound the inner enceinte with a ring of tenaille forts linked by a continuous trenchwork and further out he placed detached forts. His work occupies the second half of the eighteenth century and he died in 1773.

The New Prussian System which dominated the work in Silesia in the nineteenth century exploited a number of devices of ancient origin, modified to suit the striking power of the new more powerful guns. The Polygonal System had been advocated by Francesco di Giorgio, Castriotto and De Marchi, and it was revived by the French engineer, Montalembert, who found it so difficult to get his ideas accepted by his colleagues. The system was used at Swidnica, and in a more fully developed form after 1827 at Poznan and Torun, so that it became one of the standard methods of defence throughout the nineteenth century. Then there was the reintroduction of caponiers. Francesco di Giorgio was the first to illustrate these in the second half of the fifteenth century, and later Dürer used them with considerable effect in his designs. They were reintroduced in a modified form in the designs of Montalembert and adopted by the Prussians where, housing massed guns of much greater power, they became active aggressive elements within the defensive ring of the enceinte. The third feature was the reuse of keeps. These were strong last retreats containing barracks and accommodation for the garrison, and they were the descendants of the medieval keep, *donjon* and *mastio*. They were reintroduced into Poland in 1824, first at Torun.

One of the best Prussian examples of a central keep can still be seen at Srebrna Gora where the fort is preserved as an artillery museum. Standing on a ridge in the foothills of the Giant Mountains, its core consists of a four-leafed clover-shaped keep with walls of immense thickness and pronounced batter. Upon each leaf is a soil mound sloping gently to the parapet of the stone walls. In appearance it looks medieval.

Along the hillside stretch powerful hornworks and beyond these extend advanced lunettes, placed well beyond the perimeter of the fort. Srebrna Gora was built in great secrecy and no visitors were allowed in the vicinity.

The Montalembert tower, a powerful free-standing structure housing many guns on several floors, was popular with the Austrians, but it was used by the Prussians like a detached fort, part of a defensive ring. There is a good example built in 1805 at Kozle, and in form it is similar to the multi-gun keeps built within the forts.

Finally, the saw plan was in regular use. In this the covered-way was formed like the teeth of a saw, an idea that can be traced back through the works of Walrave, Montalembert, Landsberg, Speckle to those Italian military engineers who first ruminated on the problems of modern fortification.

Each successive development of the science of war brought modifications to the forts and fortified towns of Prussian Silesia, Western Pomerania and East Brandenburg. Changes came from the introduction of rifled guns and, as a result of the Franco-Prussian War, standard forts began to ring the central systems of fortifications, standing some four to five kilometres out from the main enceinte. Many were built of earth and have long since disappeared under the expanding suburbs of the towns they once guarded. Poznan, between 1872 and 1883, was surrounded by a ring of nine main forts and nine smaller forts. Torun, about the same time, had seven main and six smaller forts. Many of the other towns followed suit. A typical design consisted of a front of two faces joined at an obtuse angle, with two wings running back at equal obtuse angles to the faces, the fort being closed by a re-entrant hornwork with a diamond-shaped ravelin in the gorge. The gorge contained the barracks and on the raised terreplein stood armoured cupolas, protected by steel plate, guarding observation and battery positions.

AUSTRIA IN POLAND

The Austrians built in Galicia and their engineers were more eclectic than the Prussians. They drew their ideas freely from German, French and Belgian schools. Austria had a large frontier to defend and, as one might expect, the work in Poland is somewhat similar to the defences they constructed in the 'Quadrilateral' of Italy and in the Alpine passes. There is still the same sturdy construction and good detailing, but brick construction or earthworks tend to replace the fine masonry found in Italy.

In the nineteenth century two systems predominated. From the cessation of the Napoleonic Wars up to the Crimean War most of the designs were polygonal enceintes modelled on the Old Prussian System and inspired by Montalembert. The Russian General Todleben learned from experience at Sebastopol that it was best to push detached forts well forward of the main enceinte in order to enlarge the defensive perimeter, and his ideas were adopted by Brialmont in his influential scheme for the re-defence of Antwerp.

As a result of the appearance in 1850 of the Hesse Report of the Central Commission on Fortifications, the Austrians declared that part of Galicia which lay north of the Carpathian Mountains to be an area of manoeuvre and decided to establish two powerful ring fortresses at Krakow and Przemysl, with smaller fortified towns dotted elsewhere in the province. Przemysl was to be turned into a fortified camp for the Austrian army, consisting of a continuous inner enceinte which enclosed the town punctuated by five forts, an intermediate line mainly south of the river consisting of eight forts of various sizes joined by trenches, and an outer ring placed from five to eight kilometres beyond the enceinte consisting of some forty-two forts built to a variety of designs. The inner forts were begun in 1850 and the outer ones constructed between 1877 and 1883. The defences of Krakow were even more extensive. In the centre lay the old royal castle of Wawel which was stiffened by new Austrian walls and a semi-circular multi-gun caponier to enable it to be used as a last stand retreat or keep. Around the old city ran the medieval walls. In 1859, General Caboga planned to encircle the central area with a six-sided polygonal bastion trace. Where it touched the Vistula River it was pinned by the old castle at one side and to Fort Krzemionzach on the other, providing a strong front against a possible Russian attack from the north. South of the river, Caboga built a wider trace using a more traditional bastion system where the city was less vulnerable, swinging it in a big semi-circular arc to touch the Vistula further

Below: *Fort Kleparz III at Krakow; a large double caponier built in the form of a pair of 'cat's ears'.*

Bottom: *Fort Kleparz III; a double caponier.*

gained by looking at three examples. Fort Kleparz III, a polygonal fort in the internal ring, was completed in 1863. It consists of two outer faces joined at an obtuse angle, with two wings that run back parallel to each other. Between the faces and the wings lie large caponiers in the form of 'cats' ears'. These are double caponiers designed to cover the ditch, separated by a curved centrepiece in which are powerful casemates with guns firing forwards. Inside the fort and centred on the gorge is a large semi-circular keep with casemates covering its own ditch, the whole concept modelled on the traditional *basteja*. The gorge is covered by a ravelin with a central entrance between two rounded caponiers whose casemates cover the approaches. Above the entrance the wall is pierced by thin, tall musketry loopholes firing down on the ground in front. The ravelin is linked to the fort by a triangular caponier which covers the ditch of the gorge and provides a direct communication to the *basteja*-type keep.

Fort Krakus built during the same period south of the Vistula is an eighteen-sided Maximilian tower, a favourite device of the Austrians, free-standing on the hillside of the inner ring. At this period military engineers were still content to introduce military symbolism into their work. The entrance has a gothic arch crowned by a heraldic head-piece. At roof level there is crenellation and a group of drop-boxes which, if not used for boiling oil, might provide useful positions for musketeers covering the ground in front of the entrance. The tower has three floors with musketry loopholes on the ground floor which, separated from the rest of the building by a string course, forms a plinth for the design. Large gun casemates and embrasures occupy the first floor, strengthened by brick relieving arches and equipped with smoke vents.

Fort Kosciuszko, lying north-west of Krakow in the outer ring of defences, is one of the most interesting and unusual examples. Its shape is partly dictated by the artificial hill built by the Polish people between 1820 and 1823 which, with bucket upon bucket load of earth, rose to a conical height of 34 metres (110ft). The hill was lovingly constructed to the memory of Tadeusz Andrjez Kosciuszko (1746–1817), soldier, fighter for Polish freedom and patriot who had also fought with brilliance in the American War of Independence. The fort was designed around the hill. The main defences were destroyed after 1945,

out than the points of contact of the northern trace. The work was completed in 1865. Thus the inner ring incorporated two systems: the northern one modelled on Antwerp, had polygonal forts with multi-gun caponiers capable of both defending the ditches and firing forward across the country; the southern front had bastions with orillons and flat earth terrepleins. The whole defensive ring took years to complete. It does not follow a neat chronological pattern. Broadly speaking, there was a second, or inner ring of detached forts, mainly designed by Franz von Scholl, constructed at the same time as the inner enceinte. As the range of guns increased, a third or outer ring of over sixty detached forts was designed by Salissoglio and Brunner the younger and built in the period from 1878 up to the outbreak of the First World War. There is great variety in the designs as each fort was tailor-made to fit the peculiarities of the terrain.

Some idea of the general concepts can be

Krakow; the main entrance facade to Fort Krakus, an eight-sided Montalembert tower.

but it originally consisted of a six-sided figure with three bastions facing west and a semi-fortified barrack block on the east side looking over the city of Krakow. Each bastion enclosed a multi-gun caponier with its own ditch. Covering the centre of both re-entrant curtains stood a powerful multi-gun ravelin. The barracks comprised three blocks of three-storied brick accommodation with freestanding caponiers placed between them and joined to them by bridges on the top floor. The architecture of the barracks is symbolic, decorated with medieval devices such as crenellation, machicolation and decorative brick string courses.

The Austrian fortifications were continuously modernised and enlarged. Halicz was surrounded by a double line of earthworks in 1885 and Jaroslaw was similarly treated in 1890 so that both towns formed bridgeheads, and single forts were built to guard roads and railway lines. Concrete came into general use after 1870 and the first armoured cupolas

were being built in the 1880s. The Austrian School in Poland represents the height of European fortification, helping Przemysl, when the blow fell in the First World War, to make a notable stand against the Russian advance.

RUSSIA IN POLAND

The Russians had by the nineteenth century shown remarkable ability in the field of military architecture. The modern defences of Warsaw date from 1831. Gradually the Russians threw two rings of fortification around the city, consisting of detached forts, the inner rings being joined along much of its length by entrenchments. Within this lay the citadel built to subjugate a city restless with nationalist fervour, for the Poles rose up unsuccessfully in 1831 and 1863. The citadel had its own ring of six detached forts and a perimeter of brick and stone constructed in the form of Carnot walls backed by earth bastions. Both in the outer forts of the citadel and in the powerful defences of towns like Modlin, the Russians favoured triangular forts similar to the work of Brialmont, with a counter-scarp gallery at the point covering the ditches and faces, supported by large caponiers at the shoulders and a defensible block in the gorge.

COAST DEFENCE THEORY

Coastal defence has often been a primary problem for the British. Edward I's castles were victualled from the sea, Bodiam was designed to counter French naval raids up a navigable river, Henry VIII's forts lined the foreshores of southern England, and the fort at Tilbury was built to prevent a repercussion of the alarming raid by the Dutch in 1667. A powerful naval nation would seem to have least need of coastal defences, but no fleet, however large, could be everywhere at once. Before the middle of the nineteenth century the disposition of the fleet was largely dictated by the direction of winds and, although the introduction of steam power gave it greater manoeuvrability, the advantage was largely offset by the need to patrol ever-increasing areas of the world's oceans to protect the outposts of the British Empire.

Up to the time of the Spanish Armada the use of hand-to-hand weapons had predominated and ships were designed primarily as mobile infantry platforms, but from about 1588 the gun became the main naval weapon. The one great advantage that ships had over shore defences was that they could swing round to bring a heavy broadside to bear and then make haste to move out of range of retaliation. The number and size of guns was gradually increased so that a ship of the line at the time of Nelson was capable of delivering a broadside of 50–60 guns. However ships suffered from three disadvantages. They were to some extent at the mercy of the weather, their rolling decks making accurate gunfire difficult, and the ships themselves were combustible. On the other hand, coastal defence batteries fired from stable platforms, could be given bombproof protection, and their faces, which as targets were equivalent to the hulls of ships, could be constructed of durable materials such as brick, stone and later iron. Gradually more and more guns were introduced to a point when any vulnerable stretch of coast could be defended by multi-gun towers. This situation continued until a time when the

advantages were slowly eroded by the introduction of shellfire and the application of steam as motive power for ships of war. Shell-firing guns were adopted by the French navy in 1837. Britain and America soon followed suit. Steam power began to be used about 1830. In 1841 the defences of Gibraltar were modified by the introduction of steamships. In 1843 the Americans launched their first screw warship and the Royal Navy followed with the commissioning of HMS *Amphion* in 1844. The efficiency of the screw-driven ship was proved in the famous tug of war with a paddle steamer carried out in a Royal Navy test in 1845.

As naval gunnery improved, coast defence guns had to be supplemented by underwater obstacles. In 1805 Robert Fulton had shown that it was possible to destroy ships by detonating a charge against their hulls below the waterline. Gradually the number of guns in coast batteries dropped until in some instances at the end of the nineteenth century the British were using one-gun batteries.

GIBRALTAR AND JERSEY

Two British strongholds were developed at this time which, if not primarily intended for coastal defence, had to consider the possibility of naval bombardment. Gibraltar had been annexed for Britain by Sir George Rooke in 1704 and had withstood three serious sieges in which enemy ships had successfully collaborated with forces trying to penetrate the defences of the landfront. Above the plain towered the North Front and in the rocky face deep casemates were excavated to provide overwhelming fire on the only ground of approach across which an attacking force could advance. The British gunners had been so successful that Montalembert, on the raising of the siege in 1783, cited Gibraltar to support his theory in favour of the use of casemated artillery. Although the land approaches could be held without great difficulty, the sea defences of the town and the line of coast running to Europa Point needed a traditional fortified trace. King's Bastion, a fine masonry work with parapets 3 to 4.5 metres (10–15ft) thick, was constructed in 1770 and Orange Bastion was built during the siege of 1779. In the ensuing years various reports were submitted for improving the defences and modernising the armament to counter the threat of screw-driven, and later iron-plated vessels. The report of 1859 described

Plan of Gibraltar in 1789; after Drinkwater.

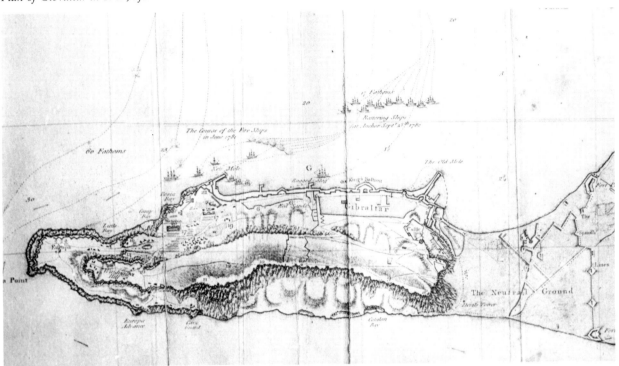

'measures to be taken to place the fortress in a reasonable state of preparation to meet a sudden attack from the sea'.

The only other important British fortress to be constructed in the early nineteenth century was at Jersey. Fort Regent was designed by Colonel John Humfrey to form the main stronghold of the island on Tower Hill above St Helier. It was part of a comprehensive scheme for the defence of Jersey which included new military roads and Martello towers along the coast. Fort Regent was begun in 1806 to prevent the recurrence of a French invasion which in 1781 had nearly captured the place. The fort was irregularly shaped, taking full advantage of the precipitous nature of the site. Its long flanks were guarded by bastions and the north and south approaches were each

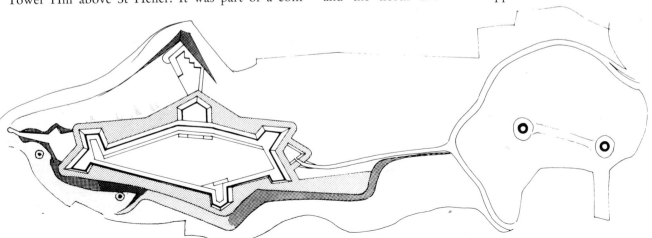

Fort Regent on the island of Jersey; from a project of 1805.

A 68-pounder gun: the last of the large smooth-bores used at the time of the Crimean War.

Fieldworks protecting a mortar battery at the siege of Sebastopol; after a drawing by William Simpson, 1855.

defended by two redans which joined at rather more than a right angle to form a tenaille front and which, through the introduction of flanks on their outer faces, became demi-bastions. This was a strange device, perhaps inspired by Montalembert whose influence can be seen in an unexecuted project for placing two round towers to defend an adjacent hilltop. The south front was covered by a counterguard, separated by a ditch from a long smooth glacis which sloped away to the south.

THE CRIMEAN WAR

The Crimean War had a profound effect on the development of coastal defences. In 1854 Franco-British forces landed in the Crimea and slowly closed for the investment of Sebastopol. The town was defended by a fortified trace at the head of which stood the Malakoff, a large stone tower flanked on either side by the Redan and the Little Redan. The coastline was held by a series of forts, started in 1783 and strengthened in

Fort Nicolas at Sebastopol; plan.

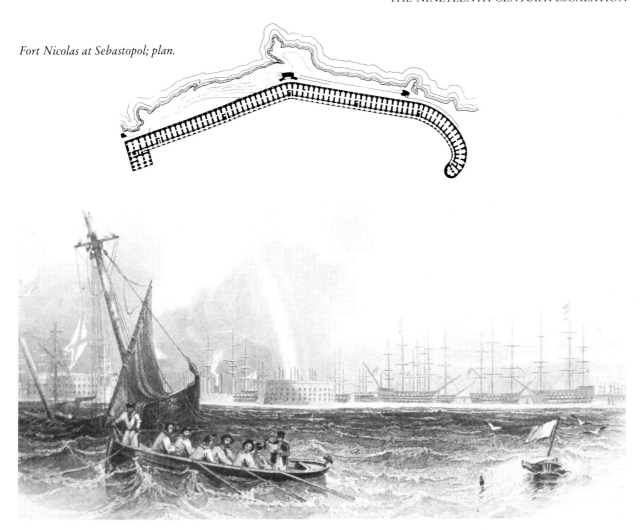

Taking soundings under the Russian batteries off Kronstadt: in the background are three-decker forts; after Nolan.

1834 by the addition of several coast forts and batteries, work on which was incomplete on the outbreak of war.

The harbour entrance was sealed by sunken ships and General Todleben was appointed engineer in charge. Todleben's magnificent defence has been so well described as to need no amplification. The ingenuity with which he faced each fresh situation and the originality with which he fashioned the improvised earthworks, held in check the allied armies through the cruel winter of 1854–55. From the beginning the allies argued about the method of attack, the French preferring the slow methodical scientific approach they had learnt from Vauban, the British putting their faith in a sudden assault which on 18 June 1855 went in with disastrous effect and horrible loss.

The battle for the Russian coastal defences, though less well known, was equally important and the Russian fortifications, which proved so effective, later became models for British practice. The Franco-British fleet moved into the Black Sea and on 28 April 1854 arrived before Sebastopol to reconnoitre the defences. During the summer, in a lightning raid, two British ships had destroyed batteries at the mouth of the Danube, so that when, on 16 October, the fleet closed in for the attack, there was a feeling of confident expectation aboard the ships. The French attacked from the south and the British from the north, the inshore squadron closing to 660 metres (700yds) to engage Fort Constantine. This was a powerful fort mounting over 100 heavy guns which soon got the range of the British ships. HMS *Queen* was quickly set on fire; *Rodney* grounded and had to be towed off, and several other ships were so badly damaged that they had to return to Malta for repairs. By evening, nothing achieved, the British squadron retired having lost 44 killed and 262 wounded. No more naval attacks were undertaken against Sesbastopol. The coastal forts had proved their worth.

The naval campaign in the Baltic had mixed results. In terms of the development of warfare it was an influential portent of coming events and a demonstration of the impact of the rapidly changing technologies on the conduct of battles. The destruction of a Turkish squadron by Russian ships mounting French Paixhans shell-firing guns before the Anglo-French declaration of war had had a disturbing effect and, to some extent, the Crimean War was considered by those in control of the British Navy as a temporary

Main fort on the island of Bomarsund; plan.

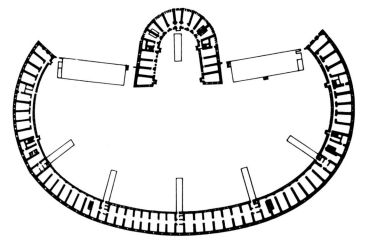

diversion from the long-term rivalry with France. Those in authority thought that war with France was inevitable, hastened by the reconstruction of the French navy with screw-driven armoured vessels. But there was also a fear the Russian navy might break out of the Baltic and attack Britain. So the prime naval aim of the war was to bottle up the Russian fleet and prevent its egress.

Faced by the threat from France, the Royal Navy was not slow to adapt to the new situation and modernise its fleet. It had particular requirements: the ability to maintain fleets in distant waters and on long blockades could best be done with traditional square riggers, yet the ability to manoeuvre in difficult conditions and confined waters called for steam propulsion. The large scale use of paddle steamers for the main warships was ruled out because paddles were vulnerable to gunfire, necessitated an awkward disposition of the main masts and seriously restricted the use of broadside fire. Iron hulls, though technically possible and then being seriously developed in merchant vessels, were not viable simply because the quality of iron to withstand the impact of shot, certainly at the low temperatures sometimes encountered in European wars, was not available. So the solution lay in adapting the existing ships-of-the-line to screw propulsion with powerful auxiliary steam engines set deep and well protected within the hull of the ship, assisted and supplemented by sail for long voyages and blockading purposes. Without too much difficulty new ships could be built to this specification. So the fleet that sailed against Russia was primarily a fleet of screw-driven sailing ships, admirably suited to the task of containing the Russian fleet. However, by the end of the campaign it was clear to the Admiralty that these ships needed to be supplemented with an adequate supply of armour-plated shallow-draught vessels mounting heavy guns. By July 1854, the French considered that the great problem of subduing masonry coastal forts had been solved by the use of steam floating batteries; impervious to counter-bombardment, 'the shells broke against them like glass'.

On all fronts the war was bungled by aged commanders who had last seen active service in the Napoleonic Wars some forty years earlier. The fleet, consisting of 28 ships-of-the-line, many of them fitted with auxiliary screws, entered the Baltic and sailed for the great Russian naval base at Kronstadt. A careful reconnaissance soon revealed that the port was too strong to attack. Shore-based batteries were supplemented by a number of variously designed forts scattered across the open waterways. In addition to square and pentagonal designs, there existed round stone forts containing three tiers of casemated gun positions armed with heavy weapons. So the fleet departed in search of less suspecting prey.

The Russians had three important naval stations in the Baltic. Sveaborg, the 'Fortress of Sweden', built by the Swedes in 1747, consisting of a series of separate linked forts on the main islands of the chain across the mouth of the harbour in front of Helsinki, was to fall to the Russians in 1809. By 1854 it had been grossly neglected and could not have withstood a bombardment by the Anglo-French fleet, but, because of poor reconnaissance and command indecision, the Royal Navy was not to know this. By the following year the fortress had been greatly strengthened. The most important naval base lay at Kronstadt covering St Petersburg. The island of Kronstadt and the naval base were protected by land fortifications and the group of coastal forts built in the sea so that at least 300 large calibre guns, including shell-firing Paixhans, covered the channel. Many of the forts were multi-tiered, built in stone and packed with guns better protected than those on wooden men-of-war, capable of matching shot for shot. For example, the Menchikoff Battery was built of granite masonry with four tiers of casemates armed with 44 Paixhans. In front of the forts lay a web of submarine mines, 'as

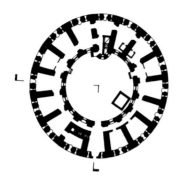

*Fort Nottick;
plan and section.*

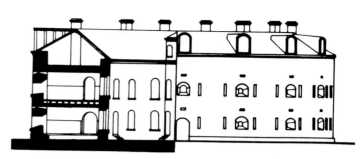

*The Russian fort and towers at Bomarsund in the Åland
Islands being attacked by the allied fleet in 1854.*

thick as daisies'. The Russians were the first to develop this kind of warfare having, in 1839, established a committee on underwater experiments. They used three types of mine: those fired by electricity from the shore; those by electricity in contact with the hull of a ship; and the chemical contact mine, which was most common in the Baltic, exploded when a lead and glass tube, projecting from the mine, was broken by a passing ship. They were a deterrent although they did no great damage. Some were detonated at the wrong time, others had charges too small to do real harm, although one did seriously wound a British admiral who poked his finger in when it had been lifted on deck. HMS *Merlin* hit three mines and suffered extensive but not vital damage.

The third Russian naval base was further north, at Bomarsund in the Åland Islands. In 1809, Lieutenant-General Steinheil visited them and prepared a report on their defence. Eventually plans and a model were approved and work began in earnest in 1832. The advantages of this station lay in the fact that the sea there froze less solid, and, in some years, not at all, so that a Russian fleet based there would have more freedom of action. The plan was to cover the anchorage with a group of granite forts, the main

fort being a large semi-elliptical work with guns in two tiers of casemates. The vaults of the casemates were covered with 2 metres (6.5ft) of sand and above that there was a timber roof shod with iron sheets to throw off the snow and to protect the timbers from hot shot and Congreve rockets. (William Congreve had begun experimenting with launchers in 1804, and his rockets soon developed an extreme range of 3000 metres – 3330yds – and were used successfully in the attack on Boulogne in 1806. Congreve himself must have been convinced from the start of their effectiveness for in 1805 he began experiments on applying armour plate to warships.) The main fort was to be linked to a ring of five circular towers on the hillside behind, connected by fortified walls and a military road nearly one kilometre (⅝ mile) in length. On two peninsulas further north, covering one of the channels, they built two strong circular gun towers, one to be protected by a screen of seven smaller detached towers. All the masonry was granite, constructed in polygonal form similar to the method used by the Austrians at Verona. It would have been a formidable defensive system if completed, but by the early 1850s only the main fort and the two northern towers were ready and the foundations of others laid. There was still no curtain walls and no outlying towers to the east and north. Bomarsund had a garrison of 1700 men.

In August Anglo-French troops were landed on the Russian-held Åland Islands. Isolated and far from home, the Russian garrison did not put up much of a defence. Their embrasures proved vulnerable to accurate artillery which had been landed on the shore and gunners in the main Russian work had difficulty in bringing more than six of their guns to bear on an attacking ship at any one time. But it was hardly a fair test of the capabilities of coastal defence for the allies knew that the forts had been constructed with shoddy workmanship.

In the following year a powerful fleet under the command of Admiral Dundas again sailed into the Baltic and prepared to bombard Sveaborg. Its five fortified islands presented an almost unbroken line of batteries. Although the allied naval losses were nominal, their bombardment, which continued through the night, did little more than destroy public buildings, for the fortress remained unsubdued, once again confirming the traditional belief in the superiority of forts over ships.

THE AMERICAN STATES

In 1794 the Americans, with their extended coastline and innumerable cities lying on or close to it, started to look to their defence. This young nation was soon to become, with Britain and Russia, one of the three most advanced exponents of the art of coastal defence. The early American forts were traditional, consisting of open works and earth parapets. Some had scarps revetted with timber and others had stone defences. Most followed the work of the French school of engineers. Fort McHenry guarding the approaches to Baltimore was typical. Built on the site of an earlier fort, it was constructed in 1794 as a 20-gun battery comprising a pentagonal fort with angle bastions, a ditch and covered-way and a ravelin covering the entrance gate. An outer battery approximately following the southeast trace of the fort was added about forty years later.

On the threat of another war with Britain new works were initiated in 1807 and American engineers began to adopt the ideas of Montalembert. The

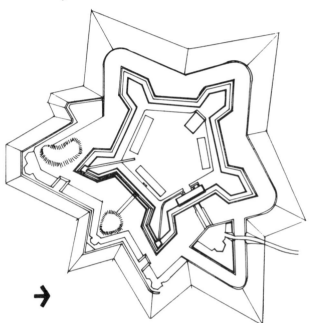

Fort McHenry.

multi-gun fort constructed entirely of masonry with its guns housed in well-ventilated casemates, rising in several tries somewhat resembling the broadside armament of a man of war, became the recognised method of defending the coast. Joseph G Totten was appointed Chief Army Engineer in 1838, a post which he held until his death in 1864. He was instrumental in carrying out the recommendations of the Bernard Board which in 1821 has proposed an integrated national defence system for the harbours of the United States. Eighteen first class works and thirty-two smaller ones were planned, including open batteries and a few Martello towers. The large forts, like Sumter, Pulaski and Fort Jefferson in Florida could bring a concentration of fire which matched anything that a man of war could fire on to the fort. In the 1850s stone walls were reinforced with iron, and Totten was in the forefront, experimenting with an iron throat which could close across the mouth of an embrasure after its gun had fired. The Russians at Kronstadt soon introduced a system of iron laminates where bars 30 centimetres (11.8in) thick were tongued and grooved. And in 1861 the British introduced the 'Gibraltar shield' which could withstand the fire of 38-centimetre (15in) guns at 360 metres (395yds) range. As will be seen, iron was to become one of the major materials in defensive works.

Fort Sumter.

A model of Fort Sumter as it stood on the outbreak of the American Civil War.

THE AMERICAN CIVIL WAR

Fort Sumter in Charleston harbour was planned in the form of a pentagon, its salient angle to the front and each of its corners blunted to deflect shot. It was designed in 1827 and modified during construction so that on the outbreak of the Civil War it was uncompleted. When on 12 April 1861 Fort Sumter came under a murderous bombardment from Confederate batteries it was under-armed and unprepared for battle. It capitulated on the following day and passed into Confederate hands. Fort Sumter's major battle came two years later when it took on two ironclad ships in a 40-minute duel which ended in a victory for the fort, one ship being sunk and the remainder of the Union fleet withdrawing The casemated guns were undamaged; the only ones that suffered being those in barbette positions on the terreplein. A determined siege then followed from land batteries supplemented by a naval attack at night which also failed. Fifteen-inch shells were pumped into the fort until it became a mass of ruins. In seven days it received 315 direct hits.

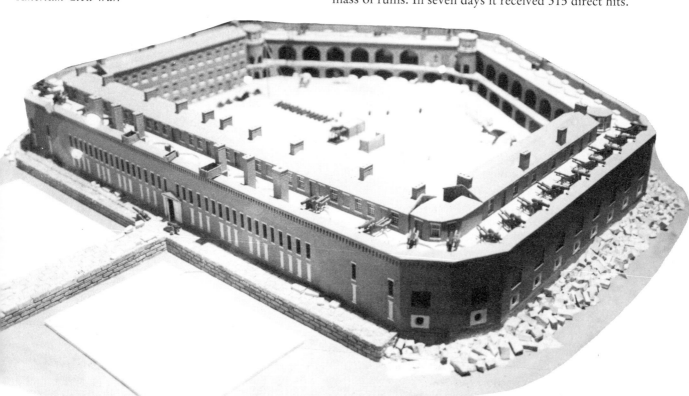

Fort Sumter in Charleston Harbour; one of the reconstructed casemates armed with a 7-inch RML gun formed from a 42-pounder conversion.

This brave defence showed that, with the muzzle-loading smooth-bore guns then available, a stone case-mated fort was capable of holding off the strongest naval attack and could resist for a considerable period a land-based siege. The experience of the Civil War shaped the plans of the future.

Fort Pulaski on the approaches to Savannah was a somewhat similar design. It was originally planned in 1827 as a three-tier fort, but the foundations proved too unstable to support so massive a structure. Four years later the design was modified and Robert E Lee, then a young engineer officer, was involved in its construction. Almost completed by 1847, the fort was shaped in the form of a pentagon, its faces and flanks consisting of one floor of casemates with guns firing through embrasures and with bar-bette guns above on the roof. The gorge was slighly recessed and contained the barrack accommodation and the main gate, which was approached by a draw-bridge from a ravelin. The ravelin replaced an earlier demi-lune whose half-moon shape covered the gorge, and the whole system was surrounded by a broad moat 14 metres (46ft) deep, reduced to 10 metres (33ft) around the ravelin, or demi-lune as it is sometimes called. Its full armament was 150 guns and in January 1862, when during the American Civil War it was besieged, it held 48 guns. The siege was important because it was the first major siege of a fort using the new rifled cannon which was to revolutionise warfare. The siege proved that it was possible, using three

breaching batteries at a mean distance of 1550 metres (1700yds), to make a practical breach in a wall over 2 metres (7ft), standing obliquely to the line of fire and backed by heavy counterforts and arches, whereas before, using smooth-bore guns, it was possible to breach from between 460–640 metres (500–700yds). If one could get within 900 metres (1000yds) it was sometimes possible, but only after some four to seven days of bombardment. Various experiments had been carried in Britain under peacetime conditions against Martello towers when it was deemed that 68-pounder and 32-pounder smooth-bores were altogether a failure at 944 metres (1032yds). The British experiments at Eastbourne proved that rifled guns could be a complete success, whereas smooth-bores were an utter failure. At Fort Pulaski rifled guns were put to the test in wartime. Their success was to demonstrate fully their power and effectiveness for breaching fortifications at long range, rendering obsolete all smooth-bore artillery.

At Hatteras Inlet and Port Royal, Union ships were successful in attacking earthwork batteries because their concentration of fire was heavier and their gunnery superior, but most of all because the ships directed high-angle fire against the shore. Confederate engineers learned from this experience and built large earthwork traverses over bombproof accommodation into which the gunners could retire when the fire from the ships became too heavy, only to return to their guns when there was a lull. In contrast, Fort Jackson, a permanent fort below New Orleans, subjected to continuous bombardment by a mortar flotilla as the fleet passed, was rendered helpless and capitulated.

Fort Powell, built on an oyster bank, was low lying. Its terreplein rose no more than a metre (3ft) above the waters of the high tides, but its guns, three in each face, were set into round pits 5.5 metres (18ft) in diameter at the base and 7.3 metres (24ft) at the top. Between the guns stood earthen traverses covering bombproof chambers and there were covered passages between the gun pits, each of which had its own expense magazine. The channel to the west of the fort was obstructed by 'torpedoes' (what we now call mines) and *chevaux-de-frise* made of railway lines driven into the sand. The fort was bombarded by ships under the command of Admiral Farragut from 22

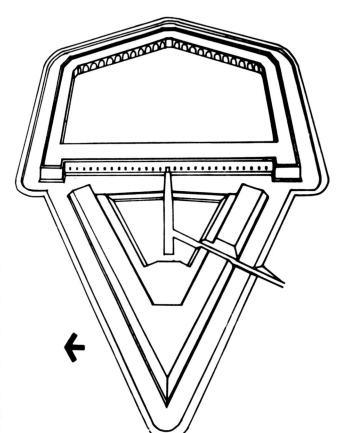

Fort Pulaski; bird's eye view.

February to 2 March 1864 with accurate fire, particularly from 15-inch mortars, which would have reduced a brick or stone fort to rubble. Although shells penetrated to a depth of 1 metre (3.5ft) into the earthwork covers of the bombproof chambers, not a single gun was dismounted, nor a traverse damaged. One man was killed and one wounded. This action was to prove the value of earthworks in absorbing bombardment.

At the start of the American Civil War, Washington, the capital, lay open to an attack. Almost completely without defences, the city lay sprawled along the low lying banks of the muddy Potomac, threatened if not dominated by high ground in nearby Virginia to the south. Clearly the city needed fortifying rapidly for, if the Army of the Potomac was the 'sword', a series of fortifications around the capital would be the 'shield'. The first step was to occupy the heights and then, in August 1861, Major (later Brevet Major-General) John Gross Barnard took charge of the construction of a ring of detached earthwork forts with batteries and supporting troops in the intervals. By the end of the year a total of forty-eight defensive works encircled the city, rich in variety and shape, each designed to take the maximum benefit from its site. In form they were more like redoubts than what we normally think of as forts. Mostly irregular in shape, they remind one of the works built at Torres Vedras half a century later earlier, but the detail plans were up to date, mostly provided with broad gun platforms firing forwards, the faces sometimes protected by bastionettes or caponiers and, in one case, by fully flanked bastions. The model was Dennis Hart Mahan's *A Treatise on Field Fortifications* which Barnard used and acknowledged for the setting out of his profiles. In fact, Chapter Two of this book consists of Barnard's report on the defences of Washington giving full and useful information about profiles, revetments, bombproofs, gun platforms, embrasures, blockhouses and many other features of contemporary earthwork construction. Barnard was an interesting engineer for, in addition to building this ring of fortifications, his most important task, he wrote books on coast defence and the use of iron for defensive purposes. A commission set up in October 1862 came to the conclusion that 25,000 infantry, about 9000 gunners and 3000 cavalry were needed to garrison the capital and support the fortifications. The weak link was the river estuary

where, should Britain and France come into the war against the Union, a fleet could easily penetrate the defences and bombard Washington. Two forts were constructed facing each other across the river, mounted with 200-pounder Parrotts, the type of rifled guns which had, a decade earlier, deterred the allied fleet before Kronstadt.

By the end of 1863, 60 forts, 93 batteries and 830 guns encircled the city with the intervals covered with batteries of artillery and rifle pits. The perimeter stretched some 21 kilometres (13 miles) and 1421 guns had been emplaced – a formidable undertaking and much to Barnard's credit. At the end of the war it was nearly all scrapped for, unlike Europe's capital cities and enclosed camps which remained engirdled by permanent forts, some in being up to this day, Washington returned to the status of an open city.

To summarise the impact of the American Civil War upon the development of fortification and upon coast defence, it became clear that, 'In no single instance did a naval attack succeed where the channel had been obstructed; and in no single instance did it fail where the channel had remained open.' The war saw the extensive use of underwater obstacles and it began to be realised that torpedoes or sea mines 'would occupy the place in naval warfare as mines in land warfare'.

Secondly, exposed masonry of a fort was incapable of withstanding the fire of modern rifled artillery, but earthworks were remarkably resilient to its fire. In many cases it was found that, although powerful well directed fire from ships could silence shore batteries, it did little damage to the guns, and their gun crews, after taking shelter in bombproof accommodation, could return to their guns and retaliate; bearing in mind that ships had a greater difficulty in carrying a large supply of ammunition than did coastal forts.

Finally, the evidence of the value of high-angle or vertical fire from mortars was mixed. There were some successes and some failures. However, the Americans placed great reliance on the use of concentrated mortar batteries from then on, well covered and sunk in pits, whereas the British tended to abandon their use in coast defence, considering them too inaccurate to be effective.

NEW TECHNOLOGY

The American Civil War of 1861–65 threw up more ingenious innovations than almost any previous campaign. Both sides started ill-equipped and were forced to rely on their inventiveness. A number of devices emerged which were to reshape the conduct of war. The final destruction of Fort Sumter proved that masonry alone was incapable of withstanding the force of

modern artillery. Muzzle velocity and accuracy were both increased by the introduction of rifling (its use with studded shot was being developed in 1842 by Colonel de Beaulieu in France) and by the explosive power of shells which had begun to replace solid shot in the French navy in 1837. Breech-loading, as opposed to muzzle-loading, was developed by Johann Dreyse and adopted by the Prussians in 1842, soon to revolutionise both the handling and the efficiency of big guns. Each year saw new developments and inventions which rapidly changed the face of war.

The Civil War also proved that, even though forts might easily withstand a naval bombardment, they were powerless to prevent a large fleet from penetrating any channel unless the defence was aided by underwater obstacles. With these obstacles in position and kept under fire from heavy batteries, no fleet could force a passage. The use of underwater obstacles is as old as naval warfare itself, but science and technology now stepped in to improve their efficiency. The torpedo and the mine were introduced in defence

Union armoured vessels attacking a coastal tower during the Civil War.

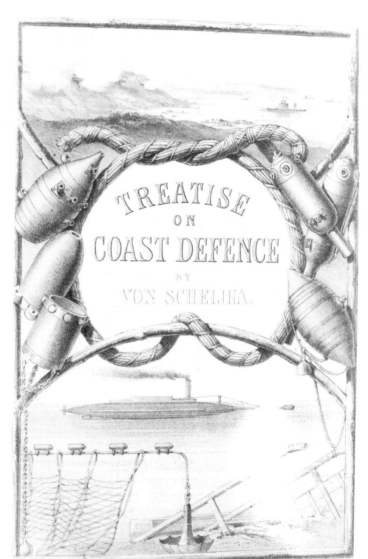

Von Scheliha's Treatise on Coast Defence *illustrates the new underwater obstacles in use in 1868.*

to supplement the use of sunken vessels, rocks, piles, booms and chains. The first large scale use of these devices occurred in the Civil War. The submarine mine, originally called a torpedo, could be fired in a number of ways, but the two most efficient methods caused it to explode either on contact with a ship or by remote electric detonation from an observation post on the coast.

The torpedo-boat, later to become submersible, was invented during the war, and after a number of disastrous failures it successfully attacked one of the ironclads in October 1863. Coast defences were supplemented later by torpedo rockets which could be fired, operated and detonated from the shore, and by the introduction of searchlights to illuminate a vulnerable channel. Electric beacons had been used in 1857 at South Foreland and in 1862 at Dungeness, and from these innovations there developed the concentrated and dispersed beams of the search- and fixed lights used in defence. The guided, locomotive torpedo was introduced by the British to provide underwater protection for the entrance to harbours. There were three types, called Lay, Sims-Edison and Brennan. The last type, invented by an Australian and developed in great secrecy, was launched down a ramp into the sea. Carrying a high-explosive charge, it travelled under the water and was propelled by unwinding two drums or reels of fine steel wire within the torpedo. The rotation of the reels was communicated to the propellers causing the torpedo to advance. The ends of the wire were connected to an engine on shore to give rapid unwinding and increased speed to the torpedo. It was steered by varying the speed at which either wire was unwound. The Brennan torpedoes were installed in the late 1880s.

In the second year of the American Civil War two iron-plated ships fought out a thrilling duel. At the battle of Hampton Roads the Confederate ironclad *Virginia* (known to history by her earlier name of *Merrimac*) was engaged in pitched battle by the Union *Monitor*. Although the *Merrimac* had created havoc with the timber hulls of the Union fleet, its guns blazed ineffectually against the *Monitor* whose rotating turret retaliated with equal lack of effect. In 1860 Captain Cowper Coles, RN, had written a paper advocating the use of revolving gun turrets. Later they became all-important in naval architecture. The

encounter, if not conclusive, at least highlighted the remarkable properties of armour plating.

After the success of the *Monitor* the United States used armoured ships extensively. On one occasion the armoured vessel *Montawk* attacked Fort McAllister. The guns of the fort and the earthwork batteries replied and the ship was hit thirteen times during its first attack and sixteen during its second, but it suffered no serious damage. In some desperation the gunners on shore christened the low freeboard turret ship 'a cheese-box on a plank'.

IRON FORTIFICATIONS

From the middle of the nineteenth century the emphasis began to shift from the protection of forts against bodily assault to the protection of heavy guns from destruction by bombardment. It had long been an axiom in fortification that 'masonry, if seen, will be destroyed'. With the growth of permanent fortifications in that century, their major parts had to be concealed or covered, but what remained might be given an added protection, like a man in armour, by applying an outer coat of greater strength. Several experts had long advocated the use of steel cladding. Gustavus Adolphus (1594–1632) had proposed to fortify with blocks of iron and General D'Arcon (1733–1800) had wished to plate with iron the floating batteries he used against Gibraltar. General Henri Joseph Paixhans, writing in *Force et faiblesse militaires de la France* in 1829 had argued that, if iron could be used for building bridges, churches, factories and roads, why not fortifications? But it was not as easy as all that! Cast iron, the most simple form to use in large sheets as a cladding material, although very strong in compression, was brittle and tended to shatter under the impact of shot. Wrought iron was, like a fibre, strongest in tension and could sustain impact along the length of its fibres. It was ideal for resisting the expansion of a gun barrel when wrapped around a gun, but it was difficult to place in the right direction to withstand bombardment, and it was expensive, even though the naval ironmaster, Henry Cort, had in 1784 introduced two processes for puddling and rolling the material which greatly increased the quantities of wrought iron available.

The first recorded experiments against an iron-cased wall of granite blocks covered with a mesh of iron bars were made by Major-General Ford, RE at Woolwich in 1827, but were not at all successful. In 1846 Colonels Colquhoun and Sandham tried with wrought iron plates set obliquely to the line of fire, applied first in front of a ship's gun carriage, then against a granite wall and finally in front of oak beams. Between 1850 and 1854 there were naval experiments at Portsmouth without much success. The need for effective iron cladding on ships was even more apparent than its necessity on coastal forts.

In America, General Joseph G Totten, army chief engineer from 1838 to 1864, began in mid-century a series of controlled tests to assess the resistance of material to bombardment with the result that he contemplated the construction of works of coast defence clad in iron and, where necessary, built entirely of iron. His Totten Embrasure was an iron throat that closed when the gun had fired.

In 1856 General Sir John Burgoyne collected information about what had been done in the matter of applying iron to the parapets of batteries, both floating and on shore, and moved the British government to take action to give better cover to guns and, by using iron, to reduce the external apertures of embrasures. The result was the production of the 356-millimetre (14in) Thornycroft Shield, more experiments in Britain and France and the setting up of a number of committees – the Special Committee on Plates and Guns (1859), and the Special Iron Committee (1861). In that year Captain Cowper Coles, RN tested his revolving cupola which was to become important in naval artillery. In coast defence the British and the Americans concentrated on laminates of iron and wood, from 1877 using steel-faced armour plate, to protect their gun embrasures, whereas continental powers in Europe tended to go for the production of immensely expensive iron and steel cupolas sometimes on retractable mechanisms which will be described later.

The problem was side-tracked by the introduction of the disappearing gun for coast defence, loaded and worked under cover and invisible to an attacking fleet except during the brief moments when the gun fired. Iron protection in coast defence became superfluous with the introduction of Captain Moncrief's gun carriage whose gun, under the force of recoil, sank into a pit, the force being used against a heavy counterpoise to raise the gun once more after it had been loaded. Once the disappearing system had been applied to heavy coast guns using hydro-pneumatic power, most British coast forts at home and abroad were re-equipped with these weapons. Some were fitted with overhead shields but all were expensive to build and to repair so that they in turn were superseded by barbette mountings at the end of the century with guns protected like those on ships against splinters and rifle fire by steel shields. The Americans continued to use heavy 381-millimetre (15in) disappearing guns until the eclipse of coast defence artillery well after the Second World War.

THE DEFENCE OF BRITISH PORTS

The Crimean War held together an uneasy alliance between Britain and France. The peace which followed was apprehensive as Britain watched the French navy being built up, equipped with the latest technical devices and armed with the new screw-driven ships, their hulls sheathed in iron. The bombardment of Kinburn at the mouth of the Dnieper in 1855 by three

Casemates and iron embrasures on Fort Bovisand at Plymouth.

French floating batteries, which emerged unscathed after a four hours' engagement during which the French ships were hit repeatedly, proved conclusively the value of armour plating. To make matters worse for the British, the French began to equip a great naval arsenal at Cherbourg, menacing the English south coast ports, and ringed it with a formidable defensive screen. By 1858 Britain, her navy largely dispersed at overseas stations and her home defences hardly touched for over a hundred years, stood in peril of invasion. It is still unknown whether the threat of a sudden attack was serious, but Palmerston feared that the two countries might inadvertently become involved in a state of war. In December 1858 a committee, set up to investigate the relative strengths of the French and British navies revealed the frightening fact

Fort Perch Rock at the entrance to the Mersey.

Fort Hubberstone guarding Milford Haven.

that France already had superiority of capital ships in the Channel. Immediately steps were taken in an attempt to safeguard the main British naval arsenals and deep water anchorages to which a fleet might have to withdraw to rearm and repair the scars of battle. It was to be an expensive undertaking, unpopular with Parliament and criticised by those who believed that the Royal Navy formed an impenetrable shield for the defence of Britain.

The Royal Defence Commission report came out in 1860 with recommendations for works at the royal dockyards of Portsmouth, Plymouth, Pembroke and Chatham, plus protection for the harbours at Portland, Dover and Cork. Work had already begun on some schemes when the government axed the recommended expenditure from £10,350,000 to £6,570,000. As the work progressed costs inevitably rose. In some cases foundations proved to be more expensive than anticipated, new heavy guns cost more and the considerable use of iron plating was expensive. The price of labour and materials rose and the commission of 1861 recommended an improvement in barrack accommodation. Higher standards of ventilation, drainage and water supply were called for, while space allocated for each soldier was to be increased from 37 square metres (400sq ft) to at least 56 (600sq ft). Only after considerable opposition did the govern-

ment get its way and the Fortifications Act was passed in 1867. Work was already well under way at all the main naval ports.

The defences consisted of three types each with its own distinctive characteristics. Coastal defence forts were constructed close to the shore. They were modelled on Russian designs in the Crimea, each irregularly shaped in the form of a long hooked arm with casemated batteries. Built some distance away, the barrack accommodation usually consisted of a large defensible horseshoe. Secondly, there were forts built in the sea. The British had already experimented at Fort Perch Rock, built at the entrance to the river Mersey between 1826 and 1829 to the designs of Captain Kitson. Except at low tide this fort is surrounded by seawater. But most of the new forts – multi-gun circular structures modelled on the Russians' work in Kronstadt harbour – were placed in mid-channel. The third type of defence consisted of detached forts forming elements in a major fortress and strongly influenced by Montalembert. These were intended to repel an army which had landed somewhere down the coast and was now circling to attack the port from the rear. Each land fort was to be supported by neighbours. Of the seventy-six forts in course of construction or completed by 1867, nineteen were land forts and the remainder either coastal defence forts or sea forts.

The report on the sea defences of Milford Haven was published in 1858 and work began immediately to safeguard the great anchorage at the head of which lay the naval dockyard of Pembroke. In addition to forts placed in the sea, there were three major coastal forts with barracks widely separated from the gun positions. Fort Hubberstone was ready to receive her armament in 1860 but, because modifications were carried out to provide iron shields, it was not completed until 1863 at a cost of £73,600. The battery lay on the cliff edge 6.5 kilometres (4 miles) from the dockyard and originally consisted of twelve casemates, later supplemented by barbette positions on the roof. A horseshoe-shaped barrack block placed on the crest of the hill secured the rear of the gun positions, and beyond the barracks lay a dry ditch defended from its counterscarp by granite galleries placed to flank the ditch. The barrack block was modified during construction to provide bombproof accommodation and was not completed until 1865. This type of fort was

Below: *Counterscarp galleries flanking the ditch at Fort Hubberstone.*

Below: *The old gun emplacements at Fort Popton, Milford Haven.*

never intended to withstand a full scale siege but should have been capable of resisting a sudden assault by enemy marines landed on the coast.

Sea forts were a different proposition. They depended for their defence upon unscaleable walls rising sheer from the water's edge. Stack Rock (1859–61) at Milford Haven was the least successful as it was built on a rocky outcrop which might under certain circumstances have provided a tenuous foothold for an attack. All four forts in the Solent guarding the approach to Portsmouth were round structures rising directly from the sea. They were partly clad with iron, although they were at one time intended to be fully sheathed with this material. The Solent forts were begun in 1863 against considerable opposition originating mainly from those who wished to put their whole trust in the navy and its deployment of floating batteries. But those who advocated the sea forts carried the day and the forts were built at great expense

The west battlements at Fort Popton before alterations.

caused largely by foundation difficulties. The largest one was completed in 1880 having cost over £242,000, a sum which might be compared with the more meagre cost of the coast defence forts at Milford Haven, the most expensive of which was Fort Popton at £75,600 and the cheapest, South Hook Fort, costing £44,000.

First Portsmouth, then Plymouth and Chatham in the 1870s, were ringed by detached forts. At Portsmouth a group of forts was built to cover the approach to Gosport. Fort Brockhurst (1858–62), the best preserved, consisted of a polygonal fort with case-

Design for a fort at Spithead with 49 guns in two tiers and ten guns in revolving turrets, the whole of the exterior clad in iron; after Jervois.

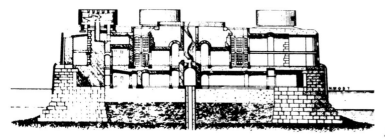

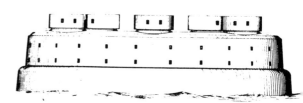

Spitbank fort guarding Portsmouth.

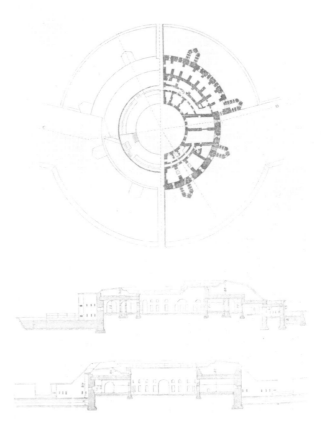

Plan and section of the circular keep at Fort Brockhurst; after Lendy.

mates from which guns could fire directly across the countryside. It was surrounded by a wet ditch, flanked by three caponiers, the central one being a powerful work of the type advocated by Montalembert and then currently being used by the Prussians. The gorge wall was pierced for musketry defence, and in its centre stood a circular keep armed with artillery in casemates and with a series of small bastions from which muskets could flank the ditch.

Behind Portsmouth lies the Portsdown hill, its crest providing a remarkable panorama of the naval port and the surrounding countryside. An enemy in possession of this hill could have pounded the naval installations into a mass of rubble. To foil him, four large forts and three minor works were constructed, the last and the most ambitious land fortification project to be built in Britain. Fort Wallington was typical, its guns firing from barbette positions on earth ramparts supplemented by a mortar battery at the northern angle. The fort was designed in the shape of a polygon surrounded by a dry ditch flanked by caponiers firing in one direction and a two-storey

Fort Brockhurst at Portsmouth.

Plan of one of the forts in the Gosport lines, Portsmouth; after Lendy.

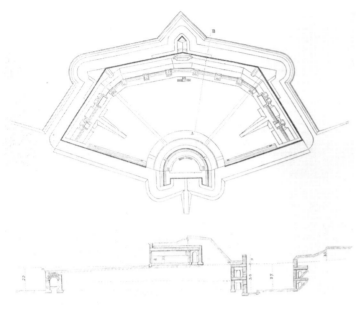

counterscarp gallery which covered the two northern arms of the ditch. The barracks were in the gorge, situated in a tall brick structure loopholed for musketry defence with a large loopholed redan projecting in the direction of the town. Fort Wallington, started in 1861, was completed in 1874 at a total cost of just over £100,000.

Although never tested in war, there can be no doubt that the forts were as advanced as anything on the Continent and by this time British engineers like Burgoyne, Jervois and Lefroy were fully aware of the changing nature of warfare and its implications for permanent fortification.

With the extension of imperial power Britain's defence commitments stretched across the world. By 1856 she had major military responsibilities in Gibraltar, Malta, Corfu, Bermuda and Mauritius, with lesser liabilities at St Helena and Ascension Island. India, Canada, the West Indies, the Cape of Good Hope, Ceylon and Australia, whilst requiring defensive measures, were capable of financing them from their own resources. The task of defending the British Empire was a prodigious one. Discounting the 100,000 troops required for the defence of Britain, of which 27,000 were needed in Ireland, and the fairly heavy requirements for the defence of the Channel Islands, the main emphasis in imperial defence fell upon Gibraltar and Malta. Other places made their demands.

BERMUDA

Bermuda lay much further away than Gibraltar and Malta, some three thousand miles from Britain, but was strategically placed well off the North American continent and almost mid-way between the British fortified bases in the West Indies and the strongly defended naval port at Halifax. From 1612 the British colonists built a large number of coastal forts and batteries, but the defences constructed around the naval base at the northern end of the islands became a necessity during the Napoleonic Wars as the result of the establishment by the British of the naval dockyard in 1809. Some of the works that followed are of great interest for they show the innovative characteristics of the Royal Engineers towards the end of, and after, the Napoleonic Wars. One Martello tower was built on Bermuda in the early 1820s but, more interesting, Captain Thomas Cunningham, RE proposed placing a Martello tower in the middle of a ditch which ran across the peninsula, forming the landward defences of the dockyard in 1811. Although the French had been inclined to use their *tours modèles* strung along defensive lines for land fortification, this was unusual with British engineers where most of the Martellos were designed to protect the coast from a landing. In 1808 four had been built as land forts to bar the approaches to the Heights of Abraham in front of Quebec, each tower being capable of mutually flanking its neighbour, but without the ditch proposed at Bermuda. Fort St Catherine, designed by Captain Cunningham in 1811 and finished in 1826, is also interesting for it shows the reintroduction of the keep, in this case a regular figure curved towards the front, flanking its own ditch but incapable of being flanked in front, placed, almost like the keep-gatehouse of the Edwardian castles in North Wales, in the forefront, facing any possible direction of attack.

In 1809 a naval dockyard was established at Bermuda and between 1822 and 1843 an enceinte was thrown around the dockyard, fortifications which, soon after completion, would be outdated. This enceinte consisted of a land front of two bastions with a short curtain, a ravelin tower, and a counterguard. In the 1820s counterscarp galleries were popular with English engineers and they were provided in the counterguard in front of the ravelin tower, and beyond, in the salient

The 100-ton gun at Napier of Magdala Battery, Gibraltar; after Inglis.

angle of the ditch. The extremities of the land front were strengthened by a *couvre porte* (now demolished), with counterscarp galleries, and the last work to be constructed, the Right Advance of the land front which is a curious double platform of guns firing out to sea and down the glacis. It is formed of two isolated positions placed beyond the north-western bastion. At the seaward end of the dockyard there stands a keep, a large fortified area with an impressive coastline of bastions and curtains and a land front of two large bastions, so that it acted rather as a retrenchment. As one might expect, most of the subsequent improvement of the defensive position at Bermuda was carried out by updating the ordnance rather than making major modifications to the fortifications.

CANADA

Halifax in Canada, founded in 1749 as a new British fortress town on the shores of Chebucto harbour, guarding the approaches from the north Atlantic, was laid out as a grid plan surrounded by a palisade and a ring of five square earthwork bastioned forts, one of which was termed 'the citadel'. Other citadels followed, the third built after the outbreak of the war with France in 1793. All were earthworks and had a comparatively short life span. The Duke of Wellington's commission of 1825 recommended the construction of permanent fortifications in British North America and the construction of a major citadel at Halifax. The present fort was designed by Colonel

Below: *Sliema Point Battery at Malta.*

Below: *Interior of a British casemate at Fort St Lucian, Malta.*

Gustavus Nicholls and begun in 1828, but construction dragged on for twenty-eight years. The result was an imposing regular fort, basically tenaille in plan with two demi-bastions on the long front, plus the additional protection of three ravelins. In the gorge was placed a cavalier, with two-storey casemates and guns on the roof, a building later modified to provide extra barrack space. All around the town and on the islands in the harbour, numerous forts and batteries were constructed to create a web of fortified positions of great interest. One in particular, the Prince of Wales Tower, built in 1796, is important as an early example of the English development of the circular tower which was to be brought to some form of standardisation in the Martello towers on the English coast. This one is broad, circular and low, with four drop boxes protecting the doorway and portions of the base of the tower. On the islands, Fort Charlotte is interesting: a coast defence fort, an irregular octagon in plan, the guns ranged on a horseshoe mound and the deep ditch protected by caponiers.

BRITISH FORTS ON MALTA

There is no better place than Malta to study the changing pattern of permanent fortification from the time of the assumption of control by Britain in 1800 to the outbreak of the First World War. At first the army was overawed by the prodigious expanse of the fortifications inherited from the Knights of St John. Mile upon mile of yellow limestone bastions and curtains seemed to stretch into the distance and the sheer task of manning them let alone modifying them, daunted the British. Up to the 1860s the task lay mainly in modernising the armament and improving barrack accommodation, but in 1871 the army began a new continuous line to cover the landward approach to the naval dockyard. From then on there was an unbroken policy of modernisation and new building as more and more coastal forts sprang up in defence of the Island. With the opening of the Suez Canal in 1869 the pace quickened and the tendency was towards providing forts with no more than four or five large guns, at first housed in casemates and after 1878 mounted in the open, *en barbette*. Gradually there was a separation of the observation position from the gun position made possible by the introduction of field telephones. Colonel Watkin invented a position finder so that guns could be laid and fired by electricity from a distant position finder station.

The diversity of design in the British forts in Malta is amazing; hardly any two are alike. The early ones, like Sliema Point Battery (1872–76) are erect and richly decorated with carved gothic motifs like some medieval fortress. The plan is fan-shaped with four casemates for 25- and 38-ton muzzle-loading guns. Begun in 1876, Fort Delimara followed an irregular site on a promontory overlooking the great bay of Marsaxlokk. The deep dry ditch with vertical scarp and counterscarp walls was flanked by counterscarp galleries and the guns, six heavy 38-ton rifled muzzle-loaders, still surviving but badly rusted, were dug into large casemates in the cliff face. But already at that time the value of casemated guns was in dispute. After the battle of Duppel in 1864 the Prussians decided that embrasures were useless. In the same year the British developed the Moncrief mounting, the first of a long line of devices which allowed the barrel of a gun to project above the parapet for firing and to recoil to a

One of the 38-ton RML guns at Fort Delimara.

point of safety concealed behind the thickness of the parapet. Eight years later designs were submitted for Fort Tombrell in Malta, with a regular hexagonal trace mounting six 64-pounder RML guns on Moncrief carriages, protected in the rear by a large traverse which ran the width of the fort. In front of the traverse and facing out to sea stood three 280-millimetre (11in) guns in barbette mountings. In those early days of the development of technology it was only possible to mount comparatively light guns on disappearing carriages, although gradually the techniques were improved to allow the utilisation of much heavier guns.

As the range of guns increased the early land

Casemates for the big muzzle-loading guns at Fort Delimara, Malta.

Proposed design of Fort Tombrell, Malta; plan.

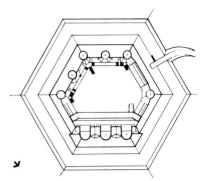

The ditch and a counterscarp gallery at Fort Delimara.

The keep at Fort Musta in the Victoria Lines, Malta.

The ditch of Fort St Leonardo from the scarp.

defences of Malta became outdated. The old Floriana and Cottonera Lines were too near the heart of the naval dockyard to be practicable and in 1866 a recommendation was made to build a line of five ring-forts to form a large semi-circle around the capital and the port. However the rate of improvement in gun design was so rapid that hardly had this recommendation been made than it was outdated. In that very year the French army decided to adopt Chassipot's greatly improved breech-loading gun and in the following year Krupps exhibited a 50-ton breech-loader capable of firing a 454-kilo (1000lb) shell. At the same time

Britain was experimenting with coiled barrels which greatly increased muzzle velocity and thus range. So in Malta the first plan was abandoned, and in 1873 the Victoria Lines were projected on an escarpment much farther to the north. There half a dozen new forts and casemated batteries were joined by a continuous line of infantry positions.

Meanwhile the work on the coastal forts forged ahead. Fort St Leonardo was completed in 1878 on a triangular plan with barbette guns firing out to sea along one face of the triangle, and a strong keep, completely detached from the rest of the fort by a

A gun emplacement at Fort Musta designed to minimise the chance of shot entering the fort.

moat, was placed in the opposite angle. On the landward side the fort was protected by a spur, at that date still a favourite device of British engineers, its long pointed shape stretching back like a tail from the fort.

Between then and the outbreak of the First World War some dozen new forts were constructed on the island and many of the earlier ones like Fort Delimara converted to take large breech-loading guns and quick-firing guns on barbette mountings as the old muzzle-loaders were gradually phased out. Britain had pioneered the introduction of breech-loading guns but, after some failures, had reverted to the old muzzle-loaders. In 1882 she changed back to the breech-loading guns; 234-millimetre (9.2in) BL guns

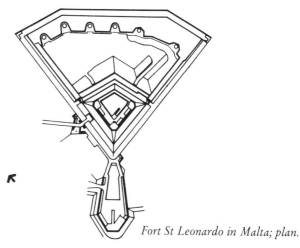

Fort St Leonardo in Malta; plan.

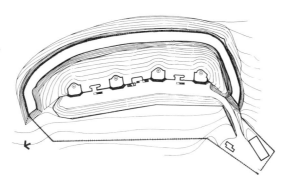

Wolseley Battery, Malta; plan.

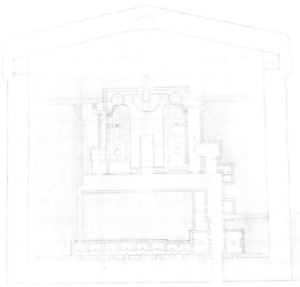

The 100-ton gun battery at Fort Rinella, Malta; plan.

The mighty 100-ton gun at Fort Rinella on Malta.

were placed in the open above the casemates which in places had to be strengthened to take the load. Fort Delimara was re-equipped in 1888.

Of the new forts in Malta, at least two types show significant development. In the last decades of the nineteenth century Britain was still experimenting with larger and larger muzzle-loading guns. In 1875 an 80-ton gun had been completed at the arsenal at Woolwich, to be followed soon by the 100-ton gun with a calibre of 17.72 inches (450mm). The Italians had ordered these giant weapons to be fitted to their newest battleships and the British suddenly became apprehensive of the possibility of the Italian navy standing outside the maximum range of the guns of Malta and Gibraltar and bombarding the naval installations with impunity. A decision was taken to despatch four of these weapons to the Mediterranean bases. In each case a new fort was designed to house just one gun. In 1884 Fort Rinella was completed in Malta and the heavy gun landed in the harbour to be hauled with considerable difficulty up the tortuous road into its position in the fort. Like its sister guns at Fort Cambridge in Malta and Napier of Magdala Battery in Gibraltar, it was never fired in anger, but it gave the authorities considerable anxiety. These were the only guns of the British army which could not be laid by hand, traversing, elevating and depressing being

carried out by steam power. Maybe the British need not have worried for the end of the big muzzle-loading guns was in sight.

The final development of the fort lay in the substitution of the Twydall Profile for the traditional ditch flanked from caponiers or counterscarp galleries. A good illustration is Wolseley Battery, built between 1897 and 1899 to mount four 152-millimetre (6in) quick-firing guns. The ground in front of the barbette mountings sloped gently forward to terminate in a shallow scooped out arc which embraced the whole front of the gun positions. This depressed area was filled with loose barbed wire and its outer edge secured by a barbed wire fence. Except for the entrance gate the back of the fort was defended by a spiky steel palisade 3 metres (10ft) high. In this design flanking fire was completely abolished and the defence of the fort depended on frontal fire from rifles, which could quickly be reloaded, and from machine-guns. The British army had adopted the Martini-Henry rifle in 1871; Hiram Maxim invented the belt-loading machine-gun in 1883, and the British introduced the Vickers-Maxim machine-gun in 1891. Barbed wired obstacles and rapid fire from small arms were to re-establish the superiority of defence, a superiority which culminated in the stagnation of trench warfare in the First World War.

THE IMPACT OF TECHNOLOGY

Gradually the gun as a defensive factor began to assume greater importance than the bricks and mortar of the fortifications which housed it. The casemate was abandoned, its position usurped by two diametrically opposed systems. On the one hand there was the growing popularity of the open gun position, especially in coastal defence work, helped by the introduction of smokeless gunpowder by the French in 1884; and at the other extreme lay the development of the armoured cupola with the gun and its mechanisms sunk deep into the earth. In coast defence work large puffs of smoke no longer revealed the exact positions of the guns, which were dispersed, being laid and fired electrically from a position-finder station. At first the disappearing gun was popular, the barrel sometimes sliding below an overhead metal shield providing some protection for the gunners, but with the introduction of effective breech-loading guns (the British began to use them after about 1882) it was possible to use high-angled rifled ordnance. The guns placed behind the continuous parapet on a cliff were completely obscured from any attacking ships. Not only did the guns develop greater accuracy after 1855 but gradually their range was extended. With the introduction of the magazine rifle forts could be more easily defended and in any case there was less likelihood of their being attacked by landing parties because warships in the

An 8-inch BL gun on a hydro-pneumatic mounting, in its firing position.

The same gun lowered to the loading position; after Sydenham Clarke.

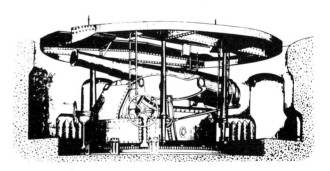

later nineteenth century before the introduction of assault craft had little space to spare for landing parties.

In America the Endicott Board, formed in 1885, shifted the emphasis from the structure of the fort to the weapons contained within it. Forts became simple low-lying structures in reinforced concrete blending with the countryside. Earlier the guns of a fort had cost anything between a sixth and a tenth of the total cost, but now they began to assume three-quarters of the overall cost of a fort. Their numbers were also reduced (the days of the multi-gun fort were over) and by 1906 the United States was also installing single gun batteries in some of her overseas possessions.

A revolving armoured cupola operated by hand; after Hennebert.

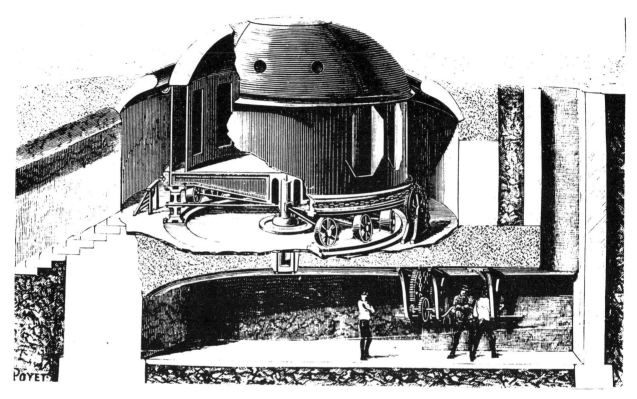

British military engineers like Sydenham Clarke, O'Callaghan, J F Lewis, B R Ward and E R Kenyon began to take an active interest in continental developments, visiting the armament manufacturers and whenever possible the sites of military installations. For in Europe the stage was being set for the last great demonstration of the defensive power of permanent fortifications. Old faiths were rudely shaken as the technocrat usurped the position of authority previously held by the geometrician.

The armoured cupola now began to attract the attention of military planners. It was immensely expensive and under certain conditions of attack its occupants could be momentarily blinded. Being encased in this shell of iron, sandwiched between the sharp edges of an exploding gun and the dripping surfaces of the outer skin where the condensation ran down in rivulets, the psychological effect cannot have been healthy. But in the event of bombardment, the protection afforded by the dome of iron formed a powerful compensation for the claustrophobic conditions. There were many solutions. Mougin invented a cupola with a completely new system of fortifica-

tion. His fort consisted of huge blocks of concrete buried deep in the earth from which rose three cupolas each manned with two 150-millimetre (5.9in) guns. Supporting these and providing close defence were four disappearing machine-gun cupolas supplemented by observation domes and all the paraphernalia of forced ventilation and electric lighting. The entrance was covered by an armoured plate which could be raised and lowered by an hydraulic ramp and from there the path into the fort twisted and turned like those in an ancient Greek fortress, so that the enemy on penetrating the structure would be caught at a number of right-angled turns. The ditch was now abolished and the machine-gun, firing 700 rounds a minute, was intended to keep enemy infantry at a distance. Around the outside of the fort ran a railway track so that trucks carrying guns, which could be raised by hydropneumatic power, could be moved forward and withdrawn as the tactical situation required: an ingenious method and a strong pointer to future developments.

In 1887 Colonel Voorduin of the Dutch corps of engineers produced a simple fort consisting of

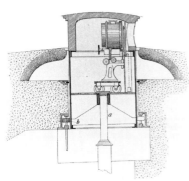

*A disappearing searchlight cupola;
after Cramwinckel.*

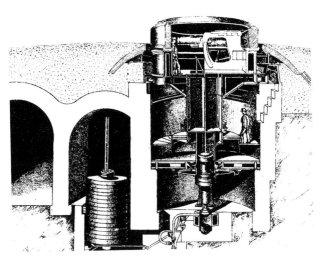

*A Chatillon and Commentary disappearing gun turret in
the raised position; from Clarke's Reports.*

*Section through an underground fort designed by Mougin;
after Sydenham Clarke.*

a low mass of concrete from which projected iron
cupolas housing twin guns. The ends of the concrete
contained caponiers from which guns fired across the
intervening space between forts, and the scheme had
the merit of being cheap because its trace was comparatively short and enclosed very little interior space.
In early forts the need had been to provide sufficient
interior space for a comparatively large garrison
cumbrously manning inefficient cannon. With the introduction of quick-firing guns and pre-prepared shell
and cartridge ammunition the garrison could be drastically reduced.

The munition factories of Europe advertised
their wares and their products were sold to anyone
prepared to pay. For example, Colonel Schumann's
armoured front was built into the Sereth Line in
Rumania between 1889 and 1892. Germany and
France produced the goods and, rather pathetically,
the most avid purchaser was little Belgium.

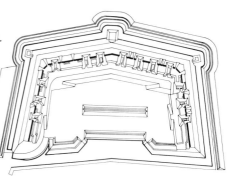

Redoubt des Hautes Bruyères at Paris; plan.

Fort Issy defending Paris; plan.

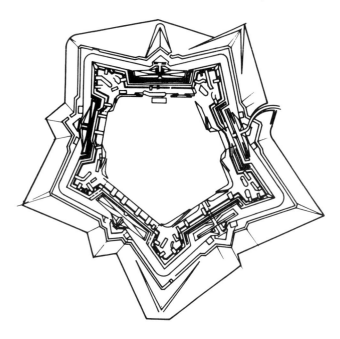

THE DEVELOPMENT OF PERMANENT FORTIFICATIONS IN THE LATE NINETEENTH CENTURY

The Franco-Prussian War of 1870 saw France ill-prepared to withstand the assault of determined well-trained troops. Leaving isolated outposts of resistance the French fell back on the capital which was protected by a circuit of detached forts forming a perimeter of nearly 48 kilometres (30 miles), its design still conforming to the bastioned trace rationalised by Vauban two hundred years earlier. Fort Issy was a typical example of a conservative French attitude to defence. Dating from the 1840s when one school of French thought wanted to bastion Paris with a complete enceinte some 16 kilometres (10 miles) out from its centre, only the sheer scale and expense of the undertaking prevented its implementation. So detached forts like Issy were built. Sydenham Clark described it as a fort built on a traditional bastion trace mounting 60 guns, 'which may have flanked everything flankable, but were utterly unable to cope with siege batteries, on which a mere fraction of them could be brought to bear'. Fortunately for the French they were quick to learn, and as the siege of Paris materialised they threw up polygonal redoubts which were modelled on current German practice. The Redoubt des Hautes Bruyères was an efficient solution to the problem. The guns still fired through embrasures, their flanks protected by traverses, but the ramparts were of earth and the ditch enfiladed from caponiers. If it did nothing else for the French, the Franco-Prussian War shook the dust from the higher echelons of the French command and tolled the death knell of the bastioned trace.

THE RING-FORTRESSES OF WESTERN EUROPE

Of all the great ring-fortresses of western Europe, Antwerp was the mightiest; yet when put to the test it was one of the least successful. It was designed to be a base for operations, a refuge for the government and a *reduit* for national survival. At various times four lines of defence had been built at Antwerp. The Duke of Wellington supervised the construction of the old enceinte between 1815 and 1818 and its citadel, defended by General Chassé, bravely withstood a two-year siege in 1830. By 1859 its bastions and curtains were thoroughly outmoded and were dismantled. In that year Henri Brialmont (1821–1903), the most noteworthy of the Belgian engineers, was called in to design a continuous new enceinte with, 4 kilometres (2½ miles) farther out, a string of eight detached polygonal forts, to which four more were later added, making Antwerp the most powerful fortress of its day. Brialmont's trace was complex but its defensive power hinged on the use of large pointed caponiers armed with many guns, becoming forts in their own right, faced by a complex ravelin and backed by a short curtain in the middle of which stood a rectangular block of defensible barracks. As time passed even this extensive defence system was not considered adequate to safeguard the town and, between 1878 and 1898, five new ring-forts were built some 9.5 to 14 kilometres (6–9 miles) farther out. Thus the circumference of forts was extended from a mere 43 kilometres (27 miles) in the case of Brialmont's forts to an enormous perimeter of 106 kilometres (66 miles) for the ring-forts. The Belgians went on adding more and more forts to close the gaps, but, as quickly as they built, the problem changed. With the development of mighty new mobile howitzers (the Russians were using one with a calibre of 280 millimetres or 11 inches in 1912) the ancient 150-millimetre (5.9in) guns in the forts were sadly outmatched. All the forts had been clearly

Below: *Trace of Brialmont's enceinte at Antwerp; after
Lewis.*

Bottom: *Fort de Broechem, one of the ring forts of Antwerp.*

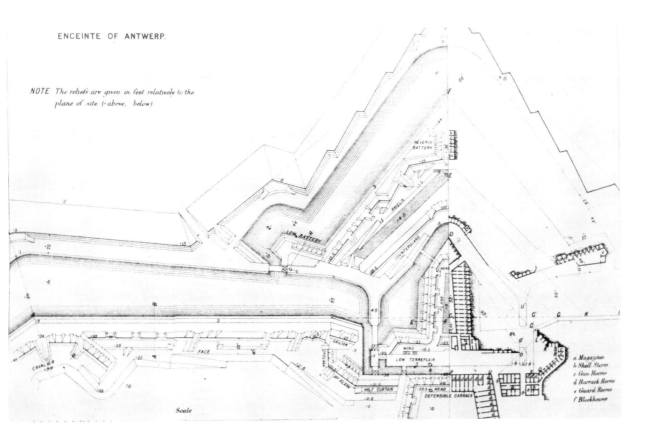

Plan and section of a Liège fort.

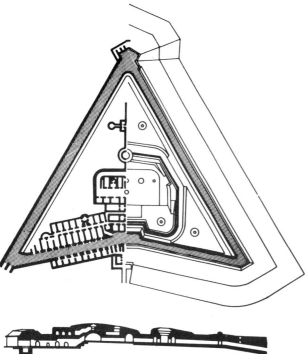

The ditch of Fort Lonçin at Liège.

marked on innumerable drawings. Their silhouettes were plainly visible and their structures could not be moved, so that every German gunnery officer had the location of each one pinpointed on his maps. Their fate was inevitable. The turn of the century saw the Belgians moving their heavy guns from the forts and deploying their effective artillery in the intervals. The position was thus reversed. Instead of the forts being strongpoints in the line of battle, supported by a field army, they were utilised to provide flanking fire for the guns in the intervals. Some forts were equipped with *traditore*, that is with guns facing only to the flanks and the rear in order to sweep the intervals.

When the First World War began and German troops flooded into Belgium many of the Antwerp forts were unfinished. Some lacked cupolas and most had old guns firing black powder and only effective over short ranges. The forts too were badly ventilated and their interiors soon filled with the poisonous fumes from their own guns and from the German shells which burst upon them causing fissures in the concrete. The concrete was poor and soon broke under the bombardment of General von Beseler's heavy Skoda and Krupp siege artillery. The Belgian troops

on seeing so many of their cherished forts collapse before their eyes were soon dispirited. On 14 August 1914 the Belgian government withdrew to the city. Its bombardment lasted eleven days and its surrender followed. So collapsed the greatest of the ring-fortresses. But it was not alone. Liège and Namur were similarly defended and shared a similar fate. Liège was surrounded by twelve forts, the best work of Brialmont. They were built in the 1880s to a uniform plan and originally designed to withstand a pounding from 21-centimetre (8.25in) guns. It is hardly surprising that they crumbled a quarter of a century later to the mighty 42-centimeter (16.5in) howitzers rapidly brought up by the Germans. The Liège forts were triangular, surrounded by a dry ditch protected by counterscarp galleries in the angles of the triangle. The rear side of the triangle was recessed into a bastion trace with a short central curtain and through this lay the gate. The triangular fort, including the scarp wall, was built of earth into which were sunk deep concrete magazines, barracks and gun positions so that the only things that protruded above the level of the ground were the iron cupolas with howitzers in the middle and the rear, and quick-firing guns with a searchlight

Below: *An armoured cupola at Fort Lonçin.*

Bottom: *An observation cupola at Fort de Vaux.*

and observation cupola in front. The forts lay between 5 and 6 kilometres (3–4 miles) from the city centre and were spaced about 4 kilometres apart. Fort Loncin is preserved as a national monument for it was there that in 1914, under heavy bombardment, the fort's magazine blew up, ripping out the iron cupolas like so much waste paper and slaughtering many of the gunners.

By the beginning of 1914 the reputation of permanent fortifications had suffered such a severe blow that it seemed unlikely that anyone would in future trust his defence to them and, had it not been for one fortress, this would probably have been the end of the line. As it turned out Verdun in 1916 was a very different proposition for the German army.

Verdun is an ancient city and has seen many sieges. Its second citadel was designed by Vauban. Its detached forts were erected in 1874 by Brialmont to form part of the general defensive curtain devised by General Séré de Rivières for the protection of the French frontier. Most of the forts were pentagonal with ditches filled with barbed wire and protected from caponiers. Although their construction was excellent the French were worried about the ability of

the forts to withstand heavy bombardment and in 1888 tested Fort Malmaison to destruction. As a result they modified the designs, replacing or facing masonry with reinforced concrete so that when war broke out forts like Douaumont had a covering of one metre of reinforced concrete separated from the main structure by one metre of sand. This fort, which was trapezoidal in shape, mounted twin 55-millimetre guns in a salient

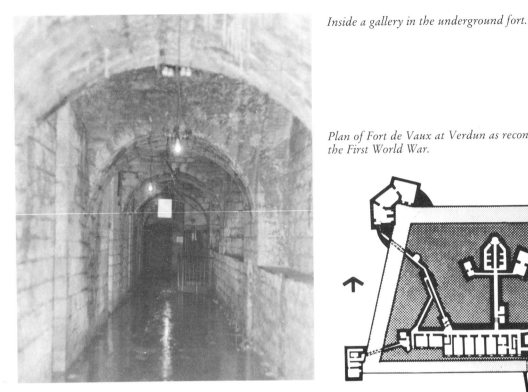

Inside a gallery in the underground fort.

Plan of Fort de Vaux at Verdun as reconstructed just before the First World War.

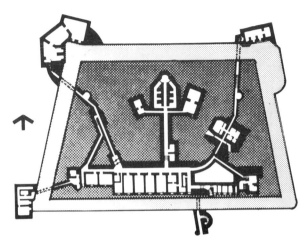

angle and two single 155-millimetre (6.1in) guns on the flanks set in iron cupolas which were raised for firing by counterweights. Close defence depended upon two outer belts of barbed wire with wire and railings in the ditch covered by machine-guns. However, with the fall of the Belgian forts the French army lost confidence in the ability of the Verdun forts to withstand a German advance and withdrew from them nearly all their main armour, with the result that when, on 21 February 1916, they faced a massive German bombardment from 'Big Berthas', the great 42-centimetre German howitzers, the forts were hardly equipped to reply. Instructions were muddled and Fort Douaumont fell to a small party of Germans with hardly a shot being fired. Then almost overnight the situation changed. General Petain issued his famous order, 'They shall not pass'. The remaining advanced forts were pounded into a mass of rubble and mud yet strangely they did not collapse and the troops were able to survive deep in the concrete dugouts. The 42-centimetre shells, whose shock in ordinary ground penetrated to a depth of 14 metres (6ft), now hit the mass of concrete and its cushion of sand without appreciable impression. The forts were well-ventilated by filtered air drawn in under slight pressure from some distance away and life was able to continue.

'France must be regarded as a great fortress,' wrote Schlieffen. With the jagged peaks of the Alps to the south, the defences ran north from the great fortress of Belfort through the high hills of the Ballon to Epinal, Toul and Verdun, the gaps in the passes filled with barrier forts. Then to the north the country was studded with powerful fortresses.

THE NEW DUTCH WATER LINE

The Dutch, like the Belgians, feared more that their country might lie in the path of the great right hook which the German army would be forced to take to outflank the fortresses in any attempt to break in upon the French citadel, than by the fear of direct invasion for the purposes of occupation. Holland had an ally – water – but not all the Dutch provinces were low-lying and capable of being flooded. In the late 1860s a plan was evolved to cut off from attack the major cities of the country. From the old fortified town of Heusden, lying to the north-east of Amsterdam close to the waters of Zuiderzee, a line of forts and water obstacles was to be drawn to Utrecht, acting as a pivot, and beyond to the broad rivers which snake to the sea across the lowlands of southern Holland. This was the New Water Line. Two of the largest works covered the approaches to Utrecht. Fort Rhijnauwen was begun in 1868 and Fort Vij Vechten in the following year. Their construction continued until about 1880.

Fort Rhijnauwen was a lopsided pentagon surrounded by a broad ditch of placid water some 6–8 metres (20–26ft) deep and about 50 metres (164ft) wide. Its front was protected by a powerful caponier completely surrounded by the ditch and at its rear, in the middle of the gorge, stood a powerful keep, or last stronghold, also pentagonal in shape with boldly projecting brick caponiers on each corner The advanced faces of the fort were terminated at their extremes by projecting caponiers and by flanks with orillons close to the main caponier. The guns were everywhere placed in barbette positions on the terreplein up to

Plan of Fort Rhijnauwen outside Utrecht.

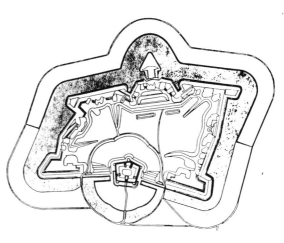

Loopholes in the caponier and the wet ditch at Fort Rhijnauwen.

Entrance to the keep-reduit at Rhijnauwen.

Fort Vij Vechten at Utrecht; plan.

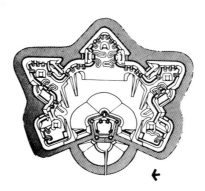

Below: *Loopholes inside the cental gallery of the keep-reduit.*

Bottom: *The underground barracks at Fort Vij Vechten.*

which they were hauled along shallow ramps. As usual in Holland, the standard of the brickwork is superb. Fort Vij Vechten was both more complex and more traditional. The same type of wet ditch surrounded the fort and the keep occupied the gorge, standing on its own small glacis resembling a stunted Norman motte. But the trace consisted of broad bastions with blunted angles.

      Brialmont had been strongly in favour of the last stand keep, but later opinion was divided. Some maintained that the keep stiffened resistance and allowed the garrison to withdraw to a position from which it might later sally out and recapture the major work. Others thought is encouraged the idea of retreat.

A French fort with guns on a cavalier, sited independently of the trace and protected by traverses: in front is a low parapet for infantry: the ditches are defended by caponiers; after Hennebert.

THE GERMAN FESTE

In the area around Strasbourg and Metz the Germans developed their most advanced thinking on fortification in the era between the Franco-Prussian War and the outbreak of the First World War in 1914. Three examples will trace this evolution. Guarding Metz in the year 1869, Fort de Queuleu is the first. It was started by the French and considerably modified by the Germans so that it consisted of a pentagonal bastion trace with masonry scarp and counterscarp walls, but the whole of the terreplein was raised as an immense earthen cavalier armed with guns for distant defence only. The only significant difference in the main French forts constructed after the war of 1870 lay in the fact that the guns no longer lined the parapets of the bastion trace, but were pulled back and grouped on the large cavalier. The bastion trace no longer fulfilled its flanking function. The ditch of Fort

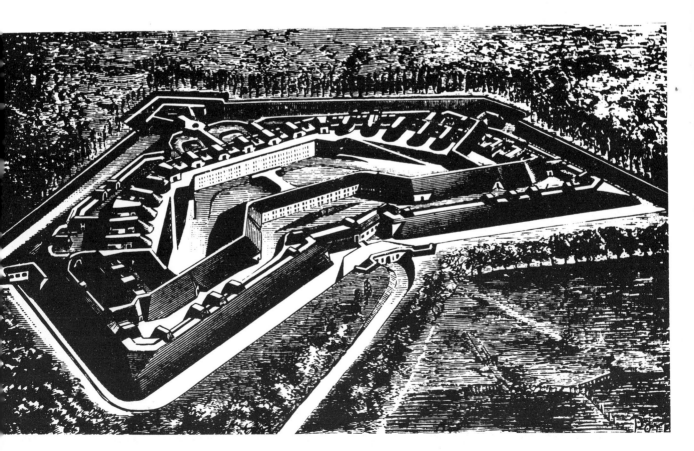

Opposite: Gun embrasure in the keep-reduit at Fort Vij Vechten.

Fort de Queuleu at Metz; plan.

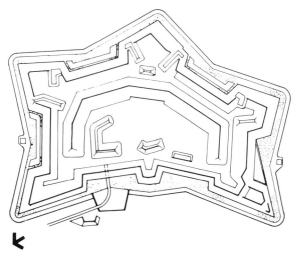

de Queuleu was flanked by counterscarp galleries beyond which were dug countermines. The gorge and the landward face of the bastion were occupied by barracks which, although loopholed on the flanks, look remarkably vulnerable to an attack from the rear. The fort was essentially somewhat conservative.

By 1893 the defensive situation had changed and the Germans, however reluctant they might have been to think in terms of fixed defences, were using their ingenuity. The new works lay at Muttzig-Molsheim on a hill not far from Strasbourg. Schlieffen had himself suggested fortifying this area, remarking 'however much it goes against our tradition to build fortifications, we cannot, as the weaker side, reject the means used by our opponent to paralyse our military plans.'

Loopholes in the rear of the barrack block covering the ditch of Fort de Queuleu.

Fort Blotten at Mutzig-Molsheim; plan.

Iron railings on the counterscarp at Fort Blotten.

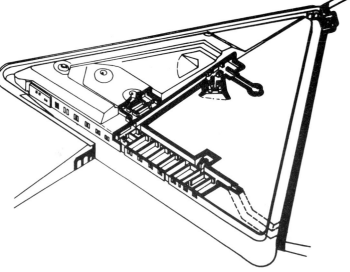

An underground passage leading to the infantry parapets, Fort de Queuleu.

At Molsheim the influence of Brialmont is apparent. Fort Kaiser Wilhelm II and Fort Blotten were both designed in the form of an equilateral triangle. The forts were surrounded by dry ditches with vertical masonry scarps and counterscarps, the ditches being covered from counterscarp galleries in the points of the triangles. There was no covered-way, but instead a high spiky iron fence enclosed the perimeter, resting on and secured to the crest of the counterscarp

An iron door seals the counterscarp gallery.

Left: *Two of the four 6-inch howitzer cupolas at Fort Blotten.*

Below: *Muzzle of a howitzer.*

wall. The middle of the triangle consisted of a compact mass of earth and concrete with four shallow-domed iron cupolas carrying the main armament of 38-centimetre (15in) howitzers in rotating turrets. Round the main armament were six quick-firing guns similarly designed but for use in close defence, and at the corners of the triangle there were iron-armoured lookouts.

Plan of a German feste, fortified Group Guentrange (Fort Ober-Gentringen) at Thionville.

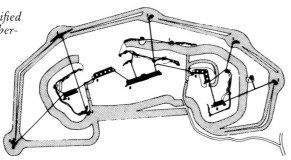

The Molsheim forts were built between 1893 and 1899, after which their surroundings were slowly modified. They show in embryonic form the group or *feste* principle of defence which was to become the most notable German contribution to permanent fortifications. The main forts mutually supported each other, but there were other batteries scattered across the hillside, the whole top of which was taken over and strung round with barbed wire emplacements. Barracks and infantry trenches were woven into the pattern of mutual defence.

The fully developed German feste was initiated about 1900 in the area around Metz and Thionville.

An underground passage joining two gun battery positions: electric cables run along the wall and the trunking of the air conditioning plant can be seen suspended from the ceiling.

An underground diesel engine room at Thionville.

A heavy steel door closes a rifle embrasure guarding a searchlight position at Thionville.

Each group occupied a large area, and there were three around Thionville: feste Ober-Gentringen (1899–1909), now given the French name of Fort de Guentrange, the feste at D'Iltrange (1903) and the fortified group Königsmacker (1908–13) forming a triangle of defence around the town.

Each occupied a large irregular area on a hilltop, surrounded by a broad ditch, in places deep and elsewhere shallow, filled with barbed wire entanglements. Lying within the wire, armoured observation posts and machine-gun emplacements communicated back to the main forts through a long deep tunnel. From the air practically nothing showed, for the forts were dug deep into the ground and encased within thick concrete. Each fort had its own concrete barracks built deep underground and independent, although joined by tunnels to its neighbours. The electricity supply was central, powered by nine diesel engines, but in all other respects the batteries could function independently. Each had a hand-operated system which controlled the ventilation and moved the armoured turrets. Each had separate 48-volt armoured searchlight positions to illuminate the approaches, flanked by concealed rifle positions. Everything could be worked from inside. Even the gun barrels could be changed and the cartridges recalibred so that they could be re-used. The telephone system was duplicated with speaking tubes running from the command post to the gun positions and the observation posts.

The merit of the feste solution lay in the fact that it could contain all the elements required for defence within a loosely grouped and irregular layout. The heavy weapons were sufficiently deployed and independently worked to prevent their being obliterated by a concentrated enemy bombardment, and flanking weapons were sufficiently closely assembled to allow adequate mutual defence. Finally close defence, in the form of entrenched infantry, was supported by the other two weapons.

CHAPTER SEVEN

A New Century: Old Concepts

Although there were occasions in the First World War when permanent fortifications such as Tsingtao and Przemysl put up a stout resistance, the final establishment of a long period of stalemate was due to the exploitation of field fortifications stiffened by wire entanglements and criss-crossed by the rapid fire of machine-guns.

Tsingtao Fortress was the pride of the German colonies in the Far East. The port lay on a peninsula of the China coast and in front stood four armoured forts constructed at great expense with cupola batteries of 70-centimetre (27.5in) howitzers and 60- and 38-centimetre (23.6in and 15in) guns. Beyond these stretched the minefield and the wire entanglements, illuminated by searchlights in disappearing cupolas, and beyond all that infantry trenches. The Japanese attacked on 27 August 1914 but it took them a month to reduce the German positions during which

time the Germans carried out, for the first time, an aerial bombardment on the Japanese ships that were shelling the forts.

Przemysl was the Austrian Verdun, fortified by a ring of nineteen large forts and twenty-three smaller works designed after the manner of Brialmont and stretching in a circuit of 48 kilometres (30 miles). The forts, originally constructed in stone in the 1880s, were later modified by the addition of heavy concrete as those at Verdun had been treated. The Russian siege opened on 11 November 1914 but the fortress stood firm for over four months until all food was exhausted.

The value of field fortifications had been known from earliest times. They had been used with effect in the Italian wars at the turn of the fifteenth century, but the long period which had seen the growth of the most elaborate systems of permanent fortification had tended to cloud any assessment of the value of their more temporary relative. The Russo-

A Russian field fort one mile south of Liao-Yang, 1904.

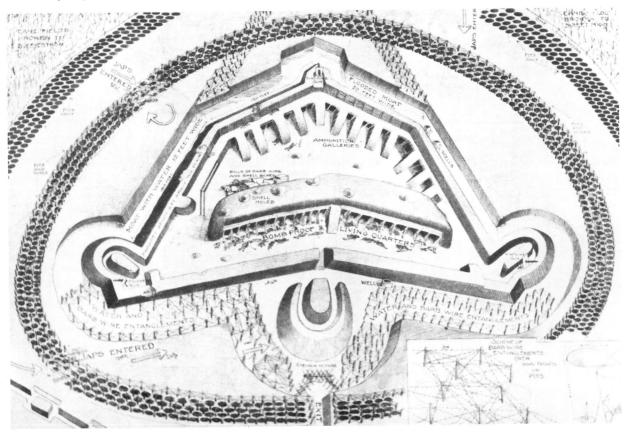

*The Russians constructing field fortifications and laying out
barbed wire entanglements at Port Arthur; after Cassell's*
History of the Russo-Japanese War.

Turkish War of 1877 redressed the balance and brought to the attention of the western army commands the value of hastily improvised earth defences which received the name 'provisional fortification'. In about six weeks around Adrianople the Turks threw up a chain of twenty-four provisional redoubts, and farther back, barring the road to Constantinople, Bluhm Pasha, with equal rapidity, constructed the famous Lines of Tschataldscha. General Montgomery has summed up the contribution: 'The success of the resistance put up by the Turks astonished contemporary Europe. Osman Pasha's field fortifications pointed to the character of future fighting between armies armed with rifles.'

The Russo-Japanese War of 1904 only acted to strengthen the conviction that the immediate future lay with field fortifications. The military textbooks had to be largely rewritten. The forts south of Liao-Yang were well-prepared earthworks surrounded by wet ditches and meshed with wire entanglements, and beyond lay two rings of deep circular pits each with a sharp spike upon which to trap a fallen man, and the inner ring was criss-crossed with barbed wire. Machine-guns covered the obstacles from the angles of the fort and the garrison had well-protected bomb-proof living accommodation. Eleven similar redoubts guarded the town and the Japanese paid dearly for their capture. One redoubt alone took a death toll of 3000.

The main defences of Port Arthur stretched in a zone 5 kilometres (3 miles) deep. Locked in a web of permanent forts was a tangled mass of hastily thrown-up redoubts and excavated trenches which kept the Japanese at bay for six months. The Japanese infantry were held up on barbed wire, mown down by machine-gun and rifle fire and illuminated by star

shells and searchlights when they sought the concealment of darkness. Only after recourse to extensive
sapping and mining could General Nogi's men slowly
break through to the town with heavy loss of life:
60,000 were killed and over 33,000 wounded. Both the
price they paid and the effort they expended in finally
overcoming the defence forecast the holocaust of the
Western Front.

LESSONS OF THE FIRST WORLD WAR

As it turned out it was a very different war to what
had been expected. From the rapid movement in the
early stages, the First World War ground to a halt in
an entangled impenetrable mass in which the attackers
became enmeshed, a stalemate of improvised trenches
and barbed wire entanglements which stretched from
the Swiss border to the Channel ports. It became the
largest concentration of field fortifications the world
had ever known.

The opening phases were all movement. The
line of the old traditional French fortresses, many of
which had been modernised, made its impact on German strategy. Fearful of the failure of a frontal attack
on those forts, the German army instead drove fast
into Belgium and, on the first day of hostilities, the
blow fell on Liège. Its girdle of forts had been modernised at enormous expense, armed with revolving
and retracting guns in steel cupolas, but the Germans
drove through the ill-prepared gaps between the forts,
not one of which fell, and captured the city. Then,
bringing up heavy howitzers, the lightest of which was
more powerful than anything against which the forts
had been designed, they pounded them into submission. Namur, similarly ringed by forts and Antwerp
with its circuit of over 95 kilometres (60 miles) and a
garrison of 100,000 troops suffered similar fates.
Mauberge, the only French fortress to be attacked,
despite its age and antiquated character, stood for elev-
en days mainly because its garrison was able to conduct an active defence and there were adequate forces
in the intervals.

When the war settled down to stalemate,
every effort was made by both sides to break through
to victory – every device was tried. Aircraft were used
to spot targets for the guns so that the nature of concealment changed from a use of cover to a use of camouflage. Bomber aircraft began to destroy areas in the
rear containing stores and ammunition previously safe
from bombardment. Guns of larger calibre were
mounted on railway trucks. Concentrations of artillery firing shrapnel laid down creeping barrages to cut
barbed wire and destroy machine-guns in the path of
an advance. Hand grenades were used in quantity to
increase the lethal effect of close fighting. Poison gas,
one of the oldest weapons, was used in new, frightening concentrations but, when its surprise use failed to
achieve a break-through, it lost much of its power
against protected troops. However, it did have the advantage that it could penetrate into the deepest shelter.
Large explosive mines were used, of a power never
seen before. And finally, the tank, a weapon of ancient
origin in a new guise, was thrown into the battle to
trample barbed wire entanglements and enemy
machine-gun posts. But the machines were at first un-
reliable, hindred by adverse ground conditions and
not used in sufficient concentrations to achieve the
critical break-through.

In defence, the intricate interwoven lines of
earthwork trenches, laced with barbed wire entanglements, were strengthened with reinforced-concrete
pillboxes, difficult to hit and largely resistant to shell
fire. Deep dugouts, often made of concrete on the
German side, provided bombproof casemates from
which the troops could emerge as soon as the creeping
barrage had passed, to arrest with devastating effect
the waves of advancing infantry who had expected a
'walk-over'. And so, until both sides were exhausted,
the slogging match went on.

IMPACT OF THE FIRST WORLD WAR

Curiously, nations reacted differently to the conditions brought about by the long periods of stalemate
experienced in the First World War and to the heavy
losses incurred in capturing each yard of ground.
Whereas France sought to take advantage of what
appeared to be a situation biased in favour of defence,
Germany searched for a method to break through or
circumvent any lines of defence in a future lightning
war which would paralyse her enemies. Benefiting
from the development of two weapons, the fast tank
and the dive-bomber, she prepared to implement a
modified Schlieffen Plan which had failed in 1914
largely through lack of speed on the part of the attackers. Germany had not been able to advance on two

General Nicolas standing beside a Mougin turret armed with twin 155-millimetre guns at Fort Barbonnet.

selves in with well designed modern fortifications.

For France it was an urgent task to build new fortifications, mainly along the north-eastern border but also in the north facing Belgium and the south-east facing Italy. The system proposed by Séré de Rivière consisted of strong, entrenched camps (usually towns surrounded by a ring of forts), lines of forts spaced 5 to 10 kilometres (3–6 miles) apart and acting as defensive curtains, plus isolated forts covering road and railway approaches or mountain passes. Older forts were incorporated into the system. There was a second line and some safety positions set further back, and three screens to cover the capital at Paris.

The forts were polygonal in shape, surrounded by narrow dry ditches protected by caponiers, and they mounted twenty to thirty guns firing in the open, separated by traverses and placed on top of the central barracks or around the perimeter of the fort. There was considerable variation in design, some of the larger forts holding sixty guns and some with armoured casemates with guns protected by cast iron shields. In other forts a rotating Mougin turret, first proposed in 1876, covered twin 155-millimetre (6.1in) guns fired by electricity.

It was an impressive programme. By 1885, 166 main forts, 43 smaller ones and about 200 batteries had been built. In the following year they began to update them to resist the more powerful shells filled with melinite and lyddite. Most of the guns were then moved into the intervals between the forts which became observation posts and infantry strongpoints, their masonry covered with sand and an outer layer of rounded masses of concrete. After 1897 reinforced-concrete was used.

sides of a triangle as fast as France could move her armies into position across the shorter base of the triangle by means of an efficient railroad system.

The French answer to the threat of invasion was the construction of the Maginot Line, the most ambitious and the most thorough piece of permanent fortification the world had ever seen. It was to be misjudged by public opinion and used as a scapegoat for the rapid defeat of France in the Second World War.

THE SÉRÉ DE RIVIÈRE LINE

The defence of the frontier had occupied French military minds for generations. Louis XIV, using Vauban, had built a large number of individual fortresses at enormous cost. In 1874 General Séré de Rivière proposed the construction of a barrier to run all the way from Calais to Nice with, behind it, a general defensive scheme stretching in depth as far as Paris. The idea was to cover the whole line of frontier, to absorb the initial shock of attack and provide time for the full mobilisation of the French army. This defensive thinking was deep-rooted in France. The line of 1874 was to follow the most easily defensible ground, the heights above the Meuse and the Moselle, rather than to attempt to defend the artificially created frontier of the country. This was particularly important as France, having been defeated by the Prussians in the war of 1870–71, lost Alsace and a large part of Lorraine where the Germans soon began to dig them-

THE MAGINOT LINE

The purpose of the Maginot Line was quite different. Primarily intended to defend the industrial basin of Lorraine with its iron and steel works, an area that had passed back to France at the end of the First World War and which lay outside the defensive belts of earlier generations, the Maginot Line was extended west to the Belgian frontier and south-east through the Alps and along the frontier with Italy to join the Mediterranean coast at Menton. Further casemates and blockhouses were built on Corsica. The Maginot Line was not of even strength. The first part of the Line

Fort L'Agaisen: on the left is a steel raising turret for a 75 millimetre howitzer.

The Maginot Line forts in the Alpes Maritime: a machine-gun cupola with a periscope on the gros-ouvrage *of L'Agaisen.*

followed the north-eastern border with Germany from Longwy, some 50 kilometres (30 miles) west of Metz, to the River Rhine. The most strongly held sector was in the area of Metz and Thionville. East of this there was a gap to be protected by inundation to the River Sarré and by the field army. To the west the Ardennes provided more rugged terrain which needed to be less strongly held and the Vosges Mountains had smaller, lighter blockhouses. In the high Alps the main task was to cover the approaches through the alpine passes with separate forts, but the line was almost continous for about 55 kilometres (34 miles) to the coast of the Mediterranean. Wherever possible older forts were modernised there and brought into the system of defence. To the west the ideal line of defence was not available for fortification by France for it lead through neutral Belgium and the forts around Liège, Namur and Antwerp to the Channel ports.

The line got its name from André Maginot, who as Minister of War was the driving force who got the project accepted. The basic design was worked out in 1927 by General Belhague, Inspector General of Fortifications, with the help of Frossard. Its design can

be seen as a culmination of the long process of development which had evolved by way of the strongly protected underground fort with guns firing from heavily armoured cupolas. The French were fully conversant with the German feste at Metz.

Work began in 1929 and, with the exception of the defences in the Alps, was largely complete on the outbreak of the Second World War. Subsequently defences in depth were added and were being built when the Germans and Italians attacked in 1940.

The long gap to the Channel ports should

The gros-ouvrage *of Sainte Agnes: the majestic form of the reinforced-concrete gun casemates. This fort is on the hillside above the coast of the Mediterranean.*

have been defended by older fortresses and the main French and British field armies. Many Frenchmen agreed with Petain that 'the northern frontier can only be defended by advancing into Belgium'. For political reasons such a step could not be taken by the French without the wholehearted collaboration of the Belgians, who were reluctant to compromise their neutrality for fear of offending Germany. In the event their attitude gave them no protection against Germany and no co-ordinated assistance from the allies. In a *blitzkrieg* attack the German armies in 1940 flooded through Belgium into France, splitting the French army and isolating the British in the great right hook which had been the essence of the Schlieffen Plan of 1906. Its success exceeded all expectations, even those of the German General Staff. From the Maginot Line the French moved out their remaining field armies and thinned down the garrison. But left half naked, the defences still proved their capabilities. In a series of frontal attacks the German army was able to make no progress except on the little fort of La Ferté which, lying on the extreme left of the line and being partly unsupported, fell to the Germans on 19 May 1940. No other fort on the Maginot Line fell to German attack and none was seriously damaged. Only after the downfall of France and on instructions from the French government did the Maginot Line surrender. It had achieved its purpose, to defend Alsace-Lorraine and to force the Germans to concentrate their attack at the one point where the French field armies should have been ready and able to hold them. If the French nation was lulled into a feeling of false security, it was due largely to the misleading articles in the press which falsely suggested that the whole line of the French frontier was invulnerable. The main cause of the collapse of France must be sought in the thoroughness of the German preparations and the brilliance and audacity of their attack.

In June 1940 the Italians attacked with a numerical superiority of more than three to one but were unable to capture a single Maginot Line fortification. They suffered heavy casualties, even from the old 155-millimetre nineteenth century guns in the Mougin turret at the Séré de Rivière Fort Barbonnet which were still able to fire with effect.

The purposes of the Maginot Line had been threefold: to try to prevent a major war being fought

on French soil, to protect the industrial basin of Alsace-Lorraine, and to provide an armoured shield behind which the French army could mobilise. French manpower, decimated in the First World War, was in a critical state. The population of France was falling whereas that of Germany was rising and it was realised that the shortage of manpower in the important age groups would become apparent after 1935 and would be serious by 1939. Any system that could conserve manpower would help France – thus the need for new fortifications.

With this in mind the Maginot Line was designed. In the front of the Line there were fortified houses at the border crossings to delay any surprise attack. Then further back lay the *avant-postes*, stronger reinforced-concrete blockhouses shielded by anti-tank obstacles – either pieces of railway line set into the ground or chunks of concrete. The main line of resistance began some 5 to 10 kilometres (3–6 miles) back from the border and consisted of a line of reinforced-concrete casemates which, wherever possible, followed the ridge lines. Designed to a standard plan, they were modified to suit individual sites and consisted of two storeys – a basement for the garrison of up to about one officer and thirty soldiers, and a casemated ground floor with embrasures for infantry weapons firing to the flanks and screened from enemy view. The concrete walls were up to 3.5 metres (11½ft) thick, covered with earth or built into a hillside. In front of the embrasures there was a ditch protected by grenade chutes. The only things visible to the enemy were the dome-shaped cast steel observation cloches which projected from the flat roof. They could also have machine-guns in them. Each casemate was self-supporting for about a month with its own electric power and water supply. To exclude poison gas and expel smoke from the weapons the air was filtered and maintained at a pressure higher than outside. This was the system adopted throughout the Maginot Line.

The *avant-postes* were encircled by barbed wire entanglements and anti-tank obstacles. In areas of strength, the *avant-postes* were supported by the main forts called *ouvrages*, named according to the armament they contained. They consisted of the smaller *petit-ouvrages* which contained infantry weapons, and the *gros-ouvrages* with infantry and artillery weapons, sometimes holding a garrison of more than 1000 men.

The *ouvrages* consisted of standardised reinforced-concrete components modified to suit individual sites so that no two are identical.

A typical *petit-ouvrage* might consist of three spaced out blockhouses surrounded by barbed wire and railway lines as anti-tank obstacles. There would be two casemates with machine-guns and anti-tank guns firing from one of their long sides to the flanks, and one turret block sunk into the ground with a revolving retracting trunk with raising and rotating mechanism. In addition there were usually one or two steel observation cloches on the roof. The casemates and the turret block were joined by underground galleries to the barrack accommodation set some twenty to thirty metres below ground. The garrison usually consisted of from 2 to 4 officers and 100 to 150 men.

The *gros-ouvrages* were the strongest works with garrisons from 500 to over 1000 strong. Usually the works consisted of a number of combat blocks on the line of resistance with, behind and some 20 or more metres (+65ft) below ground, a support area and two entrance blocks. All were joined by underground galleries of communication. The fighting zone consisted of reinforced-concrete infantry blocks rather like those used on the *petit-ouvrages*, artillery casemates, artillery turret blocks and observation blocks. Only the small armoured cupolas of the retractable turrets and the fixed domed observation cloches, some with projecting periscopes, showed above the ground. The artillery was housed on the upper floor of the two-storey blocks, firing either through steel turrets on the roof, or through embrasures in the walls of the casemates. All the guns were purpose-made for the Maginot Line. The gunners remembered how those in the Verdun forts had been removed early in the First World War and used elsewhere as field pieces. They were not going to let that happen again. The new guns could only be used in the Line. They were specially designed to fit into the steel turrets, or to be anchored by means of a tight ball joint to the mouth of an embrasure thus preventing enemy splinters and bullets entering the casemates.

The main armament consisted of 81-millimetre (3.2in) breech-loading mortars, 135-millimetre (5.3in) howitzers called *lance bombes*, or bomb throwers, and 75-millimetre (3in) mortars, four 95-millimetre (3.7in) naval guns in one casemate, and even

A detail of the elaborate form of the concrete above an armoured casemate, designed to deflect shot.

some nineteenth century weapons which were to prove still effective in action. Each turret mounted two guns which fired in the raised position through embrasures in its face and were covered by a shallow steel dome some 30–35 centimetres (11.8–13.8in) thick. Turrets had all round fields of fire, casemates flanked the Line and supported neighbouring forts, except in the Alps where some guns fired forwards into the passes. By using supporting fire it was possible to kill paratroopers who had landed on top of adjoining forts, something which could not be done to help the Belgians in Fort Eben-Emael when it was attacked by that method in 1940.

Although mounted in pairs, each turret gun had its own arms hoist and the pair could be raised,

rotated and lowered by electricity or by hand if necessary. To minimise the effect of fumes, empty shell cases were discharged into the depth of the *ouvrage* through long chutes.

For their protection, the casemate blocks were built into the reverse slope of hills or artificial mounds and their concrete faces were stepped back in a serrated manner.

From each combat block a staircase and lifts descended to the gallery level some 20 or more metres (+65ft) below ground. The only connection between the combat blocks was at that lower level which contained the main command post for co-ordinating the defence and directing the fire of the weapons, both infantry and artillery. At this lower level ammunition

Fort L'Agaisen; two 81-millimetre breech-loading mortars, each mounted at a fixed angle of 45 degrees and secured to the embrasure by means of a ball joint.

was stored in metal cages and moved about on overhead rails.

The support area, like a small town set deep underground, was located several hundred metres to the rear, joined by a gallery and usually serviced by an electric railway or *metro*, which forked to the barracks and the quite separate main magazine. This could be blocked off by a massive blast door. The barracks contained all the facilities needed for living, sleeping, feeding and washing, and also had a hospital – but there were no recreational facilities. It must have been a damp, unpleasant place in which to live, but in peacetime the soldiers were quartered in ordinary barracks behind the lines, only moving underground on the outbreak of war. Each *ouvrage* drew electricity from the national grid, but also had its own independent generators.

Near the support area but on the surface stood two entrance blocks – one for the barracks and power station, the other for the magazine. They were strong, fortified reinforced-concrete blockhouses screened from enemy view and fire and approached over ditches on steel draw- or rolling bridges. Each had a vehicle entrance and a small pedestrian entrance with its own bridge.

The largest *ouvrage* was at Hackenberg and one can get some impression of its size from the 10 kilometres (6 miles) of underground galleries and over 300 kilometres (186 miles) of railway lines.

The Maginot Line should not be thought of as an isolated phenomenon, but as part of the logical development of European fortifications which, under the threat of ever heavier bombardment, were sunk lower into the ground, covered generation after generation by a greater thickness of protection in reinforced-concrete, sand and other materials.

THE BENES LINE

Other nations had been convinced of the validity of the Maginot Line and had sought to copy it. Realising the vulnerability of their long frontier with Germany when Hitler came to power, Czechoslovakia, on French advice, began in September 1937 to build a fortified line, called in the West the Benes Line, consisting of fourteen *ouvrages* or artillery strongholds stretching from Ostrava to the Giant Mountains (Krkonose). After the Munich Agreement work was stopped and the system remained unfinished. The Czechs had modelled their defences on the Maginot Line so that when the Germans marched into the country they were able to study its construction at leisure. The Dobrosov artillery stronghold was one typical example of the work. It had a garrison of 500 soldiers in underground barracks joined by 750 metres (820yds) of galleries. Its steel turrets housed twin 100-millimetre (3.9in) guns or 100-millimetre howitzers in curved revolving cupolas only a small portion of which projected above ground. The single 100-millimetre howitzers and the 76-millimetre and 47-millimetre cannon in the casemates swivelled on close fitting ball-bearings in the apertures, and the steel-lined embrasures were serrated to deflect enemy splinters. The walls and the roof were up to 3.5 metres (11½ ft) thick. Bren guns and grenade chutes covered the ditches. The border lay about two kilometres (1¼ miles) in front of Dobrosov and between it and the stronghold stood eight infantry blockhouses.

The Poles began to fortify with lines in 1931 and the Yugoslavs in 1936. In Holland and Belgium there were less powerful versions of the Maginot Line in the Grebbe, Peel and Dyle Lines, but they should have been formidable obstacles.

A revolving machine-gun cupola on the Benes Line.

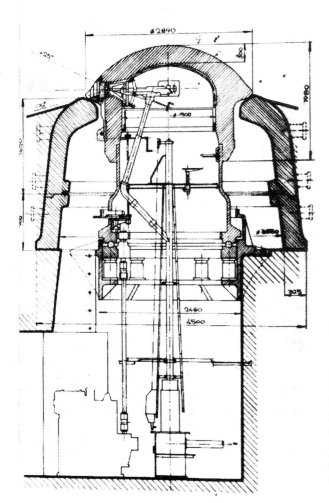

FORT EBEN-EMAEL

The story of the fall of Fort Eben-Emael in Belgium is most interesting. The fort lay at the end of a line of modern Belgian forts, its task to defend the River Meuse and the new cut of the Albert Canal over which spanned two bridges vital to a German army if it were to penetrate the Belgian defences.

The fort had been built in 1931 and had many features in common with the *gros-ouvrages* of the Maginot Line. It was a six-sided design protected by a ditch on the sides not parallel to the Albert Canal, but from the air it looked almost triangular in shape. It was powerfully armed with four 120-millimetre (4.7in) and four 75-millimetre (3in) guns mounted in steel turrets on the roof, and with twelve 75-millimetre

(3in) casemated guns which covered the key bridges over the the canal and the approaches. Lifts fed ammunition to the guns from galleries on two levels deep below ground. The upper one contained the magazine, command post, power station and infirmary, the lower one, some 40 metres (130ft) down, the barrack accommodation for the large garrison of 1440 men. To deceive the enemy there were also dummy cupolas on the roof. It was an impressive modern design and should have held off any German advance, but in 1940 it did not.

The Germans planned their assault in great secrecy, Hitler masterminding the operation himself. To attack the fort, the Germans had to violate Dutch territory, thus bringing that country into the war. German gliders were used because, when the towing aircraft released them over German territory, they could glide in silently to their target. Crash landing on the fort itself and in front of the two bridges, the paratroopers attacked the unsuspecting garrison of Fort Eben-Emael. Using, for the first time in warfare, hollow charges which punched holes into the thick steel armour of the turrets, causing splinters to rip off their inner surfaces, the paratroopers were able, within ten minutes, to blind the fort so that its guns could not fire on the all-important Meuse bridges. They captured the fort and held the bridges long enough to permit German tanks, sweeping through the adjoining strip of Holland, to come up and cross the Albert Canal.

THE WEST WALL

The Germans in 1936 began construction on their great West Wall. It is sometimes called the Siegfried Line, which is confusing, because that was also the name given to a defensive line built by the Germans in 1918 from Cambrai to St Quentin. By 1940 the West Wall stretched from the Swiss frontier to Aachen in the north. It was called by the British troops in France the Siegfried Line upon which they were determined to 'hang out our washing'. The line was hurried in execution and its forts were less complex than those in the Maginot Line, but it was an immensely wide fortified area stretching in places to a depth of 32 kilometres (20 miles). It consisted of a series of heavy reinforced-concrete bunkers similar in conception to the French *avant-postes*, whose fire criss-crossed the

The Atlantic Wall: a model of a German coast defence
casemate armed with a 150-millimetre gun. (Mark Grundy)

area and supported the main forts which acted as the strongpoints of the defence. The purpose of the West Wall was to hold a front with the minimum number of troops against any possible French counterattack, whilst allowing the main armies to attack Poland or the gap in the defences on the left of the French lines.

HITLER'S ATLANTIC WALL

The most ambitious project of all was begun by the Germans after the break out of their forces through Belgium, Holland and France in 1940. As a result of her conquests, Germany acquired a long coastline stretching from the northern tip of Norway to the Spanish frontier.

Work on fortifications in the Pas de Calais began as part of an offensive programme against Britain – preparations for invasion. The navy placed heavy guns there to seal off the Straits of Dover and bombard the English coast. These guns were given reinforced-concrete protection against air attack by the RAF. When the invasion of Britain was abandoned and particularly after Pearl Harbor when Hitler realised he must face the full power of the United States, in December 1941 the policy was changed to one of defence of Fortress Europe, 'designed to stand for a thousand years'. The Continent was to be sealed off with a fortified line of reinforced concrete; 300,000 troops stood guard and Hitler called for the building

of 15,000 strongpoints stretching from Norway to Spain. The target date for completion was May 1943. German industry was to be harnessed to the task with a massive output of cement and steel for reinforcement. Much of the work was undertaken by the Todt Organisation, under the direction of Fritz Todt until his death in March 1942, and then of the architect, Albert Speer.

When Rommel took over as Inspector General of Defences in October 1943 the work was far from complete. It was never intended that it should be of equal strength along the whole line, but Holland and the Belgian and French coasts, plus the Channel Islands were particularly strongly fortified. Rommel was to write, 'never in history was there a defence of such an extent, with such an obstacle of the sea. The enemy must be annihilated before he reaches our main battlefield. We must stop him in the water, not only delaying him but destroying all his equipment while it is still afloat.'

The permanent defences were supported by field fortifications and stiffened by obstacles on the beaches and in the sea. The defences had to be built to withstand both naval and air bombardment. It was thought that the Allies, if they were to invade successfully, must capture a port, so all the French ports were to be strongly held to the last man. In the event, the Allies brought their harbours with them – the prefabricated Mulberry Harbours.

The key to the successful construction of the Atlantic Wall was standardisation. The various buildings were broken down into types, each being given a code number or letter. Standard specifications described the cubic content of the concrete, the amount of steel reinforcement needed, and gave details of all the shuttering. An illustrated manual with drawings and perspectives was available to help engineers and gunners choose suitable structures for any particular site. A large labour force, most of it slave labour from conquered nations, was pressed into service. At times half a million men were working on the Wall. Some 13,000,000 cubic metres (17,000,000cu yds) of reinforced-concrete were used and over 30,000 standardised structures built.

There are six main groups: gun sites, bunkers, observation posts, command posts, U-boat pens, and V1 and V2 rocket sites.

Two views of a strong double armoured observation turret observing the coast at Noirmont, Jersey, part of a German battery command post.

The gun sites were covered by standardised casemates built to a number of sizes and shapes to house the large variety of guns collected from conquered armies. The navy tended to get the new guns and the army what was left over. Thus it was not possible to build casemates with tight fitting apertures like those on the Maginot Line. Most of the guns had to be loose fitting, their crews protected by steel shields and by the reinforced-concrete embrasure that was serrated, or stepped outwards to deflect shell and bomb splinters. In design a balance had to be struck between maximum fire power, protective cover and concealment or camouflage. Attached to the back of the casemates were bunkers for crew accommodation. These were to be blast- and gas-proof, protected by thick concrete walls and roofs of standard dimensions. Where possible steel reinforcement was used as the permanent shuttering for roofs. Units were not enlarged but standard components were repeated using modular control and mathematical precision.

The observation posts could range in size from steel armoured turrets set in concrete pits and

One of the old towers at Gorey Castle, Jersey, converted into a German observation post.

aerial bombing the ships and their crews on returning to port, and to provide large underground facilities for repair and maintenance.

The V1s or 'flying bombs' as they were called, were pilotless planes stored in reinforced-concrete structures then taken to a launching site which consisted of two reinforced-concrete ramps aimed as England with protective soil piled on each side. The launching sites were vulnerable and most were destroyed by the RAF.

A chain is as strong as its weakest link. Rommel always feared the blow would fall on the Normandy coast, which was not the most strongly held section of the Wall, whereas the High Command thought the Allies would land near Calais. For all the impressive preparations and industry, the Wall crumbled and the Allies gained a foothold on the Continent which was to lead to final victory.

In retrospect one can see the qualities of the Atlantic Wall and these were not only military for its products were architectural, consciously designed and following a long architectural tradition of German Futurism. It was more than an architectural function for it contained intrinsic qualities of design.

BRITAIN'S PRECAUTIONS AGAINST INVASION AND ATTACK

In contrast to the German Atlantic Wall with its carefully controlled modular co-ordination of all the parts and spaces, and its monumental architectural appearance, it never looked as though anyone enjoyed designing or building the British pillboxes. They were thought up and pushed up in a great rush, and they look like it. For example in May 1940 one British general telephoned a building contractor to see if he could build two hundred pillboxes along 80 kilometres (50 miles) of coastline in three weeks, bearing in mind the shortage of cement, steel reinforcement and timber.

There were some standard British designs prepared by the Directorate of Fortifications and Works, based on practice in the First World War and upon experience gained in northern France in 1939, but the standard designs were, in typical British fashion, varied by local designers and builders who either thought they knew better, or had to make adaptations to suit local conditions and the availability of materials.

equipped with periscopes and plugged apertures for small arms to multi-storey towers holding large garrisons like those found on the Channel Islands. Sometimes old towers were converted with great care to this new use and many of the posts displayed fine architectural and aesthetic qualities.

Command posts which received information and data from observation posts, radar, etc, were often multi-storey blocks consisting of slabs of reinforced concrete with thin slits for vision. There was a variety of demands – combat, signal, rangefinding and support posts, and radar stations.

At the main submarine bases U-boat pens had to be constructed to protect from the heaviest

A British naval fort built in the River Thames and mounted with anti-aircraft guns. (Model by Dale H Jennings)

By February 1942 it was all over – the threat of invasion had evaporated.

Probably the most impressive defence structures erected in Britain during the Second World War were the sea forts that were built on land, floated out to sea and sunk to rest on the bed of the Thames and Mersey estuaries. They were designed to protect the vulnerable approaches to London and Liverpool from air attack, from minelaying and against Geman E-boat raids. The idea originated in the concrete Nab Towers, two of which had been built at the end of the First World War to be taken out to sea and sunk in the English Channel to block the Straits of Dover.

Each naval fort, designed by a civil engineer, G A Maunsell, consisted of a boat-shaped pontoon cast in reinforced-concrete. On to this two large cylindrical concrete towers or drums, each with a diameter of 7.3 metres (24ft) and a height of 18 metres (60ft), were mounted. On top of these there was a steel deck which mounted two 3.7-inch AA guns and two 40-millimetre Bofors guns, plus radar and other equipment. There was also living accommodation for a crew of 120. Once in position, the water was let into the concrete pontoons which sank to the sea bed. Four

forts were placed at the entrance to the Thames estuary.

The army forts were different. They each consisted of a group of pods, each on four concrete legs which rested on foundations sank in the bed of the rivers. From a nucleus containing gun controls and garrison accommodation, steel bridges radiated to the pods on which were mounted four 3.7-inch AA guns and a Bofors – a strong armament intended to deal with heavy air raids and later used against V1 'flying bombs'. Seven army forts were built within the estuaries of the Thames and the Mersey.

CONCLUSION

The mighty fortifications of concrete provide a fitting climax to any study of military architecture. Whether they will be the last of the line of development stretching back to ancient Mesopotamia, or the beginning of a new underground world, predicted by H G Wells and occasioned by the devastating power of atomic explosion, only time can tell. Man has shown an infinite capacity to protect himself by artificial means: let us hope that this facility does not now desert him.

BIBLIOGRAPHY

JAMES ACKERMAN, *The Architecture of Michelangelo*, 2 vols (London 1961).

ALAIN ALBARIC, *Aigues-Mortes* (Chateau-de-Valence, Gard 1968).

LEON BATTISTA ALBERTI, *De re aedificatoria* (Rome 1485).

——, *I primi tre libri della famiglia*, (c1435–4). See G Mancini, *I libri della famiglia* (Forence 1908).

——, *Ten Books on Architecture*, translated into Italian by Cosimo Bartoli, into English by James Leoni, edited by Joseph Rykewert (facsimile, London 1965).

WILLIAM ALLCORN, *A Guide to the Fortifications of Northwestern Europe*, edited and illustrated by Quentin Hughes (Liverpool 1983).

——, 'The Maginot Line in Northern France' *Fort* 14, (1986), pp79–108.

——, 'The Maginot Line in the Alps', *Fort* 15 (1987), pp135–152.

GALASSO ALGHISI, *Delle fortificationi . . . libri tre* (Venice 1570).

WILLIAM ANDERSON, *Castles of Europe from Charlemagne to the Renaissance*, (London 1970).

ANON, *Sketch of the Defences of the Western and Swiss Frontiers of Germany*, (London 1988).

ANON, *Nouveau Manuel de Fortification Permanente* (Paris 1895).

ELLIS ASHMEAD-BARTLETT, *Port Arthur: the Siege and Capitulation*, (London 1906).

LT-COL BAINBRIDGE, 'Notes on the Defence of Coasts', *Professional Papers of the Royal Engineers*, new series, Vol IX (1860).

ALAN BALFOUR, *Portsmouth* (London 1970).

CORRELLI BARNETT *Britain and her Army: 1509–1970* (London 1970).

G C BASCAPE and C PEROGALLI, *Castelli del Lazio* (Milan 1968).

EVERSLEY BELFIELD, *Sieges*, London 1967.

LUCIANO BERTI, 'Studies for the Fortifications of Florence (1528–30)', in *The Complete Works of Michelangelo*, Vol II (London 1966).

CHARLES BISSET, *The Theory and Construction of Fortification* (London 1751).

JANUSZ BOGDANOWSKI, 'Fortyfikacja austriacka na ziemiach polskich', *Studia i materialy do Historii Wojskowsci* (Warsaw 1966).

M LE BLOND, *The Military Engineer or a treatise on the attack and defence of all kinds of fortified places* (London 1759).

T S R BOASE, *Castles and Churches of the Crusading Kingdom* (London 1967).

A BOINET, *Le Château de Pierrefonds* (Paris 1930).

JOSEPH BORDWINE, *Memoir of a Proposed New System of Permanent Fortification* (London 1834).

MARIANO BORGATTI, *La fortificazione permanente contemporanea*, 2 vols (Turin 1898).

JACQUES BOUDET, *The Ancient Art of Warfare*, 2 vols (London 1966).

GEORGIUS BRAUN and FRANZ HOGENBERG, *Civitates orbis terrarum (Cologne 1572)*; facsimile in 6 parts, III volumes with introduction by R A Skelton (Amsterdam 1965).

HENRI BRIALMONT, *La Défense des Côtes, etc* (Brussels 1896).

ERIC BROCKMAN, *The Two Sieges of Rhodes, 1480–1522* (London 1969).

C A DE BRUIJN and H R REINDERS, *Nederlandse Vestingen* (Bussum 1967).

GENERAL SIR JOHN F BURGOYNE, 'Coast Batteries', *Corps Papers of the Royal Engineers*, Vol I (1849–50). 'On Coast Defences, *Professional Papers of the Royal Engineers*', new series, vol. VI (1857).

JOHN BURY, 'Are Renaissance fortifications beautiful?', *Fort* 8 (1980), pp7–20.

FRANCOIS BUTTIN, *Les Propulseurs de Léonard de Vinci* (Paris 1965).

——, *Bull de la S P F* LXI, No 1 (1964).

IGNAZIO CALVI, *L'Architettura Militare di Leonardo da Vinci* (Milan 1943).

——, 'Military Engineering and Arms', in *Leonardo da Vinci* (London 1957).

LAZARE-NICOLAS MARGUERITE, COUNT CARNOT, *De la défense des places fortes. . . . Mémoire sur la fortification primitive, etc* (Paris 1810).

——, *A Treatise on the defence of Fortified Places: Written under the direction and published by command of Buonaparte*, translated by Baron de Montalembert (London 1814).

R J CASSELL, *Cassell's History of the Russo-Japanese War*, 3 vols, (London, Paris, New York & Melbourne 1904–5).

GIROLAMO CATANEO, *Opera nuoua di fortificare, offendere et diffendre . . .* (Brescia 1564).

PIETRO CATANEO, *I quattro primi libri di architettura di P Cataneo* (Venice 1554).

MARIO CEOLA, *La guerra sotteranea attraverso i secoli* (Rovereto 1939).

ANDRE CHARBONNEAU, YVON DESLOGES and MARC LAFRANCE, *Québec. The Fortified City: From the 17th to the 19th Century* (Ottawa 1982).

SIR GEORGE SYDENHAM, CLARKE, *Miscellaneous Papers, 1884–88* (Chatham 1888).

——, *Fortification: its past achievements, recent developments and future progress*, 2nd ed, (London 1907, reprinted 1989).

G S CLARKE and P O'CALLAGHAN, *Report on 100-ton Guns at Gibraltar and Malta*, War Office (London 1887).

KARL PHILIPP GOTLIEB VON CLAUSEWITZ, *Vom Kriege* (Berlin 1832–34). *On War*, translated by O J Matthijs Jolles (New York 1943).

DON SALVADOR CLAVIJO, 'Extracts from an analysis and comparison of the French and German Systems of Fortification, published in the *Spanish Royal Engineers' Annual Papers*, translated by Captain Hutchinson, RE,' in *Professional Papers of the Royal Engineers*, new series, Vol VIII (1859).

MAURICE J D COCKLE, *A Bibliography of Military Books up to 1642* (London 1957).

MENNO, BARON DE COEHOORN, *Nouvelle Fortification tant pour un terrein bas & humide que sec & élévé, Représentée en trois manieres, sur le conenu intérieur de l'hexagone á la françoise* (The Hague 1741).

——, *Nieuwe Vestingbouw . . . van de Fransche royale seshoek . . .*, (Leeuwarden 1702). *The New Method* of Fortification, translated from the original Dutch . . . by Tho. Savery (London 1705).

BENJAMIN FRANKLIN COOLING III and WALTON H OWEN II, Mr Lincoln's Forts: A Guide to the Civil War Defenses of Washington (Shippensburg 1988).

LOUIS DE CORMONTAIGNE, L'Architecture militaire, ou l'Art de fortifier, 3 parts (The Hague 1741).

——, Memorial de Cormontaingne pour l'attaque des places, etc., posthumous work, with notes by de Bousmard (Berlin 1803).

ARTHUR CORNEY, Fortifications in Old Portsmouth – a guide (Portsmouth 1968).

——, Southsea Castle (Portsmouth 1968).

CORPS ROYAL DU GENIE, Memoires sur la Fortification Perpendiculaire (Paris 1786).

J C CRAMWINCKEL, Duurzame Versterkingskunst, Leerboek voor de cadetten van alle wapens, Tweede deel, Militaire Academie (Amsterdam 1918).

J CROCKER, History of the Fortifications of Malta, General Staff, Malta Command (Malta 1920).

WILLIAM DAVIES, Fort Regent (Jersey, CI 1981).

HORST DE LA CROIX, 'Military architecture and the radial city plan in sixteenth century Italy', The Art Bulletin 42 (1960), p263–90.

——, 'The Literature on Fortification in Renaissance Italy', Technology and Culture 4 (Winter 1963).

——, Military considerations in City Planning – Fortifications (New York 1972).

VEROIL DE LA TREILLE, Maniere de Fortifier les villes et châteaux (Paris 1557).

JOHANN WILHELM DILICH, Peribologia (Frankfurt-on-Main 1640).

CHRISTOPHER DUFFY, Fire and Stone: The Science of Fortress Warfare 1660–1860, (Newton Abbot, 1975).

——, Siege Warfare: The Fortress in the Early Modern World 1494–1660, (London 1979).

——, The Fortress in the Age of Vauban and Frederick the Great

1660–1789, [Siege Warfare Vol II] (London 1985).

ALBRECHT DÜRER, Etliche underricht zu befestigung der stett, schloss und flecken, (Nuremberg 1527).

'EGYPT', Report on the defences of Alexandria and on the results of the action of 11 July 1881, War Office (London 1883).

EGON EIS, The Forts of Folly – the history of an illusion, translated by A J Pomerans (London 1959).

JEAN ERRARD DE BAR-LE-DUC, La fortification reduicte en art le demonstrée . . . (Frankfurt-on-Main 1604).

CYRIL FALLS (ed), Great Military Battles (London 1964).

ROBIN FEDDEN and JOHN THOMSON, Crusader Castles (London 1957).

NICOLAS DE FER, Les Forces de L'Europe ou Description des principales villes avec leur Fortifications, etc, 8 parts in 2 vol (Paris 1690–95).

JAMES FERGUSSON, An Essay on a Proposed New System of Fortification; with hints for its application to our national defences (London 1849).

ANTONIO FRANCESCO AVERLINO, called FILARETE, ms Florence, Bibl Naz, II.I.40.

PIETRO PAOLO FLORIANI, Difesa et offesa dell piazze (Macerata 1630).

DI GIORGIO MARTINI FRANCESCO, Trattato dell' architettura civile e militare, Siena, Bibl Comunale, S IV 4.

——, Trattati di architettura, ingegneria e arte militare, ed Corrado Maltese (Milan, nd).

CAPTAIN T FRASER, The Attack of Fortress in the Future, Royal Engineer Prize Essay 1876 (London 1877).

ADAM FREITAG, Architectura militaris nova et aucta, oder Newe vermehrte Fortification, von Regular Vestungen, von Irregular Vestungen und Aussen wercken, etc. (Leyden 1631).

TERRY GANDER, 'The explosive attack on Fort Eben-Emael', Fort 16 (1988), pp129–132.

BERTRAND GILLE, The Renaissance Engineers (London 1966).

GUSTAVO GIOVANNI, Antonio da Sangallo il Giovane, 2 vols (Rome 1959).

MARK GIROUARD, 'Castles on the Ghana Coast', Country Life (9 November 1961), pp1122–5.

I H GLENDINNING, The Hammers of Invicta; Being a History of the Martello Towers Round Romney Marsh (Hythe 1981).

BASIL GREENHILL and ANN GIFFARD, The British Assault on Finland, 1854–1855: a forgotten naval war (London 1988).

E J GRIMSLEY, The Historical Development of the Martello Tower in the Channel Islands (Guernsey 1988).

ANDREZEJ GRUSZECKI, 'Twierdze rosyjskie na ziemiach polskich', Studia i materialy do Historii Wojskowosci (Warsaw 1966).

ADMIRAL SIR F W GREY, President of Committee, Report of the Committee appointed to enquire into the construction, condition and cost of the fortifications erected, or in course of erection, under 30th and 31st Vict. and previous Statutes, presented to both Houses of Parliament (London 1869).

A GUGLIELMOTTI, Storia della fortificazione nella spiaggia romana, (Vol V della Storia della Marina Pontificia), (Rome 1887).

VIGEVANO DA GUIDO, 'Thesaurus Regis Franciae', ms Paris, Bibl Nat.

MARGARET GUIDO, Syracuse (Syracuse 1958).

DOUGLAS B HAGUE, 'Penrhyn Castle', Translations of the Caernarvonshire Historical Society', Vol 20 (1959).

JOHN R HALE, The Early Development of the Bastion – an Italian Chronology, c1450–c1534', in Europe in the late Middle Ages, ed J R Hale (London 1965).

——, Renaissance Fortifications; Art or Engineering? (London 1977).

——, Renaissance War Studies (London 1983).

DANIEL HALEVY, Vauban: Builder of Fortresses, translated by Major C J C Street (London 1924).

A HALTER, Histoire Militaire de la place forte de Neuf-Brisach (Strasbourg 1962).

JOHN HARVEY, English Medieval Architects: a Bibliographical Dictionary down to 1550 (Boston, Mass 1954).

Lt-Col Hennebert, *L'Art Militaire et la Science: Le Matériel de Guerre Moderne* (Paris 1884).

General Herment, *L'Etat des Fortresses Belges* (Paris 1913).

Geoffrey Hindley, *Castles of Europe* (London 1968).

HMSO, *Handbook for the RML 17.72-inch 100-ton Gun (Mark 1) mounted on sliding carriage and platform Land Service 1887*, HMSO (London 1887).

Oliver F G Hogg, *English Artillery, 1326–1716* (London 1963).

Ian V Hogg, *Coast Defences of England and Wales 1856–1956* (Newton Abbott 1974).

——, *Fortress: A History of Military Defence* (London 1975).

——, *The History of Fortification* (London 1981).

Major-General B P Hughes, *British Smooth-Bore Artillery* (London 1969).

Quentin Hughes, *Britain in the Mediterranean & the Defence of her Naval Stations* (Liverpool 1981).

——, 'Wellington & Fortification', *Fort* 15 (1987), pp61–90.

Captain Inglis, re, 'Application of Iron to Defensive Works', *Papers on Professional subjects by Officers of the Corps of Royal Engineers*, Vol 1 (Session 1861–62), pp144–163.

Colonel T Inglis, *Transporting, Landing and Mounting 80-ton and 100-ton ML Guns, intended for the Armament of Batteries at Dover, Gibraltar and Malta*, War Office (London 1884).

Paul Ive, *The Practice of fortification . . .* (London 1589).

Captain T S Jackson, rn, *Ships versus Forts* (nd c 1900).

Vittorio Jacobacci, 'Le fortificazioni austriache di Verona', *Castellum* 2 (1965), pp99–106.

Colonel R E Jervois, re, cb, *Coast defences and the application of iron to fortification*, reprint from the *Journal of the Royal United Services Institution*, Vol XII (1868).

Lt-General Sir Harry D Jones, 'Description of the Russian works at Bomarsund, in the Aland Islands, and Journal of the Operations which led to their surrender in August 1854, together with observations on the subject,' *Papers of the Royal Engineers*, new series, Vol V (1856).

——, *Reports relating to the re-establishment of the Fortresses in the Netherlands from 1814 to 1830*, printed for private circulation (London 1861).

Colonel John T Jones, *Journals of the Sieges carried on by the Army under the Duke of Wellington in Spain between the years 1811 and 1814*, 2 vols (London 1827).

——, *Memoranda relative to the Lines thrown up to cover Lisbon in 1810* (London 1829).

J E Kaufmann, 'The Dutch and Belgian defences in 1940', *Fort* 17 (1989), pp57–85.

Anthony Kemp, *The Maginot Line: Myth or Reality?* (London 1981).

Major R E Kenyon, *Notes on Land and Coast Fortification* (London 1894).

David J Cathcart King, *Castellarium Anglicanum*, 2 volumes (New York, London & Liechtenstein 1971).

James Kirkman, *Fort Jesus, Mombasa*, 5th edition (Mombasa 1970).

Konrad Kyeser, *Bellifortis*, c1405, ms Göttingen, University Library, cod phil 63.

Daniella Lamberini, 'Practice and Theory in sixteenth century fortifications', *Fort* 15 (1987), pp4–20.

Johann Heinrich Von Landsberg, *Nouveaux plans et projets de fortification, pour défendre et attaquer les places* (The Hague 1731).

Eric Langenskiold *Michele Sanmicheli, The Architect of Verona* (Uppsala 1938).

Giacomo Lanteri, *Due dialgohi . . . del modo di disegnare le piante delle fortezze, ecc* (Venice 1557).

——, *Delle offese et difese delle città et fortezza di G Lanteri . . . con due discorsi d'architettura militare d'A Lupicini*, 5 parts (Venice 1601).

Alain Lecomte, 'The Séré de Rivière fortifications: 1873–1914', *Fort* 17 (1989), pp43–55.

Francesco Laparelli *Codex* (c1566), ms Cortona, Laparelli-Pitti coll.

A W Lawrence, *Trade Castles and Forts of West Africa* (London 1963).

Auguste Frederic Lendy, *Elements of Fortification, field and permanent* (London 1857).

——, *Treatise on Fortification; or Lectures delivered to Officers reading for the Staff* (London 1862).

Da Vinci, ms Paris, Bibl Institut, ms. A-M Milan, Bibl Ambros, Cod Atlanticus.

Jacques Levron, *Le Château fort de la vie au Moyen Age* (Paris 1963).

Colonel Lewis, re, 'Report on the Application of Forts, Towers and Batteries to Coast Defences and Harbours', *Professional Papers of the Royal Engineers* VII (1845).

Emanuel Raymond Lewis, *Seacoast Fortifications of the United States* (Washington, DC 1970).

J F Lewis, *Fortification for English Engineers* (Chatham 1890).

——, *Textbook of Fortification and Military Engineering*, Part II (London 1893).

E M Lloyd, *Vauban, Montalembert, Carnot: Engineer Studies* (London 1887).

Niccolo Machiavelli, *Libro dell'arte della guerra* (Florence 1521).

Ian Macivor, 'The Elizabethan Fortifications of Berwick-upon-Tweed', *Antiquaries Journal* XLV (1965).

——, *Fort George*, HMSO (Edinburgh 1970).

Girolamo Maggi, *Della fortificatione delle citta, di G. Maggi e del Capitan I. Castriotto . . . Libri III* (Venice 1564).

Leone A Maggioretti, 'Architetti e architettura militari', in *L'Opera del genio Italiano all'estero*, series 4, *Gli architetti militari*, 3 vols (Rome 1933–39).

Malta, *A Description of Malta with a sketch of its history and that of its fortifications, translated from the Italian, with notes by an officer resident on the Island* (Malta 1801).

Pietro Marchesi, *Fortezze veneziane, 1508–1797* (Milan 1984).

Francesco De Capitano, *Della architettura militare . . . libri tre* (Brescia 1599).

Francesco Marchi, *Architettura militare*, 5 vols, ed Luigi Marin (Rome 1810).

GIUSEPPE MARCHINI *Giuliano da Sangallo* (Florence 1942).

PAOLO MARCONI, *I Castelli* (Novara 1978).

——, *La cettà come forma simbolica: Studi sulla teorica dell'architettura nel Rinascimento* (Rome 1973).

LE COMMANDANT MARGA, *The Art of Fortification*, revised by Albert Girard (Amsterdam 1638).

E W MARSDEN, *Greek and Roman Artillery: Historical Development* (London 1969).

COLONEL K W MAURICE-JONES, *The History of Coast Artillery in the British Army* (London 1959).

VEZIO MELGARI, *Great Sieges* (London and Glasgow 1970).

'MEMOIR', 'Memoir on the Fortifications in Western Germany compiled from various sources, *Professional Papers of the Royal Engineers*, II (1838).

MATTHAUS MERIAN the elder, *Topographia*, etc (Amsterdam 1644).

BERNARD de MONGOLFIER, *Dictionnaire des Châteaux de France* (Paris 1969).

MONGOMERY OF ALAMEIN, *A History of Warfare* (London 1968).

MARC RENE MARQUIS DE MONTALEMBERT, *La Fortification Perpendiculaire; ou, essai sur plusieurs manières de fortifier* (Paris 1776–84).

PIERRE MOREL, *The Sights of Carcassonne* (Paris and Grenoble 1951).

JOHN MULLER, *A Treatise containing the Elementary Part of Fortification: Regular and Irregular* (London 1746).

——, *A Treatise of Artillery* (London 1759).

W MULLER-WEINER, *Castles of the Crusaders* (London 1966).

LT M NATHAN, RE, 'The Fortifications of Verona', *Professional Papers of the Royal Engineers Occasional Papers*, VI (1881).

E NEAVERSON, *Mediaeval Castles in North Wales* (London 1947).

GENERAL NIEL, *Siége de Sébastopol: Journal des opérations du Génie*, 3 vols (Paris 1858).

E H NOLAN, *The Illustrated History of the War against Russia*, 2 vols (London 1857).

COLONEL SIR CHARLES NUGENT, RE, 'Fortification', in *Encyclopaedia Britannica*, IX, 9th edition (London 1898).

C W C OMAN, *The Art of War in the Middle Ages. AD 378–1515*, revised and edited by John H Beeler (Ithaca, New York 1953).

——, *A History of the Art of War in the Sixteenth Century* (London 1937).

B H ST J O'NEILL, *Dartmouth Castle and other defences of Dartmouth Haven*, reprint from *Archaeologia*, LXXXV (1936).

——, Stefan von Haschenperg, an Engineer to King Henry VIII, and his work *Archaeologia*, XCI (1945).

——, *Castles and Cannon: A Study of Early Artillery Fortifications in England* (Oxford 1960).

WILLIAM BARCLAY PARSONS, 'Leonardo da Vinci, the Military Engineer', in *Engineers and Engineering in the Renaissance*, Vol V (Cambridge, Mass & London 1968).

COLIN PARTRIDGE, *Hitler's Atlantic Wall* (Les Goddards, Guernsey 1976).

SIR CHARLES WILLIAM PASLEY, *A Course of Elementary Fortification . . . second edition*, 2 vols (London & Chatham 1822).

——, *Course of Instruction, Originally Composed for the use of the Royal Engineers Department* (London 1814–17).

A TEMPLE PATTERSON, *'Palmerston's Folly'. The Portsdown and Spithead Forts* (Portsmouth 1970).

SIR RALPH PAYNE-GALLWEY, *The Crossbow* (New York 1958).

SIMON PEPPER, 'The Meaning of the Renaissance Fortress', *Architectural Association Quarterly* 5, No 2 (1973).

SIMON PEPPER and NICHOLAS ADAMS, *Firearms & Fortifications: Military Architecture and Siege Warfare in Sixteenth-Century Siena* (Chicago and London 1986).

CARLO PEROGALLI, *Castelli della pianura lombarda* (Milan 1960).

GEORGES PERROT and CHARLES CHIPIEZ, *Histoire de l'Art dans L'Antiquité*, Vol VI: *La Grece Primitive* (Paris 1894).

HAROLD L PETERSON, *The Book of the Gun* (London 1968).

PHILIP, DUKE OF CLEVES, *Instruction de toutes manieres de guerroyer* (Paris 1558).

COLONEL G PHILIPS, *Text Book of Field Engineering* (London 1901).

CHRISTINA DA PIZZANO, *The Book of Fayttes of Armes and of Chivualrye, etc* (Westminster 1489).

H PLESSIX and E LEGRAND-GIRARDE, *Manuel complet de Fortification*, 3rd ed (Paris & Nancy 1900).

DUDLEY POPE, *Guns* (London 1955).

WHITWORTH PORTER, *History of the Corps of Royal Engineers*, 2 vols (London 1889).

PHILIP POUNCEY, 'Girolamo da Treviso in the Service of Henry VIII', *Burlington Magazine* XCV (1953).

PRO CIVITATE, *Plans en relief de villes belges, leves par des ingénieures militaires francais – XVII–XIX Siécle* (Brussels 1965).

CARLO PROMIS, *Biografie di ingegneri militari italiani dal secolo XIV alla meta del XVIII* (Turin 1891).

G REY, *Étude sur les monuments de l'Architecture Militaire des Croisés en Syrie* (Paris 1871).

PAUL E VAN REYEN, *Middeleeuwse Kastellen* (Bussum 1971).

GERHARD RITTER, *The Schlieffen Plan*, translated by A and E Wilson (London 1958).

G T ROBINSON, *The Fall of Metz* (London 1871).

WILLARD B ROBINSON, *American Forts: Architectural Form and Function* (Chicago & London 1977).

COLONEL ROCOLLE, *2000 ans de fortifications francaise*, 2 vols. (Paris 1973).

RUDI ROLF, *Atlantic Wall Typology* (Beetsterzwaag 1988).

FRANCESCO RONZANI and GIROLAMO LUCIOLLI, *Le fabbriche civili, ecclesiastiche e militari di Michele Sanmicheli* (Verona 1832).

VIVIAN ROWE, *The Great Wall of France: the triumph of the Maginot Line* (London 1959).

WILLIAM HOWARD RUSSELL, *General Todleben's History of the Defence of Sebastopol 1854–5: A Review* (London 1865).

——, *Russell's Despatches from the Crimea, 1854–56*, ed Nicolas Bentley (London 1970).

LT-COL E W C SANDES, *The Military Engineer in India*, Vol 1 (Chatham 1933).

A D SAUNDERS, 'Palmerston's Follies – A centenary', *Journal of the Royal Artillery* LXXXVII, No 3 (Winter 1960).

——, 'Hampshire Coastal Defence since the Introduction of Artillery', in *Archaeological Journal* CXXIII (May 1967).

——, *Fortress Britain: Artillery Fortification in the British Isles and Ireland* (London 1989).

VINCENZO SCAMOZZI, *L'idea dell'architettura universale, ecc*, 2 part (Venice 1615).

VON SCHELIHA, *A Treatise on Coast Defence* (London 1868).

W H SCHUKKING, *De Oude Vestingwerken van Nederland* (Amsterdam 1941).

PEDRO LUIS SCRIVA, *Apologia en ecusacion y favor de las fabricas del reino de Napoles* (1538), ms, Bibl Roy, Madrid.

SEBASTOPOL, *Guerre d'Orient: Siège de Sébastopol* (Paris & Strasbourg 1859).

R R SELLMAN, *Castles and Fortresses* (London 1954).

W DOUGLAS SIMPSON, *Castles from the Air* (London 1949).

——, *Castles in England and Wales* (London 1969).

R C SMAIL, *Crusading Warfare, 1097–1193* (Cambridge 1956).

CAPTAIN GEORGE SMITH, *An Universal Military Dictionary* (London 1779).

ALAN SORRELL, *Living History* (London 1965).

DANIELE SPECKLE, *Architectura von Vestungen* (Strasbourg 1589).

JERZY STANKIEWICZ, 'Ze studiow nad fortyfikacjami pruskimi na ziemiach polskich', *Studia i materialy do Historii Wojskowski* (Warsaw 1966).

T K STAVELEY 'Notes on Brixen and Verona in 1838', *Professional Papers of the Royal Engineers* IV (1842).

MAJOR HECTOR STRAITH, *Treatise on Fortification and Artillery*, revised by Thomas Cook and John T Hyde, 7th ed (London 1858).

LEONHARD CHRISTOPH STURM, *Le veritable Vauban, se montrant au lieu du faux Vauban qui a couru jusqu'ici par le monde ...* (The Hague 1710).

——, *Leonhard Christoph Sturms Architectura militaris hypothetico-edectica ...* (Nürnberg 1736).

SHEILA SUTCLIFFE, *Martello towers* (Newton Abbot 1972).

MARIANUS JACOBUS TACCOLA, called *De machinis libri X*, ms Paris, Bibl Nat, lat 7239.

A A TAIT, 'The Protectorate Citadels of Scotland', *Architectural History* (1965).

NICCOLO TARTAGLIA, *Sul modo di fortificare le città rispetto la forma* (Venice 1536).

——, *Nova scientia* (Venice 1537).

——, *Quesiti et inventioni diverse de N Tartalea Brisciano* (Venice 1546).

——, *Three Books of Colloquies concerning the Arte of shooting in great and small pieces of Artillerie ...* (London 1588).

ARNOLD TAYLOR, *The Welsh Castles of Edward I* (London 1986). Originally published as part of *The History of the King's Works*, Vols I and II, ed H M Colvin (London 1963), pp293–408, 1027–39.

A HAMILTON THOMPSON, *Military Architecture in England during the Middle Ages* (London 1912).

NIECEYSLAW TOBIASE, *Fortyfikacje Dawnego Krakowa* (Krakow 1973).

SIDNEY TOY, *A History of Fortification from 3000 BC to AD 1700* (London 1955).

PHILIPPE TRUTTMANN, *La Muraille de France ou la Ligne Maginot* (Thionville 1985).

ARMIN TUULSE, *Castles of the Western World*, translated R P Girdwood (London 1958).

BATTISTA DELLA VALLE, *Vallo: libro continente appertentie ad Capitanii, reternere & fortificare una Citta co bastioni, con novi artificii de fusco aggioti ... et de expugnare una Citta, etc* (Venice 1524).

SEBASTIEN LE PRESTRE DE VAUBAN, *Traité ... de l'attaque des places ... publiée ... par M Augoyat (Traité de la dèfense des places ... publié ... par M le Baron de Valazé)*, parts (Paris 1829).

——, *De l'attaque et de la défens des places*, 2 vols (The Hague 1737 42).

——, *The New Method of Forti fications practised by Monsieu de Vauban, Engineer-Genera of France*, 6th edition (Londo 1762).

FLAVIUS RENATUS VEGETIUS, *de r militari* (Rome 1494).

LEONARDO VILLENA, 'Sull'apporto italiano alla fortificazione co baluardo', *Castellum* 4, pp81–9 (1966).

E VIOLLET-LE-DUC, *Essay on the Mil itary Architecture of the Middl Ages*, translated by M Macdermot (Oxford & London 1860).

——, *Annals of a Fortress*, translated by Benjamin Bucknall (London 1875).

——, *Description et histoire du Châ teau de Pierrefonds* (Paris 1877).

——, *La Cité de Carcassonne* (Pari 1878).

——, *Description du Château de Couc* (Paris 1880).

VITRUVIUS, *de architectura* (Rome 1486).

——, *The Ten Books of Architecture* translated by Morris Hicky Morga (New York 1960).

MAJOR B R WARD, RE, *Notes on For tification: with a synoptical char* (London 1902).

GRAHAM WEBSTER, *The Roman Army* (Chester 1956).

ALBERTO A WEISSMULLER, *Castle. from the Heart of Spain* (Londor 1967).

F I WINTER, *Greek Fortifications* (London 1971).

F W WOODWARD, *Citadel – A Histor of the Royal Citadel, Plymouth* (Newton Abbot 1987).

SIR HENRY YULE, *Fortification for Of ficers of the Army and Students of Military History, with illustration. and notes* (Edinburgh and London 1851).

A DE ZASTROW, *Histoire de la Fortification Permanente*, translated from German into French by Duparecq, 2 vols and atlas (Paris 1856).

GLOSSARY

Abatis
A defence made of the branches of trees laid on top of each other facing the enemy.

Advanced works or outworks
Advanced works are placed beyond the glacis, but near enough to receive protection from the main fortifications. They are designed to force an enemy to begin a siege from a great distance, and to cover parts of the ground not easily seen from the main parapets.

Angle of the flank
The angle contained between the flank of a bastion and a curtain wall.

Approaches, zigzags, or boyaux
Siege trenches running from one parallel to the next, but lying obliquely to the fortress so that they cannot be enfiladed. *See also* Boyau.

Arrow
See Freccia.

Bailey
A court attached to a fortified enclosure.

A barba
Guns sited to fire over the tops of parapets are said to fire *a barba*.

Barbette
A platform upon which guns may be mounted to fire over the parapet instead of firing through embrasures.

Barbican
An advanced protective work placed in front of the gate of a town wall or fort, or at the head of a bridge.

Barracks
Living accommodation for soldiers.

Barrier
A strong gate built to defend the entrance of a passage into a fortified place. Normally bulletproof and protected by loopholes.

Barrier fort
Either a single self-contained fort capable of withstanding a limited siege, or one of a group of mutually supported works protecting a stretch of countryside and with each fort largely self-contained.

Bartizan (also bartisan)
A battlemented turret projecting from the angle of a fortification.

Bascule (also bacule)
A counterpoised drawbridge.

Bastionet
A diminutive masonry bastion, casemated or open, in the salient of the ditch of a detached work.

Batardeau
A dam built across a ditch, usually topped with a sharp ridge to prevent it being crossed by enemy troops.

Batter
The backward slope of the surface of a wall.

Battery
Any work, permanent or temporary, considered merely as a position for a group of guns. There are five categories: cavalier, with a platform above ground level; elevated, with a platform at ground level; sunken, placed below ground so that the gun can range just above it; half-sunken; and screen.

Beluardetto
A small bastion used on a fausse-braye.

Berm, or chemin des rondes
A space between 1–2½ metres (3–8ft) wide, on top of the scarp wall to prevent dislodged earth falling in the ditch.

Blind
A piece of wood placed over a trench in order to support a covering of hurdles.

Bombproof
A stout building capable of resisting the force of bombs and shells.

Bonnet
A small counterguard in front of a ravelin.

Boyau
Either a small gallery of a mine, or a zigzag branch of a siege trench. *See also* Approaches.

Breach
The ruin which a cannon or a mine makes in a fortification in order to take it by assault.

Brattice (also brettice or brettis)
A temporary wooden parapet used during a siege.

Brisure
An angled break in a rampart or parapet usually close to the flank of a bastion, as used in Coehoorn's first system, 1685.

Bulwark (early English for bastion)
A projecting work usually constructed in earth. Sometimes referred to as an *outwork* and also termed a *boulevard*.

Capannato
A loopholed building, usually triangular in form, constructed to protect towers or ditches.

Capital
An imaginary line bisecting the salient angle of a work such as a bastion.

Caponier
A covered passage constructed across a ditch to provide sheltered communication. Sometimes it is used to defend the ditch.

Casemate
A bombproof vaulted chamber built in the thickness of the ramparts to contain cannon or to provide barrack accommodation.

Cavalier
A work raised higher than the rampart in order to command the surrounding countryside.

Below and opposite: *Plans of traces to illustrate terms in the glossary; from the seventh edition of* Encyclopaedia Britannica.

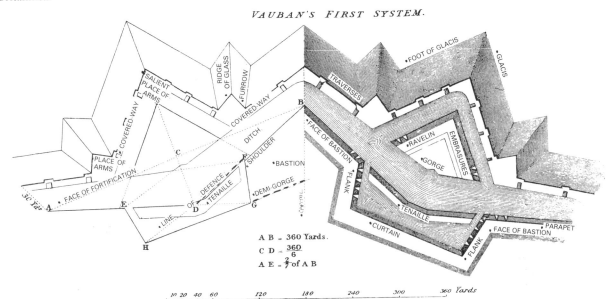

VAUBAN'S FIRST SYSTEM.

AB = 360 Yards.

$CD = \dfrac{360}{6}$

$AE = \dfrac{2}{7}$ of AB

Chandelier
A wooden-framed traverse built to protect the besiegers during sapping operations.

Chemin des rondes
See Berm.

Circumvallation
An entrenchment built around a place in order to invest it.

Coast battery
A battery erected on the coast to defend entrances to harbours and ports.

Coffer
A parapetted defensive trench built across a dry moat.

Command
When any work is raised higher than another it is said to command it.

Corbeil
A basket filled with earth and placed as protection on a parapet.

Cordon
A stone string course at the top of a scarp wall. It defines the magistral line.

Corridor
A covered-way.

Counter approach
A trench dug to hinder a besieging force.

Counterfort
An internal buttress built to strengthen an escarp or counterscarp wall.

Counterguard
A work built to cover a bastion.

Counterscarp
The outer wall of a ditch.

Counterscarp gallery
A casemate constructed in the counterscarp in order to defend the ditch.

Covered-way
A walkway on top of a counterscarp, provided with parapet and banquette to cover the glacis.

Coverport
A small defensive work in front of the gate.

Countervallation
A ditch guarded with a parapet, constructed by besiegers to secure themselves against the sallies of the garrison.

Coupure
A traverse cut in the parapet of a bastion or ravelin. Advocated by Cormontaigne.

Cremaillère
A serrated or zigzag trace in the parapet of a work.

Crenel
A gap or loophole in a parapet or a casemate.

Crenellate
To furnish a work with battlements, embrasures or loopholes.

Crochet
A passage built round the head of a traverse in order to pass troops. Used by Vauban in his first system.

Crownwork
A projecting work consisting of a bastion and two demi-bastions joined to the main body of the place by two long sides.

*a. Detached Lunette, b. Fleche, c. Lunettes, d. Bonnet, e.
Entrenched Bastions, f. Batardeau, g. Hornwork, h.
Caponier, k. Tenaillon.*

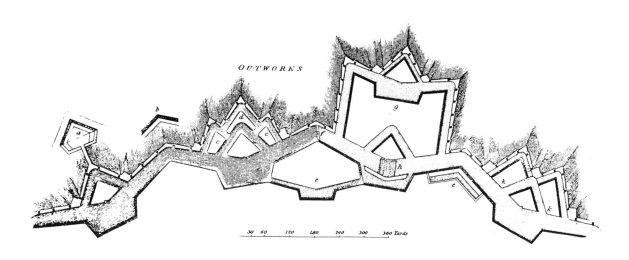

Cunette
A narrow moat along the middle of a ditch used to carry off rain water.

Curtain
The main wall of a place lying between bastions, towers and gates.

Cut
A short excavation made across a terreplein to prevent an enemy, having made a breach, from being able to penetrate further. *See also* Coupure.

Dead angle
The angle below and beyond which the ground cannot be seen and defended from a parapet or rampart.

Defilade
To raise a fortified work in order to screen it from the view of an enemy.

Dehors
A general word used to describe a variety of outworks.

Demi-bastion
A work with one face and one flank. Half the entrance to a bastion measured from the angle of its adjoining curtain. A work like half a bastion.

Demi-gorge
Half of the gorge, or entrance to a bastion, measured from the angle of the curtain to the centreline of the bastion.

Demolition system
A method proposed by Busca for successively demolishing outworks by mines if it becomes necessary to abandon them.

Detached work
A self-defensible work designed to occupy an important position or defend an approach, placed some distance outside a fortress.

Diminished angle
The angle between the face of a bastion, its line of defence and the salient of an adjoining bastion.

Ditch
A large trench excavated to provide building material for the ramparts and to form a serious obstacle to an attacker.

Drawbridge
A removable bridge in front of the gate. There are four variations: lifting, rolling, equilibrium and swing.

Echaugette
A sentrybox corbelled out from the angle of a rampart.

Embrasure
An opening in a parapet through which a gun may be fired.

Embuscade
A place where soldiers hide themselves to surprise the enemy.

Enceinte
The body or area of a place enclosed within its main line of ramparts but excluding its outworks.

Entrenchment
A fieldwork position fortified by trenches.

Epaulment
A covering mass raised to give protection from flanking fire; as for example, the shoulder of a bastion.

Escalade
The climbing of walls with the help of ladders.

Plan of the citadel at Antwerp illustrating terms in the glossary; from the seventh edition of Encyclopaedia Britannica.

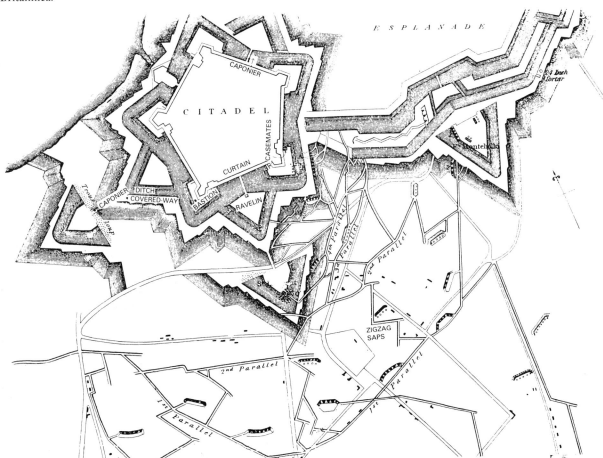

Esplanade
A place cleared of houses and obstructions between the citadel and the town, or between the town and its fortified walls.

Expense magazine
A powder magazine containing enough made-up ammunition to last for 24 hours.

Face
The front of a bastion between its salient point and its flank.

Fascine
A cylindrical bundle of brushwood to fill ditches or construct battery positions.

Fausse-braye
A continuous rampart and parapet placed in the ditch in front of the main rampart.

Feste
A group of irregular defences which includes long-range and close-suport artillery and infantry.

Flank
The portion of a bastion lying between its face and the adjoining curtain.

Flanked
Any work or outwork which is defended by another is said to be flanked by it.

Fleche-redan
A small redan placed at the foot of a glacis of a bastion or a re-entering place of arms.

Fortin
A temporary earthwork fort built to guard a passage or dangerous place, or used in circumvallation.

Fortress
A fortified city. Fortresses are classified in three classes according to size and armament.

Fougasse
A hole dug in the rock facing an enemy attack, filled with gunpowder, timber and rocks and fired like a fixed mortar

Section through a fortification by Wilhelm Dilich to illustrate terms.

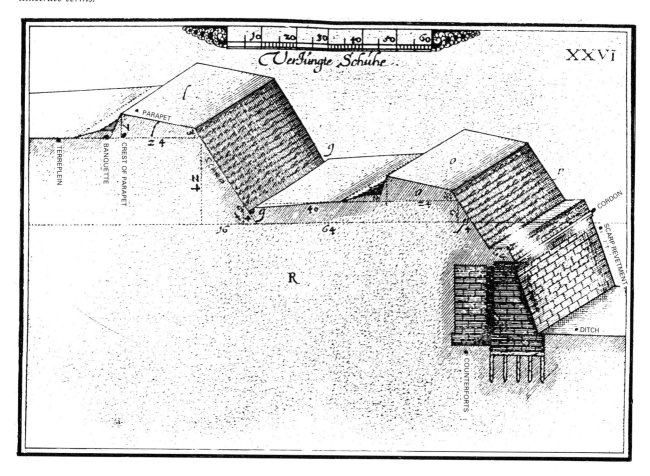

Fraise
A horizontal palisade erected around a work near its berm.

Freccia or arrow
A detached lunette joined by a long corridor or caponier to the main work.

Front
A front of fortification is the distance between the salient points of two ad-joining bastions.

Gabion
A wicker basket filled with earth.

Glacis
A long slope extending beyond the covered-way to the natural country-side, capable of being swept by fire from the ramparts.

Gorge
The neck of a bastion.

Grazon
A piece of fresh earth, covered with grass, and measuring about one foot long and six inches thick, but in the shape of a wedge to line a parapet and the traverses of a covered-way.

Guérite
A stone sentrybox or turret placed at the top of the revetment of the salient angles. It projected over the ditch and was used by Vauban. *See also* Echaugette.

Haxo casemate
A vault constructed over a gun and opened at the rear, and not built over the embrasure.

Herisson or hedgehog
A barrier made in the form of a revolving beam armed with spikes.

Herse or Portcullis
A strong wooden barrier in a gateway which can be raised and lowered by machinery.

Hornwork
An outwork consisting of two demi-bastions joined by a curtain and con-nected to the main work by two paral-lel wings.

Interior slope
The inner sloping face of a rampart or terreplein.

Keep
The central tower of a fort serving to act as a last defence. *See also* Reduit.

Kernburg
The inner ward of a castle or fort.

Line capital
An imaginary line drawn from the angle of the gorge to the angle of the bastion.

Line cogrital
An imaginary line drawn from the angle of the centre to the angle of the bastion.

Line of defence
An imaginary line drawn from the angle between a curtain and the flank of a bastion to the shoulder of the opposite bastion.

Lines with intervals
Detached works placed at such intervals as to derive protection from one another, so as to cross their fire on the intervening space.

Lodgement
A temporary defensive work made on a captured portion of an enemy's fortifications.

Lunette
A permanent outwork in the form of a detached bastion, larger than a redan.

Lunette d'Arcon
A self-defensible lunette designed by General d'Arcon, its gorge strengthened by a circular keep.

Machicoulis
A projecting gallery designed to defend a curtain, gateway or ditch.

Machicolation
Openings between corbels through which missiles or other defensive material might be dropped.

Madrier
A thick plank, normally used as a prop.

Magistral line
The outline of a work following the top of the escarp wall or the cordon; it is always drawn thicker on plans.

Main enclosure
The fortified area surrounded by the main ditch.

Mantelet
A protective screen for infantrymen and gunners.

Martello tower
A British coastal tower, its design inspired by a coast defence work in Corsica.

Merlon
Like a tooth, it is the raised part of the parapet between two embrasures.

Moncrief mounting
A counterweight system for mounting guns so that they can disappear from sight after firing.

Moyenau
An indentation with flanks placed in the middle of an overlong curtain wall.

Obstacle
An impediment erected to delay an attack, such as palisade, fraise and abatis.

Orgue
A barrier made of strong balks of wood sliding through grooves and exactly closing the passage in a gatehouse.

Orillon
A projecting ear placed to protect the flank of a bastion.

Outworks
See Advanced works

Palisade
A fence made of wood or iron to delay an assault.

Parallel
A continuous entrenchment excavated parallel to the general contour of a fortress being besieged.

Parado
A traverse made to give protection from splinters or from fire from the rear, as well as to cover powder magazines and part of the garrison.

Parapet
A breastwork in stone or earth designed to cover troops from observation and fire.

Pas de souris
Staircases giving access from the ditch to the terreplein of outworks.

Passage
See Crochet.

Perpendicular
The distance between the point where lines of defence cross and the imaginary line joining the salient points of two adjoining bastions.

Perpendicular fortification
A tenaille system devised by Montalembert.

Place of arms
An open space for assembling troops. When placed on the covered-way, places of arms are either salient or re-entrant.

Plunging fire
Direct fire on an enemy from a superior position. Firing down.

Point blank
A gun is laid point blank when the production of its axis will pass through the object aimed at.

Polygonal fortification
A fortification system designed by Montalembert where the faces, forming salient angles only, or re-entering angles of small depth, are flanked by caponier constructed in the main ditch.

Pomerio (also pomoerio)
See Esplanade.

Porcullis
See Herse.

Postern
See Sallyport.

Principal magazine
The main powder magazine erected as far as possible from the fronts exposed to attack.

Raking shot
Shot which sweeps across a target.

Rampart
A protective mound of earth raised inside the curtain wall.

Rasant
Sweeping or grazing fire.

Ravelin
An outwork placed beyond the ditch. It has two faces and a gorge, and may be provided with flanks.

Redan
An advanced work, usually triangular in form.

Redoubt
A small work made in a bastion or ravelin of a permanent fortification, or, in a detached form placed at some distance beyond the glacis but within musket shot of the covered-way, or, a type of outwork built of earth in a square or polygonal shape, with little or no means of flanking defence. A chain of redoubts are detached works designed to support each other.

Reduit or keep
A stronghold to which a garrison can retire when the outworks are taken. Often in the form of a blockhouse.

Remblais
Ramparts or earthworks thrown up to defend and cover.

Retirade
A small break in the face of a work of great length to provide additional enfilading fire.

Retrenchment
An interior work constructed within or in the rear of another work in order to strengthen it, especially after a breach has been made. It is used to seal a breach from inside.

Reverse
See Gorge. A portion of a work commanding or facing towards the rear.

Revetment
The facing of a wall. Brick and stone are permanent materials used to face an escarp wall; fascines, gabions, sods, sandbags, hurdles and planks are temporary materials.

Ricochet
The method of firing a gun so that the projectile skips along the surface of the ground with a series of rebounds.

Rideau
A small trench to protect the besiegers working close to a place.

Rondel
A round tower sometimes raised at the foot of a bastion.

Roundway, berm or chemin des rondes
A pathway, about 3 metres (10ft) wide, placed below a parapet and on top of the escarp wall.

Royal (also reale)
A fortress which mounts heavy artillery, or a very strong and impressive work.

Saignor
A drainage channel to empty a ditch.

Salient
The portion of a work which juts out as, for example, the salient angle of a bastion.

Sallyport or postern
An access passage to a ditch or outside a fortified work for the passage of troops when making a sally.

Sap
A covered trench constructed when approaching a besieged place under the fire of the garrison.

Scarp
The inner wall of a ditch or the wall or bank immediately in front of the rampart.

Serpen
An articulated ladder for escalading.

Shell filling room or laboratory
A bombproof casemate or building used for filling shells and cartridges.

Shoulder
Projecting angle between the flank and the face of a bastion.

Sillon
A small rampart raised in a large moat.

Slide
The base of a heavy gun upon which it recoils.

Slope
The angle of the earth thrown up to form a rampart and a parapet. Thus exterior and interior slopes.

Spur
An angular outwork or an arrow-like projection extending from the face of a work.

Stellar trace
A work formed like a many-pointed star

Storm-proof work
A work is said to be storm-proof when, given a complete and efficient garrison, attacking infantry can be destroyed as fast as they can approach.

Talus
A sloping wall made thicker at its base.

Tenaille (also tenail)
A small outwork placed to cover a curtain between two bastions.

Tenaillon
An outwork consisting of one long and one short face, placed on each side of a ravelin.

Terreplein
The surface of the rampart upon which guns are mounted. Originally the surface of the ground above and below which rampart and ditches were made.

Tours-modèles
Coastal reduits, or towers, similar to Martello towers recommended for construction by Napoleon I of France in 1811.

Towre hollow
A rounding made of the remainder of the two brisures in order to join a curtain to an orillon. Small guns were placed there, hidden from the enemy.

Trace
The ground plan of a work.

Traverse
A raised bank usually on the branch of a covered-way to protect troops from enfilade and raking fire.

Trench cavaliers
A series of high parapets formed of three or four tiers of gabions which are pushed forward to crown the covered-way of a besieged fortress.

Twydall profile
A continuous gentle slope from the crest to 4.5 or 6 metres (15–20ft) below natural ground level, with, at its foot, a steel unclimbable palisade and wire entanglements. Used in place of a deep ditch. Named after the redoubts built in 1886 near Chatham.

Vallum
A wall of earth, sods or stone, erected as a permanent defence.

Vamure
Either a parapet erected on the outer side of a rampart, or an advanced wall or earthwork thrown out in front of the main fortification.

Wallwalk
The top of a fortified wall protected by a parapet.

Wing
One of the long sides of a projecting work such as a hornwork or a crown work.

Zigzags
See Approaches.

INDEX